Summary of Contents

Preface xvii

1. An Introduction to SQL 1

2. An Overview of the SELECT Statement 23

3. The FROM Clause 35

4. The WHERE Clause 73

5. The GROUP BY Clause 103

6. The HAVING Clause 125

7. The SELECT Clause 133

8. The ORDER BY Clause 161

9. SQL Data Types 183

10. Relational Integrity 211

11. Special Structures 237

A. Testing Environment 253

B. Sample Applications 259

C. Sample Scripts 265

D. SQL Keywords 285

Index 287

W0010507

SIMPLY SQL

BY **RUDY LIMEBACK**

Simply SQL
by Rudy Limeback

Copyright © 2008 SitePoint Pty. Ltd.

Expert Reviewer: Joe Celko

Technical Editor: Andrew Tetlaw

Technical Editor: Dan Maharry

Managing Editor: Chris Wyness

Technical Director: Kevin Yank

Printing History:
   First Edition: December 2008

Editor: Kelly Steele

Index Editor: Russell Brooks

Cover Design: Alex Walker

Latest Update: September 2010

Notice of Rights

Notice of Liability

Trademark Notice

Published by SitePoint Pty. Ltd.

48 Cambridge Street
Collingwood VIC Australia 3066
Web: www.sitepoint.com
Email: business@sitepoint.com

ISBN 978-0-9804552-5-0
Printed and bound in the United States of America

About the Author

Rudy Limeback is a semi-retired SQL Consultant living in Toronto, Canada. His broad SQL experience spans more than 20 years, and includes working with DB2, SQL Server, Access, Oracle, and MySQL. He's an avid participant in discussion forums, primarily at SitePoint (http://sitepoint.com/forums/). His two web sites are http://r937.com/ for SQL and http://rudy.ca/ for personal stuff. When not glued to his computer, Rudy enjoys playing touch football and frisbee golf.

About the Expert Reviewer

Joe Celko served ten years on ANSI/ISO SQL Standards Committee and contributed to the SQL-89 and SQL-92 standards. He is the author of seven books on SQL for Morgan Kaufmann, and has written over 800 columns in the computer trade and academic press, mostly dealing with data and databases.

About the Technical Editors

Andrew Tetlaw has been tinkering with web sites as a web developer since 1997. Before that, he worked as a high school English teacher, an English teacher in Japan, a window cleaner, a car washer, a kitchen hand, and a furniture salesman. Andrew is dedicated to making the world a better place through the technical editing of SitePoint books and kits. He's also a busy father of five, enjoys coffee, and often neglects his blog at http://tetlaw.id.au/.

Dan Maharry is a senior developer for Co-operative Web, a software development workers co-op based in the UK. He specializes in working with new technologies and has been working with .NET since its first beta. Dan lives with his lovely wife Jane and a rose bush that's trying to engulf his house.

About SitePoint

SitePoint specializes in publishing fun, practical, and easy-to-understand content for web professionals. Visit http://www.sitepoint.com/ to access our books, newsletters, articles, and community forums.

To my children, Dieter, Damon,
Anna, and Eric, my
granddaughters Claire and Norah,
and to my Mom.

Table of Contents

Preface xvii

Who Should Read This Book? xvii

The Challenges to Learning SQL xviii

What's in This Book? xix

How to Gain Help xxi

The SitePoint Forums xxii

The Book's Web Site xxii

The SitePoint Newsletters xxiii

Your Feedback xxiii

Conventions Used in This Book xxiii

Code Samples xxiii

Tips, Notes, and Warnings xxiv

Acknowledgments xxv

Chapter 1 An Introduction to SQL 1

SQL Statement Overview 1

Keywords, Identifiers, and Constants 2

Clauses 4

Syntax 5

Data Definition Language 6

CREATE, ALTER, and DROP 7

Starting Over 10

Data Manipulation Language 11

INSERT, UPDATE, and DELETE 12

The SELECT Statement 18

Standard SQL 20

Read The Fine Manual 21

Wrapping Up: an Introduction to SQL 22

Chapter 2   **An Overview of the SELECT**

Statement 23

The SELECT Statement 23

The SELECT and FROM Clauses 24

Content Management System 25

The WHERE Clause 28

The GROUP BY and HAVING Clauses 29

The ORDER BY Clause 32

Wrapping Up: the SELECT Statement 33

Chapter 3   **The FROM Clause** 35

Why Start with the FROM Clause? 36

Parsing an SQL Statement 36

FROM One Table 37

FROM More than One Table Using JOINs 37

Types of Join 38

The Inner Join 39

Outer Joins 40

The Cross Join 44

Real World Joins 46

Inner Join: Categories and Entries 48

Left Outer Join: Categories and Entries 56

Right Outer Join: Categories and Entries 61

Full Outer Join: Categories and Entries 63

Views 67

Views in Web Development 69

Subqueries and Derived Tables 70

Wrapping Up: the FROM Clause 71

Chapter 4   The WHERE Clause 73

Conditions 74

Conditions that are True 74

When "Not True" is Preferable 75

Shopping Carts 76

Conditions that Evaluate as UNKNOWN 79

Operators 79

Comparison Operators 79

The LIKE Operator 82

The BETWEEN Operator 83

Compound Conditions with AND and OR 86

Truth Tables 87

Combining AND and OR 89

IN Conditions 91

IN with Subqueries 92

Correlated Subqueries 93

EXISTS Conditions 96

NOT IN or NOT EXISTS? 98

WHERE Clause Performance 99

Indexes 100

Wrapping Up: the WHERE Clause 102

Chapter 5   The GROUP BY Clause 103

Grouping is More than Sequencing 104

Out of Many, One 109

Drill-down SQL 113

GROUP BY in Context 114

How GROUP BY Works 115

Group Rows 115
Rules for GROUP BY 117
    Columns with Certain Large Data Types 117
Wrapping Up: the GROUP BY 122

Chapter 6   The HAVING Clause 125

HAVING Filters Group Rows 125
    HAVING without a GROUP BY Clause 128
Wrapping Up: the HAVING Clause 132

Chapter 7   The SELECT Clause 133

SELECT in the Sequence of Execution 134
Which Columns Can Be Selected? 135
    Detail Rows 135
    Group Rows 136
The Discussion Forum Application 138
    The forums Table 139
    The members Table 139
    The threads Table 139
    The posts Table 140
Functions 140
    Aggregate Functions 141
    Scalar Functions 149
Operators 154
    Numeric Operators 154
    The Concatenation Operator 154
    Temporal Operators 155
The Dreaded, Evil Select Star 156
SELECT DISTINCT 157
Wrapping Up: the SELECT Clause 159

Chapter 8   **The ORDER BY Clause** 161

ORDER BY Syntax 162

How ORDER BY Works 162

ASC and DESC 164

ORDER BY Clause Performance 167

The Sequence of Values 168

The Scope of ORDER BY 173

Using ORDER BY with GROUP BY 175

ORDER BY Expressions 176

Special Sequencing 176

ORDER BY with UNION Queries 178

Wrapping Up: the ORDER BY Clause 182

Chapter 9   **SQL Data Types** 183

An Overview of Data Types 184

Numeric Data Types 185

Integers 185

Decimals 187

Floating-point Numbers 191

Conversions in Numeric Calculations 193

Numeric Functions 193

Character Data Types 194

CHAR 194

VARCHAR 195

Numeric or Character? 196

NCHAR and NVARCHAR 198

CLOB and BLOB 198

String Functions 199

Temporal Data Types 200

DATE 200

TIME 203

TIMESTAMP 205

Intervals 206

Date Functions 207

Column Constraints 208

NULL or NOT NULL 208

DEFAULT 209

CHECK Constraints 209

Wrapping Up: SQL Data Types 210

Chapter 10   **Relational Integrity** 211

Identity 212

Data Modelling 212

Entities and Attributes 213

Entities and Relationships 214

Primary Keys 219

UNIQUE Constraints 221

Foreign Keys 224

How Foreign Keys Work 225

Using Foreign Keys 226

Natural versus Surrogate Keys 232

Autonumbers 234

Wrapping Up: Relational Integrity 235

Chapter 11   **Special Structures** 237

Joining to a Table Twice 237

Joining a Table to Itself 240

Implementing a Many-to-many Relationship: Keywords 246

Wrapping Up: Special Structures 251

Appendix A **Testing Environment** 253

Download Your Database System Software 253

Bookmark or Download the SQL Reference 254

Connect to the Database System 255

    Command Line 255

    Front-end Applications 255

SQL Script Library 256

Performance Problems and Obtaining Help 257

    Obtaining the Execution Plan 257

    Seeking Help 258

    Indexing 258

Appendix B **Sample Applications** 259

Data Model Diagrams 259

Teams and Games 260

Content Management System 261

Discussion Forums 262

Shopping Carts 263

Appendix C **Sample Scripts** 265

Teams and Games 266

    The `teams` Table 266

    The `games` Table 267

Content Management System 268

    The `entries` Table 268

    The `categories` Table 270

    The `entries_with_category` View 272

    The `contents` Table 272

    The `comments` Table 273

The entrykeywords Table 274

Discussion Forums 275

    The forums Table 275

    The members Table 275

    The threads Table 276

    The posts Table 276

Shopping Carts 279

    The items Table 279

    The customers Table 281

    The carts Table 282

    The cartitems Table 283

    The vendors Table 284

Appendix D SQL Keywords 285

Index 287

Preface

This book is about SQL, the Structured Query Language.

SQL is the language used by all major database systems today. SQL has been around for about 30 years, but is enjoying a real renaissance in the 21st century, thanks to the tremendous success of database-driven web sites.

Whether your web site is written in PHP, ASP, Perl, ColdFusion, or any other programming language, and no matter which database system you want to use—MySQL, PostgreSQL, SQL Server, DB2, Oracle, or any of the others—one fact is almost certain: if you want to have database-driven content, you'll need to use SQL.

SQL is a simple, high-level language with tremendous power. You can perform tasks with a few lines of SQL that would take pages and pages of intricate coding to accomplish in a programming language.

Who Should Read This Book?

If you're a web designer or developer looking for guidance in learning SQL for your web projects, this book is for you.

In the early days of the Web, everyone was a web developer. Nowadays, the field has matured to the point where many different disciplines exist. Two broad categories emerged:

- Web designers are responsible for what web site visitors see. This includes the design, graphics, and layout of the site. It also includes designing the functionality of the site, how it *works*, with considerations for the usability of site features.

- Web developers are responsible for the code behind the site. This includes the HTML, CSS, and JavaScript that make the site functional. In addition, web developers handle scripting languages such as PHP, which are used to automate the production of HTML and other code. Scripting languages enable dynamic web site interaction, and are used to communicate with the database.

If you're a web designer, you can benefit from learning SQL—at least at a rudimentary level—because it will help you design better user interactions. Understanding how SQL works means that you can make life simpler for the developers who will implement your designs: by ensuring that the web site is organized in a way that not only serves the web site visitor, but also allows for simple SQL and good database design. We'll cover both SQL and database design in this book.

Web developers are the primary audience for the book. Using several simple web application examples, we'll explore all aspects of SQL and database design that are required by web developers to develop efficient and effective web pages. The sample applications in this book really are quite simple, and you may already be familiar with one or more of them, just by using them on the Web.

Of course, database use goes beyond dynamic web sites. For example, databases are also used in desktop and network applications. So even if you're working with a non-web-related application, the chances are good that you're still working with a database that uses SQL. The SQL you learn in this book can be applied in all situations where a database is used.

The Challenges to Learning SQL

> We are confronted with insurmountable opportunities.
>
> —Pogo

I first learned SQL in the late 1980s. At that time, there were no books on SQL, nor web site SQL tutorials because the Web was yet to arrive. I learned by practicing, and by reading the manual. In the 1990s, I solidified my own understanding of SQL by helping others learn, as well as by participating in email discussion lists with other SQL practitioners. Today, I'm hopelessly addicted to web discussion forums like SitePoint, and have interacted with literally thousands of people as they learn SQL too.

Some of the complaints about learning SQL that I've heard over the years include:

- Basic SQL tutorials just cover the syntax, but they use trivial examples and fail to explain anything in depth.

- Some SQL tutorials use a secret language (for example, DRI, canonical synthesis, non-trivial FD) that you'd need a PhD to understand.

Some SQL tutorials are tantalizingly close to what you're looking for, but fail to *close the sale*. That's because they're unable to relate their examples to your own real-world situation.

By using common web-related sample applications, this book will cover not only simple examples of SQL that are relevant to you, but also more complex concepts using terminology I hope you won't find too obscure.

What's in This Book?

This book comprises the following chapters. In the first eight chapters, we'll learn about SQL, the language, its various statements and clauses, and how to use SQL to store and retrieve database data. These chapters are organized to provide first an introduction to the SQL language, then an overview of the SELECT statement, followed by an examination of each of the SELECT statement's clauses. In the last three chapters, we'll learn how to design databases effectively, taking into consideration column data types, table relationships, primary and foreign keys, and so on.

Why this separation? Why do we postpone learning about designing tables until well after the SELECT statement has been thoroughly dissected? Because effective database design requires an understanding of how SQL works. You must walk before you can run. If you're new to SQL, you'll want to focus on learning SQL first, rather than be prematurely sidetracked on the whys and wherefores of database design issues.

The SQL Language

Chapter 1: An Introduction to SQL

This introductory chapter will put the SQL language into a perspective relevant to a typical web developer. You'll learn the difference between a statement and a clause, as well as data definition language (DDL) and data manipulation language (DML). You'll also go on a whirlwind tour through all the common SQL statements: CREATE, ALTER, DROP, INSERT, UPDATE, DELETE, and SELECT.

Chapter 2: An Overview of the SELECT Statement

If SQL is all about database queries, then the SELECT statement is where all the action is. This overview will dissect the SQL SELECT statement into its component clauses and give you a taste of what's to come. The next six chapters will look at each clause in detail.

Chapter 3: The FROM Clause

Few SQL books begin with the FROM clause, but this is where it all begins; the FROM clause is executed first and all other clauses use the tabular results it produces. That's why it's a great place to start our in-depth examination of all the clauses of the SELECT statement. This chapter will ease you through the tricky subject of database table joins, where you'll easily master the concepts of the inner join, left outer join, right outer join, full outer join, and cross join. We'll also touch on the topics of database views and subqueries (or derived tables).

Chapter 4: The WHERE Clause

The WHERE clause filters the results of the FROM clause. This chapter will teach you all about how to express conditions using the SQL keywords: LIKE, BETWEEN, AND, OR, IN, EXISTS, and NOT, as well as correlated subqueries. We'll also discuss performance issues and indexing.

Chapter 5: The GROUP BY Clause

The GROUP BY clause aggregates the result of the FROM and WHERE clauses into groups. Chapter 5 will teach you how grouping works and the rules for its use.

Chapter 6: The HAVING Clause

The HAVING clause filters the group rows produced by the GROUP BY clause. Chapter 6 will show you how to write HAVING clause conditions, and how to use the HAVING clause without a GROUP BY clause.

Chapter 7: The SELECT Clause

The SELECT clause defines the columns in the final result set. Chapter 7 will show you how to use the SELECT clause effectively, and how its scope changes in the presence or absence of the GROUP BY clause. This chapter also does a survey of the common SQL aggregate functions (like SUM and COUNT) and scalar functions (like CASE and SUBSTRING) available in most database systems.

Chapter 8: The ORDER BY Clause

The ORDER BY clause determines the order in which the result set is returned. Chapter 8 is all about sequencing the various data types, and the difference between sequencing and grouping. It'll teach you how to write effective ORDER

BY expressions, including how to use the CASE functions to implement special sequencing.

Database Design

Chapter 9: SQL Data Types

This chapter provides a detailed look at the various numeric, character, and temporal data types available for columns, and the rationales for their use. We tour the common numeric, string, and date functions available in most database systems. This chapter also contains a section on the column constraints: NULL, NOT NULL, DEFAULT, and CHECK.

Chapter 10: Relational Integrity

Chapter 10 introduces some topics that are the source of much befuddlement for many people new to databases. It's about relational integrity, the real heart and soul of effective database design. This chapter discusses the concept of identity, primary keys, and uniqueness, and also extensively covers the concept of the relationships between database entities: how they're expressed with database modelling and how they're implemented using foreign keys.

Chapter 11: Special Structures

Chapter 11 examines some of the common database structures that can be used to implement complex relationships between entities. This chapter takes a look at how to join to a table twice, join a table to itself, and how to implement the concept of keywords (or tagging)—a many-to-many relationship.

The sample applications used throughout the book are described in the appendices, and all the examples of SQL in the book are taken from these applications. Instructions are given on creating the applications and loading them with data.

How to Gain Help

SQL has been around a few decades and hardly ever changes. Despite major database systems like MySQL and SQL Server constantly upgrading themselves, the underlying SQL language is stable, so everything you learn in this book will be applicable for years to come.

However, SQL is an immensely broad topic. Of necessity, much needs to be left out of any single book that tries to cover all of SQL. Therefore, if you have any questions about SQL or database design, you might wish to seek further help. Two sources you can try are the SitePoint Forums and the web site for this book.

The SitePoint Forums

The SitePoint Forums[1] are discussion forums where you can ask questions about anything related to web development. You may, of course, answer questions, too. That's how a discussion forum site works—some people ask, some people answer—and most people do a bit of both. Sharing your knowledge benefits others and strengthens the community. A lot of fun and experienced web designers and developers hang out there. It's a good way to learn new stuff, get questions answered in a hurry, and just have fun.

The SitePoint Forums include a main forum for Databases, and a subforum for MySQL specifically (because of the immense popularity of this database system).

- Databases: http://www.sitepoint.com/forums/forumdisplay.php?f=88
- MySQL: http://www.sitepoint.com/forums/forumdisplay.php?f=182

The Book's Web Site

Located at http://www.sitepoint.com/books/sql1/, the web site that supports this book will give you access to the following facilities:

The Code Archive

As you progress through this book, you'll note a number of references to the code archive. This is a downloadable ZIP archive that contains each and every line of example source code that's printed in this book. If you want to cheat (or save yourself from carpal tunnel syndrome), go ahead and download the archive.[2]

Updates and Errata

No book is perfect, and we expect that watchful readers will be able to spot at least one or two mistakes before the end of this one. The Errata page on the book's web site will always have the latest information about known typographical and code errors.

---

[1] http://www.sitepoint.com/forums/
[2] http://www.sitepoint.com/books/sql1/code.php

The SitePoint Newsletters

In addition to books like this one, SitePoint publishes free email newsletters, such as *SitePoint Design View*, *SitePoint Market Watch*, and *SitePoint Tech Times*, to name a few. In them, you'll read about the latest news, product releases, trends, tips, and techniques for all aspects of web development. Sign up to one or more SitePoint newsletters at http://www.sitepoint.com/newsletter/.

Your Feedback

If you can't find an answer through the forums, or if you wish to contact us for any other reason, the best place to write is books@sitepoint.com. We have a well-staffed email support system set up to track your inquiries, and if our support team members are unable to answer your question, they'll send it straight to us. Suggestions for improvements, as well as notices of any mistakes you may find, are especially welcome.

Conventions Used in This Book

You'll notice that we've used certain typographic and layout styles throughout this book to signify different types of information. Look out for the following items.

Code Samples

Code in this book will be displayed using a fixed-width font, like so:

```
<h1>A Perfect Summer's Day</h1>
<p>It was a lovely day for a walk in the park. The birds
were singing and the kids were all back at school.</p>
```

If the code is to be found in the book's code archive, the name of the file will appear at the top of the program listing, like this:

```
example.css
.footer {
  background-color: #CCC;
  border-top: 1px solid #333;
}
```

If only part of the file is displayed, this is indicated by the word *excerpt*:

example.css *(excerpt)*

```
border-top: 1px solid #333;
```

If additional code is to be inserted into an existing example, the new code will be displayed in bold:

```
function animate() {
  new_variable = "Hello";
}
```

Also, where existing code is required for context, rather than repeat all the code, a ⋮ will be displayed:

```
function animate() {
    ⋮
  return new_variable;
}
```

Some lines of code are intended to be entered on one line, but we've had to wrap them because of page constraints. A ➥ indicates a line break that exists for formatting purposes only, and should be ignored.

```
URL.open("http://www.sitepoint.com/blogs/2007/05/28/user-style-she
➥ets-come-of-age/");
```

Tips, Notes, and Warnings

Hey, You!

Tips will give you helpful little pointers.

Ahem, Excuse Me ...

Notes are useful asides that are related—but not critical—to the topic at hand. Think of them as extra tidbits of information.

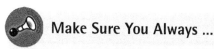

Make Sure You Always ...

... pay attention to these important points.

Watch Out!

Warnings will highlight any gotchas that are likely to trip you up along the way.

Acknowledgments

I'd like to thank Andrew Tetlaw, SitePoint's Technical Editor, and Joe Celko, the main reviewer. Both gave valuable advice that made the book better.

Joe, in particular, has been a tremendous influence on me as I learned SQL over the years. I met Joe at a database conference in the early 1990s and have been a big fan ever since, so I was very pleased that he agreed to review the book. As you may know, Joe has been an outspoken SQL advocate for decades. He helped establish the SQL standard, and has written numerous SQL columns, as well as many books on SQL and databases. In particular, his book *SQL for Smarties*[3] is a *must have* for anyone venturing into advanced SQL.

I also owe Joe an apology for willfully disregarding ISO-11179, an international standard for assigning data element names, primarily in my choice of "`id`" as the name of several of my table columns. Joe was also dissatisfied with my coding style, where I place the comma that separates items in a list—on a new line, at the front. However, it's *my* coding style and I trust that you'll not find it too disruptive; it's served me well for many years, and I write a lot of SQL.

---

[3] *SQL for Smarties* 3rd edition (San Francisco, Morgan Kaufmann, 2005)

An Introduction to SQL

Almost every web site nowadays, it seems, uses a database. Your objective, as a web developer, is to be able to design or build web sites that use a database. To do this, you must acquire an understanding of and the ability to use **Structured Query Language** (SQL), the language used to communicate with databases.

We'll start by introducing the SQL language and the major SQL statements that you'll encounter as a web developer.

SQL Statement Overview

In the past, SQL has been criticized for having an inappropriate name. Structured Query Language lacks a proper structure, does more than just queries, and only barely qualifies as a programming language. You might think it fair criticism then, but let me make three comments:

- **Structure** refers to the fact that SQL is about tables of data or, more specifically, tabular structures. A table of data has columns and rows. There are many instances where we'll encounter an alternative that isn't, strictly speaking, a table, but looks and acts like one. This tabular structure will be explained in Chapter 3.

▪ While SQL includes many different types of statements, the main one is the SE-LECT statement, which performs a *query* against the database, to retrieve data. Querying data effectively is *where the action is*, the primary focus of the first eight chapters. Designing the database effectively is covered in the last three chapters.

▪ The SQL language has been standardized. This is immensely important, because when you learn effective SQL, you can apply your skills in many different database environments. You can develop sites for your client or boss using any of today's common database systems—whether proprietary or open source—because they all support SQL.

Those three concepts—tabular structures, effective querying, and SQL standards—are the secret to mastering SQL. We'll see these concepts throughout the book.

 SQL or Sequel?

Before the real fun begins, let's put to rest a question often asked by newcomers: how do you pronounce SQL?

Some people say the letters, "S-Q-L." Some people pronounce it as a word, "sequel". Either is correct. For example, the database system SQL Server (by Microsoft, originally by Sybase) is often pronounced "sequel server". However, SQL, by itself—either the language in general or a given statement in that language—is usually pronounced as S-Q-L.

Throughout this book, therefore, SQL is pronounced as *S-Q-L*. Thus, you will read about *an* SQL statement and not *a* SQL statement.

We'll begin our overview of SQL statements by looking at their components: keywords, identifiers, and constants.

Keywords, Identifiers, and Constants

Just as sentences are made up of words that can be nouns, verbs, and so on, an SQL statement is made up of words that are keywords, identifiers, and constants. Every word in an SQL statement is always one of these:

Keywords   These are words defined in the SQL standard that we use to construct an SQL statement. Many keywords are mandatory, but most of them are optional.

Identifiers   These are names that we give to database objects such as tables and columns.

Constants   These are literals that represent fixed values.

Let's look at an example:

```
SELECT name FROM teams WHERE id = 9
```

Here is a perfectly respectable SQL statement. Let's examine its keywords, identifiers, and constants:

- `SELECT`, `FROM`, and `WHERE` are keywords. `SELECT` and `FROM` are mandatory, but `WHERE` is optional. We'll cover only the important keywords in SQL in this book. However, they're all listed in Appendix D for your reference.

- `name`, `teams`, and `id` are identifiers that refer to objects in the database. `name` and `id` are column names, while `teams` is a table name.

  We'll define both columns and tables later on in this chapter but, yes, they are exactly what you think they are.

- The *equals* sign (=) is an **operator**, a special type of keyword.

- `9` is a *numeric constant*. Again, we'll look at constants later in the chapter.

So there you have it. Our sample SQL statement is made up of keywords, identifiers, and constants. Not so mysterious.

Clauses

In addition, we often speak of the clauses of an SQL statement. This book has entire chapters devoted to individual clauses. A **clause** is a portion of an SQL statement. The name of the clause corresponds to the SQL keyword that begins the clause. For example, let's look at that simple SQL statement again:

```
SELECT
   name
FROM
   teams
WHERE
   id = 9
```

The SELECT clause is:

```
SELECT
   name
```

The FROM clause is:

```
FROM
   teams
```

The WHERE clause is:

```
WHERE
   id = 9
```

 Coding Style

You'll have noticed that, this time, the query is written with line breaks and indentation. Even though line breaks and extra white space are ignored in SQL—just as they are in HTML—readability is *very* important. Neatness counts, and becomes more pertinent with longer queries: the tidier your queries the more likely you are to spot errors. I'll say more on coding style later.

Syntax

Each clause in an SQL statement has syntax rules for how it may be written. **Syntax** simply means how the clause is put together—what keywords, identifiers, and constants it consists of, and, more importantly, whether they are in the correct order, according to SQL's *grammar*. For example, the SELECT clause must start with the keyword SELECT.

Syntax and Semantics

In addition to syntax, **semantics** is another term sometimes used in discussing SQL statements. These terms simply mean the difference between what the SQL statement actually says versus what you intended it to say; *syntax* is what you said, *semantics* is what you meant.

The database system won't run any SQL statement with a syntax error. To add insult to injury, the system can only tell you if your SQL statement has a syntax error; it doesn't know what you actually meant.

To demonstrate the difference between syntax and semantics, suppose we were to rewrite the example from the previous section like so:

```
FROM teams WHERE id = 9 SELECT name
```

This seems to makes some sense. The *semantics* are clear. However, the *syntax* is wrong. It's an invalid SQL statement. More often, you'll get syntactically correct queries that are semantically incorrect. Indeed, we'll come across some of these as we go through the book and discuss how to correct them.

Up to this point, I've alluded to a couple of database object types: tables and columns. To reference database objects in SQL statements we use their identifiers, which are names that are assigned when the objects are first created. This leads naturally to the question of *how* those objects are created.

Before we answer that, let's take a moment to introduce some new terminology. SQL statements can be divided into two types: DDL and DML.

Data Definition Language (DDL)
    DDL is used to manage *database objects* like tables and columns.

Data Manipulation Language (DML)
    DML is used to manage the *data* that resides in our tables and columns.

The terms DDL and DML are in common use, so if you run into them, remember that they're just different types of SQL statements. The difference is merely a convenient way to distinguish between the types of SQL statements and their effect on the database. DDL changes the database structure, while DML changes only the data. Depending on the project, and your role as a developer, you may not have the authority or permission to write DDL statements. Often, the database already exists, so rather than change it, you can only manipulate the data in it using DML statements.

The next section looks at DDL SQL statements, and how database objects are created and managed.

Data Definition Language

In the beginning the Universe was created. This has made a lot of people very angry and been widely regarded as a bad move.
—Douglas Adams

Where do database objects like tables and columns come from? They are created, modified, and finally removed from the database using DDL, the Data Definition Language part of SQL. Indeed those three tasks are accomplished using the CREATE, ALTER, and DROP SQL statements.

Trying Out Your SQL

It's one thing to see an example of SQL syntax, and another to adapt it to your particular circumstance or project. Trying out your SQL statements is a great way to learn. If you have some previous SQL experience, you already know this (and might want to skip ahead to Chapter 2). If you are new to SQL, and want to experiment with the following DDL statements, keep in mind that you can always start over. What you CREATE, you can ALTER, or DROP, if necessary.

Appendix A explains how to set up a testing environment for five popular database systems—MySQL, PostgreSQL, SQL Server, DB2, and Oracle—and Appendix C contains a number of DDL scripts you can try running if you wish.

CREATE, ALTER, and DROP

Of the many DDL statements, CREATE, ALTER, and DROP are the three main ones that web developers need to be aware of. (The others are more advanced and beyond the scope of this book.) Even if you haven't been granted the authority or permission to execute DDL statements on a given project, it helps to know the DDL to see how tables are structured and interconnected.

The CREATE Statement

Earlier on, I suggested that a tabular structure is one of the main concepts you need to understand when learning SQL. It's actually quite simple, and a table of data looks exactly like you would intuitively expect it to—it has columns and rows. Each table contains information concerning a set of items. Each **row** in a table represents a single item. Each **column** represents one piece of information that can be stored about each item. Figure 1.1 provides a visualization of a table called teams with three columns named id, name, and conference. The table pictured also contains some data; each row in the table represents a single team and can store three pieces of information about that individual team: its id number, its name, and its conference (its division or league).

Table Name

teams		
id	name	conference
9	Riff Raff	F
37	Havoc	F
63	Brewers	C

} Each row represents an item

Each column in a row
represents a property of the item

Figure 1.1. Tables have rows, and rows have columns

Here's an example of a DDL statement; this is the statement that creates the database table pictured in Figure 1.1:

```
CREATE TABLE teams
(
   id            INTEGER       NOT NULL  PRIMARY KEY,
   name          VARCHAR(37)   NOT NULL,
   conference    VARCHAR(2)    NULL
)
```

The CREATE TABLE statement creates the teams table—but not the data—with three columns named id, name, and conference. This is a table used in the *Teams and Games* sample application, one of several sample applications used in the book. All the applications are described in Appendix B.

 The Order of Columns

Note that while tables are represented graphically with the columns always in the same order, this is for our ease of reference only. The database itself doesn't care about the order of the columns.

It would be optimistic to expect you to understand everything in the CREATE TABLE statement above at this stage. (I'm sure some of you, new to SQL, might be wondering "What's an id?" or "What does PRIMARY KEY do?" and so on.) We simply want to see an example of the CREATE TABLE statement, and not be sidetracked by design issues for the Teams and Games application.

Note that the keywords of the CREATE TABLE statement are all in capital letters, while the identifiers are all in lower case letters. This choice is part of my coding style.

 Upper Case or Lower Case?

Although it's of no consequence to SQL whether a font appears in caps or lower case, identifiers may indeed be case-sensitive. However, I'd strongly advise you to create your database objects with lower case letters to avoid syntax problems with unknown names.

Notice also the formatting and white space. Imagine having to read this SQL statement all on one long line:

```
CREATE TABLE teams ( id INTEGER NOT NULL PRIMARY KEY,
➥   name VARCHAR(37), conference VARCHAR(2) NULL )
```

Neatness helps us to spot parts of the statement we have omitted or mispelled, like the NOT NULL that was accidentally left off the name column in the one line version of the statement above. Did you spot the omission before you read this?

Looking at the sample CREATE TABLE statement, we see that each of the three columns is given a data type (e.g., INTEGER, VARCHAR), and is also designated NULL or NOT NULL. Again, please don't worry if these terms are new to you. We will discuss how they work and what they're for in Chapter 9. This introductory chapter is not supposed to teach you the SQL statements in detail, merely introduce them to you and briefly describe their general purpose.

Are there other database objects that we can create besides tables? Yes. There are schemas, databases, views, triggers, procedures and several more but we're getting ahead of ourselves again. Many CREATE statements are for administrative use only and hence solely used by designated database administrators (DBAs). Learning to be a DBA is such a large subject, it requires a book of its own just to cover its scope! Needless to say, our coverage of Database Administration topics will be kept to a minimum.

The ALTER Statements

As its name suggests, ALTER changes an object in a database. Here's an example ALTER statement:

```
ALTER TABLE teams DROP COLUMN conference
```

The keyword DROP identifies what's being dropped, or removed, from the table. In this example, the teams table is being altered by removing the conference column. Once the column is dropped, it's no longer part of the table.

Note that if we tried to run the same ALTER statement for a second time, a syntax error would occur because the database cannot remove a column that does not exist from a table. Syntax errors can arise from more than just the improper construction of the SQL statement using keywords, identifiers, and constants. Many syntax errors arise from attempting to alter what are perceived (wrongly) to be the current structure or current contents of the table.

The DROP Statement

The DROP statement—to round out our trio of basic DDL statements—drops, removes, deletes, obliterates, cancels, blows away, and/or destroys the object it is dropping. After the DROP statement has been run, the object is gone.

The syntax is as simple as it can be:

```
DROP TABLE teams
```

To summarize, the Data Definition Language statements CREATE, ALTER, and DROP allow us to manage database objects like tables and columns. In fact, they can be very effective when used together, such as when you need to start over.

Starting Over

Database development is usually iterative. Or rather, when building and testing your table (or tables—there is seldom only one) you will often find yourself repeating one of the following patterns:

▓ CREATE, then test

First, you create a table. Then you test it, perhaps by running some SELECT queries, to confirm that it works. The table is so satisfactory that it can be used exactly as it is, indefinitely. If only life were like this more often ...

CREATE, then test ... ALTER, then test ... ALTER, then test ...

You create and test a table, and it's good enough to be used regularly, such as when your web site goes live. You alter it occasionally, to make small changes. Small changes are easier than larger changes, especially if much code in the application depends on a particular table structure.

CREATE, then test ... DROP, CREATE, then test ...

After creating and testing a table the first time, you realize it's wrong. Or perhaps the table has been in use for some time, but is no longer adequate. You need to drop it, change your DDL, create it again (except that it's different now), and then test again.

Dropping and recreating, or starting over, becomes much easier using an SQL **script**. A script is a text file of SQL statements that can be run as a batch to create and populate database objects. Maintaining a script allows you to start over easily. Improvements in the design—new tables, different columns, and so on—are incorporated into the SQL statements, and when the script is run, these SQL statements create the objects using the new design. Appendix C contains SQL scripts used for the sample applications in this book. These scripts and more are available to download from the web site for this book, at: http://www.sitepoint.com/books/sql1/.

Data Manipulation Language

In the last section, we covered the three main SQL statements used in Data Definition Language. These were CREATE, ALTER, and DROP, and they are used to manage database objects like tables and columns.

Data Manipulation Language has three similar statements: INSERT, UPDATE, and DELETE. These statements are used to manage the data within our tables and columns.

Remember the earlier CREATE statement example:

```
CREATE TABLE teams
(
   id           INTEGER      NOT NULL  PRIMARY KEY,
   name         VARCHAR(37)  NOT NULL,
   conference   VARCHAR(2)   NULL
)
```

This statement creates a table called teams that has three columns, pictured in Figure 1.2.

teams		
id	name	conference

Figure 1.2. The teams table

Once the table has been created, we say it exists. And once a table exists we may place our data in it, and we need a way to manage that data. We want to use the table the way it's currently structured, so DDL is irrelevant for our purposes here (that is, changes aren't required).

Instead, we need the three DML statements, INSERT, UPDATE, and DELETE.

INSERT, UPDATE, and DELETE

Until we put data into it, the table is empty. Managing our data may be accomplished in several ways: adding data to the table, updating some of the data, inserting some more data, or deleting some or all of it. Throughout this process, the table structure stays the same. Just the table contents change.

Let's start by adding some data.

The INSERT Statement

The INSERT DML statement is similar to the CREATE DDL statement, in that it creates a new object in the database. The difference is that while CREATE creates a new table and defines its structure, INSERT creates a new row, inserting it and the data it contains into an existing table.

The INSERT statement inserts one or more rows. Here is our first opportunity to see rows in action. Here is how to insert a row of data into the teams table:

```
INSERT INTO teams
  ( id , name , conference )
VALUES
  ( 9 , 'Riff Raff' , 'F' )
```

The important part to remember, with our tabular structure in mind, is that the INSERT statement inserts *entire rows*. An INSERT statement should contain two comma-separated lists surrounded by parentheses. The first list identifies the columns in the new row into which the constants in the second list will be inserted. The first column named in the first list will receive the first constant in the second list, the second column has the second constant, and so on. *There must be the same number of columns specified in the first list as constants given in the second, or an error will occur.*

In the above example, three constants, 9, 'Riff Raff', and 'F' are specified in the VALUES clause. They are inserted, into the id, name, and conference columns respectively of a single new row of data in the teams table. Strings, such as 'Riff Raff', and 'F', are surrounded by single quotes to denote their beginning and end. We'll look at strings in more detail in Chapter 9.

You are allowed (but it would be unusual) to write this INSERT statement as:

```
INSERT INTO teams
  ( conference , id , name )
VALUES
  ( 'F' , 9 , 'Riff Raff' )
```

We noted earlier that the database itself doesn't care about the order of the columns within a table; however, it's common practice to order the columns in an INSERT statement in the order in which they were created for our own ease of reference. As long as we make sure that we list columns and their intended values in the correct corresponding order, this version of the INSERT statement has exactly the same effect as the one preceding it.

Sometimes you may see an `INSERT` statement like this:

```
INSERT INTO teams
VALUES
  ( 9 , 'Riff Raff' , 'F' )
```

This is perhaps more convenient, because it saves typing. The list of columns is *assumed*. The columns in the new row being inserted are populated according to their perceived position within the table, based on the order in which they were originally added when the table was created. However, we must supply a value for every column in this variation of `INSERT`; if we aren't supplying a value for each and every column, which happens often, we can't use it. If you do, the perceived list of columns will be longer than the list of values, and we'll receive a syntax error.

My advice is to always specify the list of column names in an `INSERT` statement, as in the first example. It makes things much easier to follow.

Finally, to insert more than one row, we could use the following variant of the `INSERT` statement:

```
INSERT INTO teams
  ( conference , id , name )
VALUES
  ( 'F' , 9 , 'Riff Raff' ),
  ( 'F' , 37 , 'Havoc' ),
  ( 'C' , 63 , 'Brewers' )
```

This example shows an `INSERT` statement that inserts three rows of data, and the result can be seen in Figure 1.3. Each row's worth of data is specified within a set of parentheses, known as a **row constructor**, and each row constructor is separated by a comma.

teams		
id	name	conference
9	Riff Raff	F
37	Havoc	F
63	Brewers	C

Figure 1.3. The result of the `INSERT` statement: three rows of data

Next up, we want to change some of our data. For this, we use the UPDATE statement.

A Note on Multiple Row Constructors

While the syntax in the above example, where one INSERT statement inserts multiple rows of data, is valid SQL, not every database system allows the INSERT statement to use multiple row constructors; those that do allow it include DB2, PostgreSQL, and MySQL. If your database system's INSERT statement allows only one row to be inserted at a time, as is the case with SQL Server, simply run three INSERT statements, like so:

```
INSERT INTO teams
    ( id , conference , name )
VALUES
    ( 9 , 'F' , 'Riff Raff' )
;
INSERT INTO teams
    ( id , conference , name )
VALUES
    ( 37 , 'F' , 'Havoc' )
;
INSERT INTO teams
    ( id , conference , name )
VALUES
    ( 63 , 'C' , 'Brewers' )
;
```

Notice that a semicolon (;) is used to separate SQL statements when we're running multiple statements like this, not unlike its function in everyday language. Syntactically, the semicolon counts as a keyword in our scheme of keywords, identifiers, and constants. The comma, used to separate items in a list, does too.

The UPDATE Statement

The UPDATE DML statement is similar to the ALTER DDL statement, in that it produces a change. The difference is that, whereas ALTER changes the structure of a table, UPDATE changes the data contained within a table, while the table's structure remains the same.

Let's pretend that the team Riff Raff is changing conferences so we need to update the value in the conference column from F to E; we'll write the following UPDATE statement:

```
UPDATE
   teams
SET
   conference = 'E'
```

The above statement would change the value of the conference column in every row to E. This is not really what we wanted to do; we only wanted to change the value for one team. So we add a WHERE clause to limit the rows that will be updated:

Teams_04_UPDATE.sql *(excerpt)*

```
UPDATE
   teams
SET
   conference = 'E'
WHERE
   id = 9
```

As shown in Figure 1.4, the above example will update only one value. The UPDATE clause alone would change the value of the conference column in every row, but the WHERE clause limits the change to just the one row: where the id column has the value 9. Whatever value the conference column had before, it now has E after the update.

teams

id	name	conference
9	Riff Raff	F
37	Havoc	F
63	Brewers	C

teams

id	name	conference
9	Riff Raff	E
37	Havoc	F
63	Brewers	C

Figure 1.4. Updating a row in a table

Sometimes, we'll want to update values in multiple rows. The UPDATE statement will set column values for every row specified by the WHERE clause. The classic example, included in every textbook (so I simply had to include it too, although it isn't part of any of our sample applications), is:

```
UPDATE
  personnel
SET
  salary = salary * 1.07
WHERE
  jobgrade <= 4
```

Here, everyone is scoring a 7% raise, but only if their jobgrade is 4 or less. The UPDATE statement operates on multiple rows simultaneously, but only on those rows specified by the WHERE clause.

Notice that the existing value of the salary column is used to determine the new value of the salary column. UPDATE operates on each row independently of all others, which is exactly what we want, as it's likely that the salary values are different for most rows.

Finally, there is the DELETE statement.

The **DELETE** Statement

The DELETE DML statement is similar to the DROP DDL statement, in that it removes objects from the database. The difference is that DROP removes a table from the database, while DELETE removes entire rows of data from a table, but the table continues to exist:

```
                                                   Teams_05_DELETE.sql (excerpt)

DELETE
FROM
  teams
WHERE
  id = 63
```

Once again, like the UPDATE statement, the scope of the DELETE statement is every row which satisfies the WHERE clause. If there is no WHERE clause, all the rows are deleted and the table is left empty; it has a structure, but no rows.

Finally, we are ready to meet the SELECT statement.

The **SELECT** Statement

The SELECT statement is usually called a **query**. Informally, all SQL statements are sometimes called queries (as in "I ran the DELETE query and received an error"), but the SELECT statement is truly a query because all it does is retrieve information from the database.

When we run a SELECT query against the database, it can retrieve data from one or more tables. Exactly how the data in multiple tables is combined, collated, compared, summarized, sorted, and presented—*by a single query*—is what makes SQL so wonderful.

The power is outstanding. The simplicity is amazing. SQL allows us to produce complex, customized information with a minimum of fuss, in a declarative, non-procedural way, using a small number of keywords.

SELECT is our fourth DML statement, although the operation it performs on the data is simply to retrieve it. Nothing is changed in the database. This is one reason why I prefer to discuss SELECT separately from the other three DML statements. Another is that it breaks up the pleasant symmetry between the DDL and DML statements:

▨ DDL: CREATE, ALTER, DROP

▨ DML: INSERT, UPDATE, DELETE ... and SELECT

The SELECT Retrieves Data

A simple SELECT statement has two parts, or **clauses**. Both are mandatory:

```
SELECT expression(s) involving keywords, identifiers, and constants
FROM tabular structure(s)
```

The purpose of the SELECT statement is to retrieve data from the database:

▨ the SELECT clause specifies what you want to retrieve, and

▨ the FROM clause specifies where to retrieve it from.

The SELECT clause consists of one or more expressions involving keywords, identifiers, and constants. For example, this SELECT clause contains one expression, consisting of a single identifier:

```
SELECT
  name
FROM
  teams
```

In this case the expression in the SELECT clause is name, which is a column name. However, the SELECT clause can contain many expressions, simply by listing them one after another, using commas as separators. For example, we may want to return the contents of several columns from rows in the teams table:

```
SELECT
  id, name, conference
FROM
  teams
```

In addition, each expression can be more complex, consisting of formulas, calculations, and so on. Ultimately then, the SELECT clause can be fairly complex, but it gives us the ability to include everything we need to return from the database. We examine the SELECT clause in Chapter 7.

Similarly, the FROM clause can be multifaceted. The FROM clause specifies the tabular structure(s) that contain the data that we want to retrieve. In this chapter we've seen sample queries in which the FROM clause specified a single table; complexity in the FROM clause occurs when more than one table is specified. I suggested earlier that tabular structures are one of the secrets to mastering SQL. We'll cover them in detail in Chapter 3.

We'll have an overview of the SELECT statement and its optional clauses, WHERE, GROUP BY, HAVING, and ORDER BY, in Chapter 2, and then look in detail at each of its clauses in chapters of their own.

The SELECT Statement Produces a Tabular Result Set

One important fact to remember about SELECT is that the result of running a SELECT query is *a table*.

When your web application (whether it is written in PHP, Java, or any other application language) runs a SELECT query, the database system returns a tabular structure, and the application handles it accordingly, as rows and columns of data. The query might return a list of selected items in a shopping cart, or posts in active forums threads, or whatever your web application needs to retrieve from your database.

We say that the SELECT statement produces a tabular **result set**. A result set is not actually a table in the database; it is *derived from* one or more tables in the database, and delivered, as tabular data, to your application.

One final introduction will complete our introduction to SQL: a comment about standard SQL.

Standard SQL

> The nice thing about standards is that there are so many to choose from.
>
> —Andrew S. Tanenbaum

In the beginning, I mentioned that SQL is a standard language. SQL has been standardized both nationally and internationally. If you are relatively new to SQL, *do not* look for any information on the standard just yet; you're only going to confuse yourself. The SQL standard is exceedingly complex. The standard is also not freely available; it must be purchased from the relevant standards organisations.

The fact that the standard exists, though, is very important, and not just because it makes the skill of knowing SQL *highly* portable. The SQL standard is being adopted, in increasing measures, by all relational database systems. New database software releases always seem to mention some specific features of the standard that are now supported.

So as well as your knowledge of using simple SQL to produce comprehensive results being portable, there is a better chance that your next project's database system will actually support the techniques that you already know. The industry and its practitioners are involved in a positive feedback loop.

And yet, there are differences between standard SQL and the SQL supported by various database systems you'll encounter—sometimes maddeningly so. These variations in the language are called **dialects** of SQL. Numerous proprietary extensions to standard SQL have been invented for the various different database systems. These extensions can be considerable, occasionally pointless, often counterintuitive, and sometimes obscure.

There is only one sane way to cope.

Read The Fine Manual

> Never memorize what you can look up in books.
>
> —Albert Einstein

There will be occasions throughout this book where I'll suggest referring to the manual. This will be the manual for your particular database system, whatever it may be. All database systems have manuals—often a great many—but fortunately, most are of interest only to DBAs. The one you want is typically called *SQL Reference.*

After more than 20 years of writing SQL, I still need to look up certain parts of SQL. Granted, I have committed most of standard SQL to memory, but there are always nuances that trip me up, and new features to learn, and all those proprietary extensions …

Finding the Manual

Appendix A gives links for downloading and installing five popular database systems: MySQL, PostgreSQL, SQL Server, DB2, and Oracle. In addition, links are given to the online SQL reference manuals for each of these systems.

Make it easy on yourself. Bookmark the SQL reference manual on your computer, on your company server, or on the Web. Be prepared for syntax errors. But be reassured that they're easy to fix, if you know where to look in the manual.

Wrapping Up: an Introduction to SQL

In this chapter, we covered *lots* of ground. I hope you're not feeling completely overwhelmed. The purpose of the whirlwind tour was simply to put the SQL language into the perspective that a typical web developer needs; there are SQL statements for everything you need to do, and, all things considered, these statements are quite simple.

The two basic types of SQL statement are:

- Data Definition Language (DDL) statements: CREATE, ALTER, DROP
- Data Manipulation Language (DML) statements: INSERT, UPDATE, DELETE … and SELECT

If you're building your own database, you'll need to know DDL, but you should have some experience using DML first. Designing databases is the subject of the last three chapters in this book.

As mentioned earlier, SQL is mainly about queries, and the SELECT statement is *where it's at*. Chapter 2 begins our in-depth look at the SELECT statement, providing an overview of its six clauses.

An Overview of the **SELECT** Statement

In Chapter 1, our quick introduction to SQL, we briefly met the main SQL statements that we will encounter as web developers:

- CREATE, ALTER, DROP
- INSERT, UPDATE, DELETE ... and
- *SELECT*

In this chapter, we'll begin our more detailed look into SQL with an overview of the SELECT statement.

The **SELECT** Statement

The SELECT statement's single purpose is to retrieve data from our database and return it to us in a tabular result set. In Chapter 1, we saw some of its syntax:

```
SELECT expression(s) involving keywords, identifiers, and constants
FROM tabular structure(s)
```

The SELECT and FROM clauses are mandatory; what we didn't reveal in Chapter 1 is that the SELECT statement can include optional clauses used to filter, group, and sort the returned results. Let's expand our SELECT statement syntax to include the optional clauses:

```
SELECT expression(s) involving keywords, identifiers, and constants
FROM tabular structure(s)
[WHERE clause]
[GROUP BY clause]
[HAVING clause]
[ORDER BY clause]
```

We've placed each optional clause in square brackets, [...], to denote their optional status. Don't worry—we'll introduce the WHERE, GROUP BY, HAVING, and ORDER clauses in short order.

The examples we are about to discuss are fairly simple, so this chapter will be like a quick review and set the stage for the chapters that follow. We'll look at each of its clauses in turn, with some very simple examples.

 Trying Out Your SQL

If you are new to SQL, you may wish to try out the sample SELECT statements on your own computer or testing system. You don't have to—you can simply read along—but trying out the sample SQL for yourself is a good way to begin. Appendix C contains the SQL that creates and populates the databases used for the sample applications in this book. These scripts and more are available to download from the web site for this book, located at http://www.sitepoint.com/books/sql1/.

The SELECT and FROM Clauses

Only the first two clauses of the SELECT statement—the SELECT and FROM clauses—are mandatory, so our first SELECT statement will use only these.

To illustrate our SELECT statements, we'll use another sample application. In Chapter 1, the application was Teams and Games (although we used only the teams table). In this chapter, the application is a content management system, or CMS for short. Remember, the sample applications are described in Appendix B.

Content management system is a generic term that simply means a system to store, manage, and retrieve content. In most cases this means the content of a web site.

(One example is Wordpress, a popular blogging tool.[1] Our sample content management system isn't anywhere near as sophisticated.) So before we can examine and discuss our sample SELECT statements, we need to have some sample tables to select from.

Content Management System

The database portion of our CMS will be designed to store articles. (The application portion of the CMS will handle the processes of adding and updating these articles, and displaying them on web pages. We'll focus on the database portion, and how it interacts with the application.) We'll want our content—the articles—to be stored in the database, *and* also displayed on web pages after being retrieved with SQL. One way to display them would be as individual articles shown in their entirety on their own web page. Another way might be a list of articles, such as on a site map. We might also expect to have a search page to search for articles, and so on.

Actually, they don't have to be articles. The database tables in our CMS will work just as easily for stories, news updates, blog posts, journal/diary entries ...

Yes, that's it—let's call them *entries*.

The entries Table

Our CMS database, and our first sample SELECT statement, begins with a single table, the entries table. This consists of columns that hold data about each entry (article or story), such as its title, the date it was created, and so on. Figure 2.1 shows a simplified version of the table. If you look at the CREATE statement for this table in the section called "Content Management System" in Appendix C, you'll see it has extra columns: an id column to store an ID number, an updated column for the date each entry was last updated, and a content column to store the text content of each entry. But for now we'll just keep it simple.

---

[1] Others are listed here: http://en.wikipedia.org/wiki/List_of_content_management_systems

category	title	created
angst	What If I Get Sick and Die?	2008-12-30
humor	Uncle Karl and the Gasoline	2009-02-28
advice	Be Nice to Everybody	2009-03-02
humor	Hello Statue	2009-03-17
science	The Size of Our Galaxy	2009-04-03

Figure 2.1. The simplified CMS `entries` table

Now it's finally time to look at our first sample `SELECT` statement. This one returns two columns of data from the `entries` table:

```
SELECT
  title, category
FROM
  entries
```

Figure 2.2 shows the tabular result set produced by the above query.

title	category
What If I Get Sick and Die?	angst
Uncle Karl and the Gasoline	humor
Be Nice to Everybody	advice
Hello Statue	humor
The Size of Our Galaxy	science

Figure 2.2. First results—two columns of data

So our first simple `SELECT` statement produced a list of all entries, showing the title and category of each. To put it a slightly different way, the query *select*ed two columns *from* a table, producing a tabular result set.

Displaying Query Results on a Web Page

The result set produced by our first sample query could be displayed on a web page using the following HTML:

```
<h2>List of Articles</h2>
<ul>
  <li>What If I Get Sick and Die? (category: angst)</li>
  <li>Uncle Karl and the Gasoline (category: humor)</li>
  <li>Be Nice to Everybody (category: advice)</li>
  <li>Hello Statue (category: humor)</li>
  <li>The Size of Our Galaxy (category: science)</li>
</ul>
```

It could also be displayed using `<table>`, `<tr>`, `<th>`, and `<td>` tags. After all, this is tabular data.

The general strategy for displaying query results on a web page is to use the application programming language to loop over the rows in the result set, generating one or more lines of output HTML for each row.

The specific mechanics of how this is achieved depends, of course, on which application programming language you're using. The point of the example is to show a simple result set—several rows of data, in two columns—being used to create a web page.

Our first SELECT statement was a very simple case of the more general syntax:

```
SELECT expression(s) involving keywords, identifiers, and constants
  FROM tabular structure(s)
```

In our first SELECT statement, the SELECT clause's *expressions* were two simple columns, `title` and `category`, and the FROM clause's *tabular structure* was the `entries` table.

Both the SELECT clause and the FROM clause are mandatory in the SELECT statement. The next clause is optional, but it lets us be more selective about which rows to return.

The **WHERE** Clause

The WHERE clause is optional, but when it's used, it acts as a *filter*.

To demonstrate, let's take the simple query from the previous section and change it slightly. We'll select some different columns, and add a WHERE clause:

```
                                          CMS_02_Display_an_Entry.sql (excerpt)
SELECT
   title, created, content
FROM
   entries
WHERE
   id = 524
```

Notice that the WHERE clause specifies a **condition**, an expression that can be evaluated by the database system as either true, false, or in some cases, indeterminable. The condition—in this case, whether the value of the id column is 524—is evaluated against each row of the table. If, the condition is true for any given row, that row is kept in the query result set and returned when the SELECT statement finishes executing. If the condition is false for a row, it is not included as part of the results.

Figure 2.3 shows the result set produced by this query.

title	created	content
Uncle Karl and the Gasoline	2009-02-28	When I was about nine or ten, my uncle Karl, who ...

Figure 2.3. Long field values may appear abridged (but never are)

Note that the result set consists of only one row. There are three columns in the result set, corresponding to the three columns in the SELECT clause, but just one row.

The third column, the content column, is a TEXT column, containing text that includes line breaks. However, it's still just one value, even though it's quite a longish value to be revealed in its entirety—as shown in Figure 2.3. (TEXT columns can actually hold values up to several megabytes in size, or even larger. We'll learn how to choose data types when designing tables in Chapter 9.)

What's the significance of the result set consisting of only one row? It means that the WHERE clause has *filtered out* all the rows of the entries table *except* for the row that has a value of 524 in the id column. This is the id value that was assigned to the entry Uncle Karl and the Gasoline. Notice that it was not necessary for the SELECT clause to include the id column, even though the id column was specified in the WHERE clause.

To recap, the WHERE clause specifies conditions which are evaluated against the rows of the table; these conditions act as a filter that determines which rows are returned in the query result set.

We have now covered half of the clauses of the SELECT statement:

```
SELECT expression(s) involving keywords, identifiers, and constants
FROM tabular structure(s)
[WHERE clause]
[GROUP BY clause]
[HAVING clause]
[ORDER BY clause]
```

We'll look at the next two clauses together, because that's how they are used.

The GROUP BY and HAVING Clauses

The main purpose of the GROUP BY clause is to have the database examine every row in the set generated by the FROM clause, and then filtered by the WHERE clause if there is one; then it groups them together by the values of one or more of their columns to produce a single new row (per group). This process is known as **aggregation**. The GROUP BY clause identifies the column(s) that are used to determine the groups. Each group consists of one or more rows, while all the rows in each group have the *same values* in the grouping column(s). The difficulty with this concept is understanding that, after the grouping operation has completed, the original rows are no longer available. Instead, **group rows** are produced. A group row is a new row created to represent each group of rows found during the aggregation process.

Here's an example of a GROUP BY query:

```
                                    CMS_03_Count_Entries_by_Category.sql (excerpt)
SELECT
   category, COUNT(*) AS articles
FROM
   entries
GROUP BY
   category
```

The grouping column in this example is category, as specified by the GROUP BY clause. Each row in the entries table is assigned to a specific group based on the value of its category column. Then the magic happens. The grouping, or aggregation, of the rows in each group produces one row per group. Another way to think about this is that grouping collapses each group's rows, producing a single group row for every group.

Figure 2.4 shows the result set produced by the query above.

category	articles
advice	1
angst	1
humor	2
science	1

Figure 2.4. Results for a GROUP BY query

The column called articles contains a count of the number of table rows in each group. The name articles was assigned as a *column alias* for the expression COUNT(*). This expression is an example of an *aggregate function*; one that counts numbers of rows. We'll meet this function later on in the section called "Aggregate Functions" in Chapter 7.

This sample GROUP BY query produces a count of articles in each category. This seems innocuous enough, because it's so simple. The GROUP BY clause proves difficult for some people only when more complex queries are attempted. Grouping is a concept that takes a bit of effort to understand, so Chapter 5 focuses entirely on that.

The HAVING clause works in conjunction with the GROUP BY clause, by specifying conditions which filter the group rows. As a simple example, let's add a HAVING clause to the previous example:

CMS_03_Count_Entries_by_Category.sql *(excerpt)*

```
SELECT
  category, COUNT(*) AS articles
FROM
  entries
GROUP BY
  category
HAVING
  COUNT(*) > 1
```

The filtering effect of the HAVING clause is apparent when you see the result, as shown in Figure 2.5.

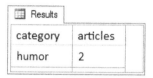

Figure 2.5. Grouped results filtered by a HAVING clause

The HAVING clause operates only on group rows, and acts as a filter on them in exactly the same way that the WHERE clause acts as a filter on table rows. In this case, it filters out rows in which the number of articles is one or fewer.

We'll conclude our quick review of the SELECT statement with the ORDER BY clause.

The ORDER BY Clause

The purpose of the ORDER BY clause is to return the tabular result set in a specific sequence. It works just as you would expect it to; it *sorts the rows* in the result set.

Here's an example:

```
                                    CMS_04_Entries_Sorted_Latest_First.sql (excerpt)

SELECT
    title, created
FROM
    entries
ORDER BY
    created DESC
```

The ORDER BY clause in the example above specifies that the results should be sorted into a descending sequence based on the created column. This is a typical requirement in a CMS context—to show latest articles first. The special keyword DESC determines that it's a descending sequence. (There's a corresponding ASC keyword, but ASC is the default and is optional.) Figure 2.6 shows the result set produced by the above query.

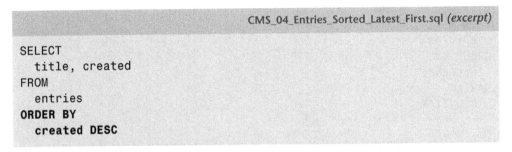

Figure 2.6. Results ordered on the created column

You may specify multiple columns in the ORDER BY clause, to give multiple levels of sequencing. Another way to describe this is to say that the ORDER BY clause allows any number of major and minor sort keys.

For instance, consider the following ORDER BY clause:

```
ORDER BY
  category, created DESC
```

In the above example, the result rows are sorted first on the category column from A to Z, and then the entries within each category are sorted on the created column, from most recent to least recent, as shown in Figure 2.7.

title	category	created
Be Nice to Everybody	advice	2009-03-02
What If I Get Sick and Die?	angst	2008-12-30
Hello Statue	humor	2009-03-17
Uncle Karl and the Gasoline	humor	2009-02-28
The Size of Our Galaxy	science	2009-04-03

Figure 2.7. Results ordered on multiple columns

Wrapping Up: the **SELECT** Statement

To summarize, in this chapter we conducted a quick review of the clauses of the SELECT statement. The syntax for the SELECT statement is:

```
SELECT expression(s) involving keywords, identifiers, and constants
FROM tabular structure(s)
[WHERE clause]
[GROUP BY clause]
[HAVING clause]
[ORDER BY clause]
```

■ The SELECT and FROM clauses are mandatory, and the other clauses are optional. SELECT determines the columns in the result set, and FROM specifies where the data comes from.

■ The WHERE clause, when present, acts as a filter on the rows retrieved from the table.

- The GROUP BY clause, when present, performs grouping or aggregation, in effect collapsing all the rows retrieved from the table to produce one group row per group. HAVING filters group rows in the same way that WHERE filters table rows.

- The ORDER BY clause is used if the rows are to be sorted and returned in a specific sequence.

Now we are ready to begin our detailed, in-depth analysis of the SELECT statement, starting with the FROM clause in Chapter 3.

Chapter **3**

The **FROM** Clause

In Chapter 2, we broke the SELECT statement down into its various clauses, but looked at each clause only briefly. In this chapter, we'll begin our more detailed look at the SELECT statement, starting with the FROM clause.

The FROM clause can be simple, and it can also be quite complex. In all cases, though, the important point about the FROM clause is that it *produces a tabular structure*. This tabular structure is referred to as the *result set* of the FROM clause. You may also see it referred to as an intermediate result set, an intermediate tabular result set, or an intermediate table. But, no matter whether the SELECT query retrieves data from one table, from many tables, or from other, similar tabular structures, the result is always the same—the FROM clause produces a tabular structure.

In this chapter we'll review the common types of FROM clause that we might encounter in web development.

Why Start with the FROM Clause?

To begin writing a SELECT statement, my strategy is to skip over the SELECT clause for the time being, and write the FROM clause first. Eventually, we'll need to input some expressions into the SELECT clause and we might also need to use WHERE, GROUP BY, and the other clauses too. But there are good reasons why we should always start with the FROM clause:

- If we get the FROM clause wrong, the SQL statement will always return the wrong results. It's the FROM clause that produces the tabular structure, the starting set of data on which all other operations in a SELECT statement are performed.

- The FROM clause is the first clause that the database system looks at when it parses the SQL statement.

Parsing an SQL Statement

Whenever we send an SQL statement to the database system to be executed, the first action that the system performs is called **parsing**. This is how the database system examines the SQL statement to see if it has any syntax errors. First it divides the statement into its component clauses; then it examines each clause according to the syntax rules for that clause. Contrary to what we might expect, the database system parses the FROM clause first, rather than the SELECT clause.

For example, suppose we were to attempt to run the following SQL statement, in which we have misspelled teams as *teans*:

Teams_06_FROM_Teans.sql *(excerpt)*

```
SELECT
  id, name
FROM
  teans
WHERE
  conference = 'F'
```

In this case, the FROM clause refers to a non-existing table, so there is an immediate syntax error. If the database system *were* to parse the SELECT clause first, it would need to examine the table definitions of all the tables in the database, looking for one that might contain two columns called name and id. In fact, it's quite common for a database to have several tables with two columns called name and id. Confusion could ensue and the database would require more information from us to know which table to retrieve name and id from. Hence why the database system parses the FROM clause first, and this is the first clause we think about as well.

FROM One Table

We've already seen the FROM clause with a single table. In Chapter 1, we saw the FROM clause specify the teams table:

```
SELECT
  id, name
FROM
  teams
```

In Chapter 2, we saw the FROM clause specify the entries table:

```
SELECT
  title, category
FROM
  entries
```

This form of the FROM clause is as simple as it gets. There must be at least one tabular structure specified, and a single table fits that requirement. When we want to retrieve data from more than one table at the same time however, we need to start using *joins*.

FROM More than One Table Using JOINs

A **join** relates, associates, or combines two tables together. A join starts with two tables, then combines—or joins— them together in one of several different ways, producing a single tabular structure (as the result of the join). Actually, the verb *to join* is very descriptive of what happens, as we'll see in a moment.

The way that the tables are joined—the *type* of join—is specified in the FROM clause using special keywords *as well as* the keyword JOIN. There are several different types of join, which I'll describe briefly, so that you can see how they differ. Then we'll look at specific join examples, using our sample applications.

Types of Join

A join combines the rows of two tables, based on a rule called a **join condition**; this compares values from the rows of both tables to determine which rows should be joined.

There are three basic types of join:

- *inner join*, created with the INNER JOIN keywords
- *outer join*, which comes in three varieties:
    - LEFT OUTER JOIN
    - RIGHT OUTER JOIN
    - FULL OUTER JOIN
- *cross join*, created with the CROSS JOIN keywords

To visualize how joins work, we're going to use two tables named A and B, as shown in Figure 3.1.

A
102
104
106
107

B
101
102
104
106
108

Figure 3.1. Tables A and B

On Tables A and B

These tables are actually oversimplified, because they blur the distinction between table and column names. The join condition actually specifies the columns that must match. Further, it's unusual for tables to have just one column.

Don't worry about what A and B might actually represent. They could be anything. The idea in the following illustrations is for you to focus your attention on the *values* in the rows being joined. Table A has one column called a and rows with values

102, 104, 106, and 107. Table B has one column called b and rows with values 101, 102, 104, 106, and 108.

To Create Tables A and B

The SQL script to create tables A and B is available in the download for the book. The file is called **test_01_illustrated.sql**.

The Inner Join

For an **inner join**, *only rows satisfying the condition in the ON clause are returned.* Inner joins are the most common type of join. In most cases, such as the example below, the ON clause specifies that two columns must have matching values. In this case, if the value (of column a) in a row from one table (A) is equal to the value (of column b) in a row from the other table (B), the join condition is satisfied, and those rows are joined:

```
                                              test_01_illustrated.sql (excerpt)
SELECT
    a, b
FROM
    A INNER JOIN B
        ON a=b
```

Figure 3.2 illustrates how this works.

Figure 3.2. A INNER JOIN B

As you can see, a row from A is joined to a row from B when their values are equal. Thus values 102, 104, and 106 are returned in the result set. Value 107 in A has no match in B, and therefore is not included in the result set. Similarly, the values 101 and 108 in B have no match in A, so they're not included in the result set either. If it's easier to do so, you can think of it as though the matching rows are actually concatenated into a single longer row on which the rest of the SELECT statement then operates.

Outer Joins

Next, we'll look at **outer joins**. Outer joins differ from inner joins in that *unmatched rows can also be returned*. As a result, most people say that an outer join includes rows that don't match the join condition. This is correct, but might be a bit misleading, because outer joins do include all rows that match. Typical outer joins have many rows that match, and only a few that don't.

There are three different types of outer join: left, right, and full. We'll start with the left outer join.

The Left Outer Join

For a **left outer join**, *all rows from the left table are returned, regardless of whether they have a matching row in the right table.* Which one's the left table, and which one's the right table? These are simply the tables mentioned to the left and to the right of the OUTER JOIN keywords. For example, in the following statement, **A** is the left table and **B** is the right table and a left outer join is specified in the **FROM** clause:

```
                                                    test_01_illustrated.sql (excerpt)

SELECT
   a, b
FROM
   A LEFT OUTER JOIN B
      ON a=b
```

Figure 3.3 shows the results of this join. Remember—left outer joins return all rows from the left table, together with matching rows of the right table, *if any*.

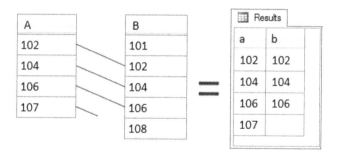

Figure 3.3. A LEFT OUTER JOIN B

Notice that all values from A are returned. This is because A is the left table. In the case of 107, which did not have a match in B, we see that it is indeed included in the results, but there is *no value* in that particular result row from B. For the time being, it's okay just to think of the value from *B* as missing—which, of course, for *107* it is.

The Right Outer Join

For a **right outer join**, *all rows from the right table are returned, regardless of whether they have a match in the left table*. In other words, a right outer join works exactly like a left outer join, except that all the rows of the right table are returned instead:

```
                                        test_01_illustrated.sql (excerpt)

SELECT
  a, b
FROM
  A RIGHT OUTER JOIN B
    ON a=b
```

In the example above, A is still the left table and B is still the right table, because that's where they are mentioned in relation to the OUTER JOIN keywords. Consequently, the result of the join contains all the rows from table B, together with matching rows of table A, *if any*, as shown in Figure 3.4.

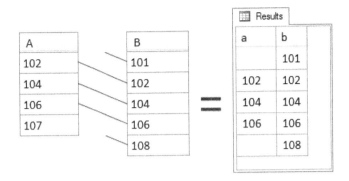

Figure 3.4. A RIGHT OUTER JOIN B

The right outer join is the reverse of the left outer join. With the same tables in the same positions—A as the left table and B as the right table—the results of the right outer join are very different from those of a left outer join. This time, all values from B are returned. In the case of 101 and 108, which did not have a match in A, they are indeed included in the results, but there is *no value* in their particular result rows from A. Again, those values from A are missing, but the row is still returned.

The Full Outer Join

For a **full outer join**, *all rows from both tables are returned, regardless of whether they have a match in the other table.* In other words, a full outer join works just like left and right outer joins, except this time all the rows of *both* tables are returned. Consider this example:

```
SELECT
   a, b
FROM
   A FULL OUTER JOIN B
      ON a=b
```

Once again, A is the left table and B is the right table, although this time it doesn't really matter. Full outer joins return all rows from both tables, together with matching rows of the other table, *if any*, as shown in Figure 3.5.

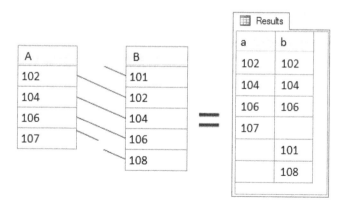

Figure 3.5. A FULL OUTER JOIN B

The full outer join is a *combination* of left and right outer joins. (More technically, if you remember your set theory from mathematics at school, it's the union of the results from the left and right outer joins.) Matching rows are—of course—included, but rows that have no match from either table, are also included.

The Difference between Inner and Outer Joins

The results of an outer join will *always* equal the results of the corresponding inner join between the two tables *plus* some unmatched rows from either the left table, the right table, or both—depending on whether it is a left, right, or full outer join, respectively.

Thus the difference between a left outer join and a right outer join is simply the difference between whether the left table's rows are all returned, with or without matching rows from the right table, or whether the right table's rows are all returned, with or without matching rows from the left table.

A full outer join, meanwhile, will always include the results from both left and right outer joins.

The Cross Join

For a **cross join**, *every row from both tables is returned, joined to every row of the other table, regardless of whether they match.* The distinctive feature of a cross join is that it has *no* ON clause—as you can see in the following query:

```
SELECT
   a, b
FROM
   A CROSS JOIN B
```

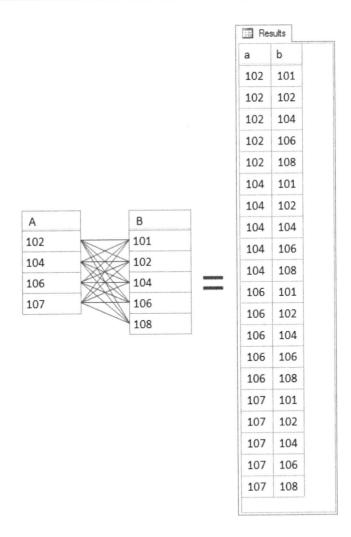

Figure 3.6. A CROSS JOIN B

Cross joins can be very useful but are exceedingly rare. Their purpose is to produce a tabular structure containing rows which rep all possible combinations of two sets of values (in our example, columns from two tables) as shown in Figure 3.6; this can be useful in generating test data or looking for missing values.

 ## Old–Style Joins

There's another type of join, which has a comma-separated list of tables in the FROM clause, with the necessary join conditions in the WHERE clause; this type of join is sometimes called the "old-style" join, or "comma list" join, or "WHERE clause" join. For example, for the A and B tables, it would look like this:

```
SELECT
    a, b
FROM
    A, B
WHERE
    a=b
```

These old-style joins can only ever be inner joins; the other join types are only possible with very proprietary and confusing syntax, which the database system vendors themselves caution is deprecated. Compare this with the recommended syntax for an INNER JOIN:

```
SELECT
    a, b
FROM
    A INNER JOIN B
        ON a=b
```

You may see these old-style joins *in the wild* but I'd caution you against writing them yourself. *Always* use JOIN syntax.

To recap our quick survey of joins, there are three basic types of join and a total of five different variations:

- inner join
- left outer join, right outer join, and full outer join
- cross join

Now for some more realistic examples.

Real World Joins

Chapter 2 introduced the Content Management System `entries` table, which we'll continue to use in the following queries to demonstrate how to write joins. Figure 3.7 shows some—but not all—of its contents. The `content` column, for example, is missing.

entries		
category	title	created
angst	What If I Get Sick and Die?	2008-12-30
humor	Uncle Karl and the Gasoline	2009-02-28
advice	Be Nice to Everybody	2009-03-02
humor	Hello Statue	2009-03-17
science	The Size of Our Galaxy	2009-04-03

Figure 3.7. The entries table

Within our CMS web site, the aim is to give each category its own area on the site, linked from the site's main menu and front page. The science area will contain all the entries in the science category, the humor area will contain all the entries in the humor category, and so on, as shown in Figure 3.8. To this end, each entry is given a category, stored in the `category` column of each row.

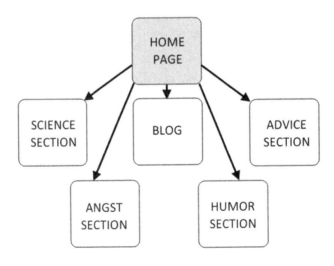

Figure 3.8. A suggested CMS site structure

The main category pages themselves would need more than just the one word category name that we see in the entries table. Site visitors will want to understand what each section is about, so we'll need a more descriptive name for each category. But where to store this in the site? We could *hardcode* the longer name directly into each main section page of the web site. A better solution, however, would be to save the names in the database. Another table will do the job nicely, and so we create the categories table for this purpose; we'll give it two columns—category and name—as shown in Figure 3.9.

categories	
category	name
advice	Gentle Words of Advice
angst	Stories from the Id
blog	Log On to My Blog
humor	Humorous Anecdotes
science	Our Spectacular Universe

Figure 3.9. The categories table

The category column is the **key** to each row in the categories table. It's called a key because the values in this column are unique, and are used to identify each row. This is the column that we'll use to join to the entries table. We'll learn more about designing tables with keys in Chapter 10. Right now, let's explore the different ways to join the categories and entries tables.

 ## Creating the Categories Table

The script to create the categories table can be found in Appendix C and in the download for the book in a file called **CMS_05_Categories_INNER_JOIN_Entries.sql**.

Inner Join: Categories and Entries

The first join type we'll look at is an inner join:

```
                         CMS_05_Categories_INNER_JOIN_Entries.sql (excerpt)

SELECT
    categories.name, entries.title, entries.created
FROM
    categories
    INNER JOIN entries
        ON entries.category = categories.category
```

Figure 3.10 shows the results of this query.

name	title	created
Gentle Words of Advice	Be Nice to Everybody	2009-03-02
Stories from the Id	What If I Get Sick and Die?	2008-12-30
Humorous Anecdotes	Uncle Karl and the Gasoline	2009-02-28
Humorous Anecdotes	Hello Statue	2009-03-17
Our Spectacular Universe	The Size of Our Galaxy	2009-04-03

Figure 3.10. The results of the inner join

Let's walk through the query clause by clause and examine what it's doing, while comparing the query to the results it produces. The first part of the query to look at, of course, is the FROM clause:

```
FROM
    categories
    INNER JOIN entries
        ON entries.category = categories.category
```

The categories table is joined to the entries table using the keywords INNER JOIN. The ON clause specifies the join condition, which dictates how the rows of the two tables must match in order to participate in the join. It uses **dot notation** (*table-name.columnname*) to specify that rows of the categories table will match rows of the `entries` table only when the values in their `category` columns are equal. We'll look in more detail at dot notation later in this chapter.

Figure 3.11 shows in detail how the result set of the query is produced by the inner join of the `categories` table to the `entries` table. Because it's an inner join, each of the rows of the `categories` table is joined only to the rows of the `entries` table that have matching values in their respective `category` columns.

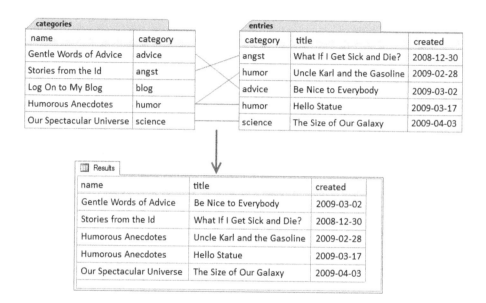

Figure 3.11. The inner join in detail

Some of the Entries Table is Hidden

The `entries` table actually has several additional columns that are not shown: `id`, `updated`, and `content`. These columns are also available, but were omitted to keep the diagram simple. In fact, the diagram would've been quite messy if the content column had been included, as it contains multiple lines of text. Since these columns were not mentioned in the query at all, including them in the diagram might have made it confusing. Some readers would surely ask, "Hey, where did these come from?"

Regarding the matching of rows of the `categories` and `entries` tables, notice that:

- The `categories` row for `humor` matched two `entries` rows, and both instances of matched rows are in the results, with the name of the `humor` category appearing twice.

- The `categories` row for `blog` matched no `entries` rows. Consequently, as this is an inner join, this category does not appear in the results.

- The other `categories` rows matched one `entries` row each, and these matched rows are in the result.

Stating these observations in a slightly different way, we can see that a single row in the `categories` table can match no rows, one row, or more than one row in the `entries` table.

One-to-Many Relationships

The *more than one* aspect of the relationship between a row in the `categories` table and matching rows in the `entries` table is the fundamental characteristic of what we call a **one-to-many relationship**. Each (one) category can have multiple (many) entries.

Even though a given category (`blog`) might have no matching entries, and only one of the categories (`humor`) has more than one entry, the relationship between the categories and entries tables is still a one-to-many relationship in structure. Once the tables are fully populated with live data, it's likely that all categories will have many entries.

Looking at this relationship from the other direction, as it were, we can see that each entry can belong to only one category. This is a direct result of the category column in the entries table having only one value, which can match only one category value in the categories table. Yet more than one entry can match the same category, as we saw with the `humor` entries. So a one-to-many relationship is also a many-to-one relationship. It just depends on the *direction* of the relationship being discussed.

Now we've examined the FROM clause and seen how the INNER JOIN and its ON condition have specified how the tables are to be joined, we can look at the SELECT clause:

```
SELECT
    categories.name
, entries.title
, entries.created
```

As you would expect, the SELECT clause simply specifies which columns from the result of the inner join are to be included in the result set.

 Leading Commas

Notice that the SELECT clause has now been written with one line per column, using a convention called *leading commas*; this places the commas used to separate the second and subsequent items in a list at the *front* of their line. This may look unusual at first, but the syntax is perfectly okay; remember, new lines and white space are ignored by SQL just as they are by HTML. Experienced developers may be more used to having trailing commas at the end of the lines, like this:

```
SELECT
    categories.name,
    entries.title,
    entries.created
```

I use leading commas as a coding style convention to make SQL queries more readable and maintainable. The importance of readability and maintainability can't be overstated. For example, see if you can spot the two coding errors in this hypothetical query:

```
SELECT
    first_name,
    last_name,
    title
    position,
    staff_id,
    group,
    region,
FROM
    staff
```

Now see if you can spot the coding errors here:

```
SELECT
  first_name
, last_name
, title
  position
, pay_scale
, group
, region
,
FROM
  staff
```

The query is missing a comma in the middle of the column list and has an un-needed, additional comma at the end of the list. In which example were the errors easier to spot?

In addition, leading commas are easier to handle if you edit your SQL in a text editor with the keyboard. Sometimes you need to move or delete a column from the SELECT clause, and it's easier to select (highlight) the single line with the keyboard's Shift and Arrow keys. Similarly, removing the last column requires also removing the trailing comma from the previous line, which is easy to forget. A *dangling* comma in front of the FROM keyword is a common error that's difficult to make using leading commas.

All Columns Are Available after a Join

In any join, all columns of the tables being joined are available to the SELECT query, even if they're not used by the query. Let's look at our inner join again:

```
SELECT
  categories.name
, entries.title
, entries.created
FROM
  categories
    INNER JOIN entries
      ON entries.category = categories.category
```

In most join queries, tables being joined usually contain more columns than those mentioned in the SELECT clause. This is true here too; the entries table has other columns not mentioned in the query. We haven't included them in Figure 3.11 just to keep the figure simple. Although the figure is correct, it could be construed as slightly misleading, because it shows only the result set of the query, rather than the tabular structure produced by the inner join.

Figure 3.12 expands on the actual processing of the query and shows the tabular structure that's produced by the FROM clause and the inner join; it includes the two category columns—one from each table. This tabular structure, the intermediate table, is produced by the database system as it performs the join, and held temporarily for the SELECT clause.

Figure 3.12. How an inner join is actually processed

When a Join is Executed in a Query

Two important points come out of the analysis of our first example join query:

- A join produces an intermediate tabular result set;
- The SELECT clause occurs *after* the FROM clause and operates on the intermediate result set.

At the beginning of this chapter, I mentioned that the FROM clause is the first clause that the database system parses when we submit a query. If there are no syntax errors, the database system goes ahead and executes the query. Well, it turns out that the FROM clause is the first clause that the database system executes, too.

You could consider the execution of a join query as working in the following manner. First, the database system produces an intermediate tabular result set based on the join specified in the FROM clause. This contains all the columns from both tables. Then the database system uses the SELECT clause to select only the specified columns from this intermediate result set, and extracts them into the final tabular structure that is returned as the result of the query.

Qualifying Column Names

Finally, let's take one more look at our inner join query:

```
                                          CMS_05_Categories_INNER_JOIN_Entries.sql (excerpt)
SELECT
    categories.name
, entries.title
, entries.created
FROM
    categories
        INNER JOIN entries
            ON entries.category = categories.category
```

Each of the column names used in this query is **qualified** by its table name, using **dot notation**, where the table name precedes the column name with a dot between them.

Qualifying column names is mandatory when there is more than one instance of the same column name in a query. (These would be from different tables, of course; more than one instance of the same column name in a single table is not possible, as all columns within a table must each have unique names.) If you don't uniquely identify each of the columns that have the same name but are in different tables, you will receive a syntax error about ambiguous names. This applies whether the query makes reference to both columns or not; every single reference must be qualified.

When there is only one instance of the column name in the query, then qualifying column names becomes optional. Thus, we could have written the following and be returned the same result set:

```
SELECT
   name
, title
, created
FROM
   categories
     INNER JOIN entries
        ON entries.category = categories.category
```

However, it's a good idea to qualify all column names in this situation because when you look at the SELECT clause, you can't always tell which table each column comes from. This can be especially frustrating if you're only remotely familiar with the tables involved in the query, such as when you're troubleshooting a query written by another person (or even by yourself, a few months ago).

 ### Always Qualify Every Column in a Join Query

Even though some or even all columns may not need to be qualified within a join query, qualifying every column in a multi-table query is part of good SQL coding style, because it makes the query easier for us to understand.

In a way, qualifying column names makes the query **self-documenting**: it makes it obvious what the query is doing so that it's easier to explain in documentation.

Table Aliases

Another way to qualify column names is by using **table aliases**. A table alias is an alternate name assigned to a table in the query. In practice, a table alias is often shorter than the table name. For example, here's the same inner join using table aliases:

```
SELECT
  cat.name
, ent.title
, ent.created
FROM
  categories AS cat
    INNER JOIN entries AS ent
      ON ent.category = cat.category
```

Here, the `categories` table has been assigned the alias `cat`, and the `entries` table has been assigned the alias `ent`. You're free to choose any names you wish; the table aliases are temporary, and are valid only for the duration of the query. Some people like to use single letters as table aliases when possible, because it reduces the number of characters in the query and so makes it easier to read.

The only caveat in using table aliases is that once you have assigned an alias to a table, you can no longer use the table name to qualify its columns *in that query*; you must use the alias name consistently throughout the query. Once the query is complete however, you're free to refer to the original table by its full name again, the same alias, or even a different alias; the point here being that a table alias is defined only for the duration of the query that contains it.

Left Outer Join: Categories and Entries

Continuing our look at join queries, the left outer join query we'll examine is exactly the same as the inner join query we just covered, except that it uses LEFT OUTER JOIN as the join keywords:

CMS_06_Categories_LEFT_OUTER_JOIN_Entries.sql *(excerpt)*

```
SELECT
  categories.name
, entries.title
, entries.created
```

```
FROM
   categories
      LEFT OUTER JOIN entries
         ON entries.category = categories.category
```

Figure 3.13 shows the results of the above query.

name	title	created
Gentle Words of Advice	Be Nice to Everybody	2009-03-02
Stories from the Id	What If I Get Sick and Die?	2008-12-30
Log On to My Blog		
Humorous Anecdotes	Uncle Karl and the Gasoline	2009-02-28
Humorous Anecdotes	Hello Statue	2009-03-17
Our Spectacular Universe	The Size of Our Galaxy	2009-04-03

Figure 3.13. The results of the left outer join query

The only difference between this left outer join query and the preceding inner join query is the inclusion of one additional row—for the category with the name Log On to My Blog—in the result set. The additional row is included because the query uses an outer join. Specifically, it's a left outer join, and therefore all of the rows of the left table, the categories table, must be included in the results. The left table, you may recall, is simply the table that is mentioned to the left of the LEFT OUTER JOIN keywords. Figure 3.14 shows the process of the join and selection in more detail.

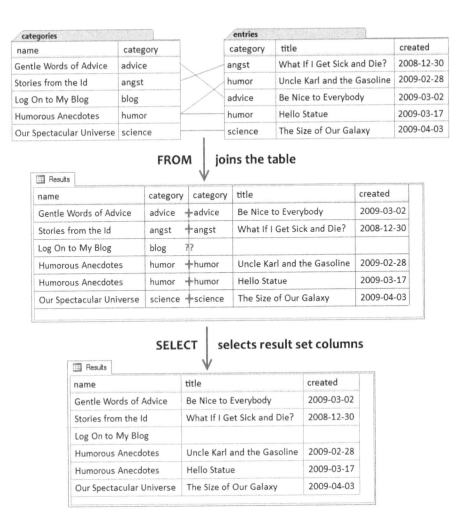

Figure 3.14. How a left outer join query is actually processed

To make it more obvious which table is the left one and which table is the right one, we could write the join without line breaks and spacing so `categories` is more obviously the left table in this join:

```
FROM categories LEFT OUTER JOIN entries
```

Let's take another look at the results of our left outer join, because there is one more important characteristic of outer joins that I need to point out.

An Application for Left Outer Joins: a Sitemap

Looking at the results of our LEFT OUTER JOIN query, it's easy enough to see how they could form the basis of a sitemap for the CMS. For example, the HTML for the sitemap that can be produced by these query results might be:

```
<h2>Gentle Words of Advice</h2>
<ul>
  <li>Be Nice to Everybody (2009-03-02)</li>
</ul>


<h2>Stories from the Id</h2>
<ul>
  <li>What If I Get Sick and Die? (2008-12-30)</li>
</ul>


<h2>Log On to My Blog</h2>


<h2>Humorous Anecdotes</h2>
<ul>
  <li>Hello Statue (2009-03-17)</li>
  <li>Uncle Karl and the Gasoline (2009-02-28)</li>
</ul>


<h2>Our Spectacular Universe</h2>
<ul>
  <li>The Size of Our Galaxy (2009-04-03)</li>
</ul>
```

If you're an experienced web developer, you can probably see how you'd make the transformation from query results to HTML using your particular application language.

Notice that the Log On to My Blog category has no entries, but is included in the result (because it's a left outer join). Therefore, the application logic needs to detect this situation, and not produce the unordered list (<ul>) tags for entries in that category. Without going into the details of application programming logic, let me just say that it's done by detecting the NULLs in the entries columns of that result row.

Outer Joins Produce NULLs

Our left outer join includes rows from the left table that have no match in the right table, as shown in Figure 3.13. So what exactly are the values in the `title` and `created` columns of the `blog` category result row? Remember, these columns come from the `entries` table.

The answer is: they are **NULL**.

NULL is a special value in SQL, which stands for the *absence* of a value. In a left outer join, columns that come from the right table for unmatched rows from the left table are NULL in the result set. This literally means that there is no value there, which makes sense because there is no matching row from the right table for that particular row of the left table.

Working with NULLs is part of daily life when it comes to working with databases. We first came across NULL (albeit briefly) in Chapter 1, where it was used in a sample CREATE TABLE statement and we'll see NULL again throughout the book.

Right Outer Join: Entries and Categories

The following right outer join query produces exactly the same results as the left join query we just covered:

```
                        CMS_06_Categories_LEFT_OUTER_JOIN_Entries.sql (excerpt)

SELECT
  categories.name
, entries.title
, entries.created
FROM
  entries
    RIGHT OUTER JOIN categories
      ON entries.category = categories.category
```

But how can this be?

Hopefully you've spotted the answer: I've switched the order of the tables! In the right outer join query, I wrote:

```
FROM entries RIGHT OUTER JOIN categories
```

In the preceding left outer join query, I had:

```
FROM categories LEFT OUTER JOIN entries
```

The lesson to be learned from this deviousness is simply that left and right outer joins are completely equivalent, it's just a matter of which table is the **outer table**: the one which will have all of its rows included in the result set. Because of this, many practitioners avoid writing right outer queries, converting them to left outer joins instead by changing the order of the tables; that way the table from which all rows are to be returned is always on the left. Left outer joins seem to be much easier to understand than right outer joins for most people.

Right Outer Join: Categories and Entries

What if I hadn't switched the order of the tables in the preceding right outer join? Suppose the query had been:

```
                        CMS_07_Categories_RIGHT_OUTER_JOIN_Entries.sql (excerpt)
SELECT
    categories.name
, entries.title
, entries.created
FROM
    categories
        RIGHT OUTER JOIN entries
            ON entries.category = categories.category
```

This time, as in our first left outer join, the `categories` table is on the left, and the `entries` table is on the right. Figure 3.15 shows the results of this query are the same as the results from our earlier inner join.

name	title	created
Stories from the Id	What If I Get Sick and Die?	2008-12-30
Humorous Anecdotes	Uncle Karl and the Gasoline	2009-02-28
Gentle Words of Advice	Be Nice to Everybody	2009-03-02
Humorous Anecdotes	Hello Statue	2009-03-17
Our Spectacular Universe	The Size of Our Galaxy	2009-04-03

Figure 3.15. The results of the right outer join query

How can this be? Is this more deviousness? No, not this time; the reason is because it's the actual contents of the tables. Remember, a right outer join returns all rows of the right table, with or without matching rows from the left table. The `entries` table is the right table, but in this particular instance, every entry has a matching category. All the entries are returned, and there are no unmatched rows.

So it wasn't really devious to show that the right outer join produces the same results as the inner join, because it emphasized the rule for outer joins that all rows from the outer table are returned, with or without matching rows, *if any*. In this case, there weren't any.

To really see the right outer join in action, we'd need an entry that lacks a matching category. Let's add an entry to the `entries` table, for a new category called `computers`, as shown in Figure 3.16.

entries

category	title	created
angst	What If I Get Sick and Die?	2008-12-30
humor	Uncle Karl and the Gasoline	2009-02-28
advice	Be Nice to Everybody	2009-03-02
humor	Hello Statue	2009-03-17
science	The Size of Our Galaxy	2009-04-03
computers	Windows Media Center Rocks	2009-04-29

Figure 3.16. A new addition to the entries table

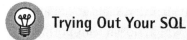

Trying Out Your SQL

The INSERT statement that adds this extra row to the entries table can be found in the section called "Content Management System" in Appendix C.

Figure 3.17 shows that when we re-run the right outer join query with the new category, the results are as expected.

name	title	created
Stories from the Id	What If I Get Sick and Die?	2008-12-30
Humorous Anecdotes	Uncle Karl and the Gasoline	2009-02-28
Gentle Words of Advice	Be Nice to Everybody	2009-03-02
Humorous Anecdotes	Hello Statue	2009-03-17
Our Spectacular Universe	The Size of Our Galaxy	2009-04-03
	Windows Media Center Rocks	2009-04-29

Figure 3.17. The results of the right outer join query—take two

This time, we see the unmatched entry in the query results, because there's no row in the categories table for the computers category.

Full Outer Join: Categories and Entries

Our next example join query is the full outer join. The full outer join query syntax, as I'm sure you can predict, is remarkably similar to the other join types we've seen so far:

CMS_08_Categories_FULL_OUTER_JOIN_Entries.sql (excerpt)

```
SELECT
  categories.name
, entries.title
, entries.created
FROM
  categories
    FULL OUTER JOIN entries
      ON entries.category = categories.category
```

This time, the join keywords are FULL OUTER JOIN, but an unfortunate error happens in at least one common database system. In MySQL, which doesn't support FULL OUTER JOIN despite it being standard SQL, the result is a syntax error: SQL Error: You have an error in your SQL syntax; check the manual that corresponds to your MySQL server version for the right syntax to use near 'OUTER JOIN entries ON …'

Figure 3.18 shows the result in other database systems that do support FULL OUTER JOIN.

name	title	created
Gentle Words of Advice	Be Nice to Everybody	2009-03-02
Stories from the Id	What If I Get Sick and Die?	2008-12-30
Log On to My Blog		
Humorous Anecdotes	Uncle Karl and the Gasoline	2009-02-28
Humorous Anecdotes	Hello Statue	2009-03-17
Our Spectacular Universe	The Size of Our Galaxy	2009-04-03
	Windows Media Center Rocks	2009-04-29

Figure 3.18. The results of the full outer join query

Notice that the result set includes unmatched rows from both the left and the right tables. This is the distinguishing feature of full outer joins that we saw earlier; both tables are outer tables, so unmatched rows from both are included. It's for this reason that full outer joins are rare in web development as there are few situations that call for them. In contrast, inner joins and left outer joins are quite common.

UNION Queries

If your database system does not support the FULL OUTER JOIN syntax, the same results can be obtained by a slightly more complex query, called a **union**. Union queries are not joins per se. However, most people think of the results produced by a union query as consisting of two results sets concatenated or appended together. UNION queries perform a join only in a very loose sense of the word.

Let's have a look at a union query:

```
                              CMS_09_Left_outer_join_UNION_right_outer_join.sql (excerpt)
SELECT
  categories.name
, entries.title
, entries.created
FROM
  categories
    LEFT OUTER JOIN entries
      ON entries.category = categories.category
UNION
SELECT
  categories.name
, entries.title
, entries.created
FROM
  categories
    RIGHT OUTER JOIN entries
      ON entries.category = categories.category
```

As you can see, the left outer join and right outer join queries we saw earlier in this chapter have simply been concatenated together using the UNION keyword. A union query consists of a number of SELECT statements combined with the UNION operator. They're called **subselects** in this context because they're *subordinate* to the whole UNION query; they're only *part* of the query, rather than being a query executed on its own. Sometimes they're also called subqueries, although this term is generally used for a more specific situation, which we shall meet shortly.

When executed, a UNION operation simply combines the result sets produced by each of its subselect queries into a single result set. Figure 3.19 shows how this works for the example above:

I mentioned earlier that a join operation can best be imagined as actually concatenating a row from one table onto the end of a row from the other table—a horizontal concatenation, if you will. The union operation is therefore like a vertical concatenation—a second result set is appended onto the end of the first result set.

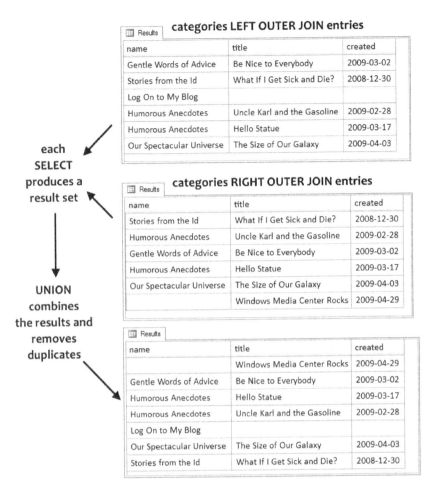

each
SELECT
produces a
result set

UNION
combines
the results and
removes
duplicates

categories LEFT OUTER JOIN entries

name	title	created
Gentle Words of Advice	Be Nice to Everybody	2009-03-02
Stories from the Id	What If I Get Sick and Die?	2008-12-30
Log On to My Blog		
Humorous Anecdotes	Uncle Karl and the Gasoline	2009-02-28
Humorous Anecdotes	Hello Statue	2009-03-17
Our Spectacular Universe	The Size of Our Galaxy	2009-04-03

categories RIGHT OUTER JOIN entries

name	title	created
Stories from the Id	What If I Get Sick and Die?	2008-12-30
Humorous Anecdotes	Uncle Karl and the Gasoline	2009-02-28
Gentle Words of Advice	Be Nice to Everybody	2009-03-02
Humorous Anecdotes	Hello Statue	2009-03-17
Our Spectacular Universe	The Size of Our Galaxy	2009-04-03
	Windows Media Center Rocks	2009-04-29

name	title	created
	Windows Media Center Rocks	2009-04-29
Gentle Words of Advice	Be Nice to Everybody	2009-03-02
Humorous Anecdotes	Hello Statue	2009-03-17
Humorous Anecdotes	Uncle Karl and the Gasoline	2009-02-28
Log On to My Blog		
Our Spectacular Universe	The Size of Our Galaxy	2009-04-03
Stories from the Id	What If I Get Sick and Die?	2008-12-30

Figure 3.19. How a union query works

The interesting feature is that duplicates are removed. You can see the duplicates easily enough—they are entire rows in which every column value is identical. The reason that duplicates are produced in this example is due to both of the sub-selects—the left outer join and the right outer join—returning rows from the same two tables which match the the same join conditions. Thus, matched rows are returned by both subselects, creating duplicate rows in the intermediate results. Only the unmatched rows are not duplicated.

You might wonder why UNION removes duplicates; the answer is simply that it's designed that way. It's how the UNION operator is supposed to work.

UNION and UNION ALL

Sometimes it's important to retain all rows produced by a union operation, and not have the duplicate rows removed. This can be accomplished by using the keywords UNION ALL instead of UNION.

- UNION removes duplicate rows. Only one row from each set of duplicate rows is included in the result set.
- UNION ALL retains all rows produced by the subselects of the union, maintaining duplicate rows.

UNION ALL is significantly faster because the need to search for duplicate rows—in order to remove them—is redundant.

The fact that our union query removed the duplicate rows means that the above union query produces the same results as the full outer join. Of course, this example was contrived to do just that.

There is more to be said about union queries, but for now, let's finish this section with one point: union queries, like join queries, produce a *tabular structure* as their result set.

Views

A **view** is another type of database object that we can create, like a table. Views are insubstantial, though, because they don't actually store data (unlike tables). Views are SELECT statements (often complex ones) that have been given a name for ease of reference and reuse, and can be used for many purposes:

- They can *customize* a SELECT statement, by providing column aliases.

- They can be an alias to the result set produced by the SELECT statement in their definition. If the SELECT statement in the view contains joins between a number of tables, they are effectively *pre-joined* by the database in advance of a query against the view. All this second query then sees is a single table to query against. This is probably the most important benefit of using views.

- They can enforce security on the database. Users of a database might be restricted from looking at the underlying tables altogether; instead, they might only be granted access to views. The classic example is the employees table, which contains columns like `name`, `department`, and `salary`. Because of the confidential nature of salary, very few people are granted permission to access such a table directly; rather, a special view is made available that excludes the confidential columns.

To demonstrate, here's how you define the inner join query used earlier as a view:

CMS_10_CREATE_VIEW.sql *(excerpt)*

```
CREATE VIEW
  entries_with_category
AS
SELECT
  entries.title
, entries.created
, categories.name AS category_name
FROM
  entries
    INNER JOIN categories
      ON categories.category = entries.category
```

This statement defines a view called `entries_with_category`. It uses the `AS` keyword to associate the name `entries_with_category` with the `SELECT` statement which defines the view. With the view defined, we can query it as if it were a table:

CMS_10_CREATE_VIEW.sql *(excerpt)*

```
SELECT
  title
, category_name
FROM
  entries_with_category
```

Of course, it's not a table—the view itself does not actually store the result set produced by its `SELECT` statement. The use of the view name here works by executing the view's underlying `SELECT` statement, storing its results in an intermediate table, and using that table as the result of the `FROM` clause. The results of the above query, shown in Figure 3.20, are quite familiar.

title	category_name
What If I Get Sick and Die?	Stories from the Id
Uncle Karl and the Gasoline	Humorous Anecdotes
Be Nice to Everybody	Gentle Words of Advice
Hello Statue	Humorous Anecdotes
The Size of Our Galaxy	Our Spectacular Universe

Figure 3.20. Selecting from a view

This result set is similar to the result set produced by the inner join query which defines the view. Notice that only two columns have been returned, because the SELECT statement which uses the view in its FROM clause (as opposed to the SELECT statement which defines the view) only asked for two. Also, notice that a column alias called category_name was assigned to the categories table's name column in the view definition; this is the column name that must be used in any SELECT statement which uses the view, and it's the column name used in the result set.

One particular implication of the view definition is that *only* the columns defined in the view's SELECT statement are available to any query that uses the view. Even though the entries table has a content column, this column is unknown to the view and will generate a syntax error if referenced in a query using the view.

Views in Web Development

How do views relate to our day-to-day tasks as web developers?

- When working on a large project in a team environment, you may be granted access to views only, not the underlying tables. For example, a Database Administrator (DBA) may have built the database, and you're just using it. You might not even be aware that you're using views. This is because, syntactically, both tables and views are used in the FROM clause in exactly the same way.

- When you build your own database, you may wish to create views for the sake of convenience. For example, if you often need to display a list of entries and their category on different pages within the site, it's a lot easier to write FROM entries_with_category than the underlying join.

Subqueries and Derived Tables

We started this chapter by examining the FROM clause, working our way up from simple tables through the various types of joins. We briefly saw a UNION query and its subselects, and we've also seen how views make complex join expressions easier to use. To finish this chapter, we'll take a quick look at **derived tables**. Here's an example:

```
                                      CMS_11_Derived_tables.sql (excerpt)

SELECT
  title
, category_name
FROM
  ( SELECT
      entries.title
    , entries.created
    , categories.name AS category_name
    FROM
      entries
        INNER JOIN categories
          ON categories.category = entries.category
  ) AS entries_with_category
```

The **derived table** here is the entire SELECT query in parentheses (the parentheses are required in the syntax, to delimit the enclosed query). A derived table is a common type of **subquery**, which is a query that's subordinate to—or nested within—another query (much like the subselects in the union query).

It looks familiar, too, doesn't it? This subquery is the same query used in the entries_with_categories view defined in the previous section. Indeed, just as every view needs a name, every derived table must be also given a name, also using the AS keyword (on the last line) to assign the name entries_with_category as a table alias for the derived table. With these similarities in mind, derived tables are often also called **inline views**. That is, they define a tabular structure—the result set produced by the subquery—directly inline in (or within) the SQL statement, and the tabular structure produced by the subquery, in turn, is used as the source of the data for the FROM clause of outer or main query.

In short, anything which produces a tabular structure can be specified as a source of data in the FROM clause. Even a UNION query, which we discussed briefly, can also be used in the FROM clause, if it's specified as a derived table; the entire UNION query would go into the parentheses that delimit the derived table.

Derived tables are incredibly useful in SQL. We'll see several of them throughout the book.

Wrapping Up: the FROM Clause

In this chapter, we examined the FROM clause, and how it specifies the source of the data for the SELECT statement. There are many different types of tabular structures that can be specified in the FROM clause:

- single tables
- joined tables
- views
- subqueries or derived tables

Finally—and this is one of the key concepts in the book—not only does the FROM clause specify one or more tabular structures from which to extract data, but the result of the execution of the FROM clause is also another tabular structure, referred to as the *intermediate result set* or *intermediate table*. In general, this intermediate table is produced first, before the SELECT clause is processed by the database system.

In the Chapter 4, we'll see how the WHERE clause can be used to filter the tabular structure produced by the FROM clause.

The WHERE Clause

The WHERE clause is the second clause of the SQL SELECT statement that we'll now discuss in detail. The FROM clause, which we covered in the previous chapter, introduced the central concept behind SQL: *tabular structures*. It is the first clause that the database system parses and executes when we run an SQL query. A tabular structure is *produced* by the FROM clause using tables, joins, views, or subqueries. This tabular structure is referred to as the *result set* of the FROM clause.

The WHERE clause is optional. When it's used, it acts as a filter on the rows of the result set produced by the FROM clause. The WHERE clause allows us to obtain a result set containing only the data that we're really interested in, when the entire result set would contain more data than we need. In addition, the WHERE clause, more than any other, determines whether our query performs efficiently.

Conditions

The WHERE clause is all about true conditions. Its basic syntax is:

```
WHERE condition that evaluates as TRUE
```

As we've learned, a condition is some expression that can be evaluated by the database system. The result of the evaluation will be one of TRUE, FALSE, or UNKNOWN. We'll cover these one at a time, starting with TRUE.

Conditions that are True

A typical WHERE condition looks like this:

```
SELECT
  name
FROM
  teams
WHERE
  id = 9
```

In this query, as we now know from Chapter 3, the result set produced by the FROM clause consists of all the rows of the teams table. After the FROM clause has produced a result set, the WHERE clause filters the result set rows, using the id = 9 condition. The WHERE clause evaluates the truth of the condition *for every row*, in effect comparing each row's id column value to the constant value 9. The really neat part about this evaluation is that it happens *all at once*. You may think of the database system actually examining one value after another, and this mental picture is really not too far off the mark. There is, however, no sequence involved; it is just as correct to think of it happening on all rows simultaneously.

So what is the end result? No doubt you're ahead of me here. Amongst all the rows in the teams table, the given condition will be TRUE for only one of them. For all the other rows, it will be FALSE. All the other rows are said to be *filtered out* by the WHERE condition.

When "Not True" is Preferable

But what if we want *the other rows*? Suppose we want the names of all teams who aren't team 9?

There are two approaches:

- WHERE NOT id = 9

  The NOT keyword inverts the truthfulness of the condition.

- WHERE id <> 9

  This is the *not equals* comparison operator. You can, if you wish, read it as "less than *or* greater than," and this would be accurate.

Notice what we've done in both cases. We want all rows where the condition id = 9 is FALSE, but we wrote the WHERE clause in such a way that the condition evaluates as TRUE for the rows we want, in keeping with the general syntax:

```
WHERE condition that evaluates as TRUE
```

More specifically, the WHERE clause condition can include a NOT keyword, and, as we shall see in a moment, several conditions that are logically connected together to form a **compound condition**.

Besides TRUE and FALSE, there is one other result that's possible when a condition is evaluated in SQL: UNKNOWN.

A condition evaluates as UNKNOWN if the database system is unable to figure out whether it's TRUE or FALSE. In order to see UNKNOWN in action, we'll need a good example, and for that, we'll use yet another of our sample applications.

A Couple of MySQL Gotchas

You would expect that with a concept as simple as equals or not equals, everything should work the same way. Regrettably, MySQL handles this slightly differently to the perceived norm. Let's recap the scenario: we want all rows where **id** is not equal to **9**.

The first way is to say **NOT id = 9**, which we expect to be **TRUE** for every row except one. Unfortunately, MySQL applies the **NOT** to the **id** column value first, before comparing to **9**. In effect, MySQL evaluates it as:

```
WHERE ( NOT id ) = 9
```

MySQL—for reasons we'll not go into—treats **0** and **FALSE** interchangeably, and any other number as **TRUE**, which it equates with **1**. If **id** actually had the value of **0** (which no identifier should), then **NOT id** would be **1**. For all other values, **NOT id** would be **0**. And **0** isn't equal to **9**.

Be careful using NOT. Unless you're sure, enclose whatever comes after **NOT** in parentheses. The following will work as expected in all database systems:

```
WHERE NOT ( id = 9 )
```

A better choice is to avoid using **NOT** altogether. Just use the *not equals* operator:

```
WHERE id <> 9
```

Also, avoid using MySQL's version of the *not equals* operator, shown below:

```
WHERE id != 42
```

Note that using **!=** is specific to MySQL and incompatible with other database systems.

Shopping Carts

So far, we've seen the Teams application, briefly, in Chapter 1, and the Content Management System application, in more detail, in Chapter 2 and Chapter 3.

Our next sample application, Shopping Carts, supports an online store for a web site, where site visitors can select items from an inventory and place them into *shopping carts* when ordering. Anyone who's ever made a purchase on the Web will already be familiar with the general features of online shopping carts. In case you're thinking that shopping carts are complex—and they are—our Shopping Carts sample application is very simple in comparison to a real one. It's not meant to be industrial strength; it's just a sample application, intended to allow us to learn SQL.

The first table we'll look at in the Shopping Carts application is the `items` table. This table will contain all the items that we plan to make available for purchase online. Figure 4.1 shows the `items` table after its initial load of data.

items		
name	type	price
thingie	widgets	9.37
gadget	doodads	19.37
dingus	gizmos	29.37
gewgaw	widgets	5.00
knickknack	doodads	10.00
whatnot	gizmos	15.00
bric-a-brac	widgets	2.00
folderol	doodads	4.00
jigger	gizmos	6.00
doohickey	widgets	12.00
gimmick	doodads	9.37
dingbat	gizmos	9.37
thingamajig	widgets	
thingamabob	doodads	
thingum	gizmos	
contraption	widgets	49.95
whatchamacallit	doodads	59.95
whatsis	gizmos	

Figure 4.1. The `items` table

Notice that some of the prices are *empty* in the diagram. These empty values are actually NULL. I haven't discussed NULL in detail yet, although we met NULL briefly in Chapter 3: NULLs were returned by outer joins in the columns of unmatched rows.

To Create the `Items` Table

The SQL script to create the `items` table and add data to it is available in the download for the book. The file is called **Cart_01_Comparison_operators.sql**. It's also found in the section called "Shopping Carts" in Appendix C.

What does it mean that the price of certain items is NULL? Simply that the price for that item is not known—yet. Obviously, we can't sell an item with an unknown price, so we'll have to supply a price value for these items eventually. NULL can have several interpretations, including *unknown* and *not applicable*. In the case of outer joins, NULLs in columns of unmatched rows are best understood as *missing*. In the items table example, the price column is NULL for items to which we've not yet been assigned a price, so the best interpretation is *unknown*.

How does all this talk about NULL relate to conditions in the WHERE clause? Let's look at a sample query:

Cart_01_Comparison_operators.sql *(excerpt)*

```
SELECT
   name
, type
FROM
   items
WHERE
   price = 9.37
```

Here the WHERE clause consists of just one condition: the value of the `price` column must be 9.37 for that row to be returned in the result set. And the result set, shown in Figure 4.2, produced by this query is exactly what we'd expect.

Figure 4.2. Using a simple WHERE clause

As we learned earlier, the condition in the WHERE clause is evaluated on each row, and only those rows where the condition evaluates as TRUE are retained. So what happens when the WHERE clause is evaluated for items that have NULL in the price column? For these rows, the evaluation is UNKNOWN.

Conditions that Evaluate as UNKNOWN

A condition **evaluates as UNKNOWN** if the database system cannot figure out whether it is TRUE or FALSE. The only situations where the evaluation comes out as UNKNOWN involve NULL.

When the WHERE clause condition, price = 9.37, is evaluated for items that have NULL in the price column, the evaluation is UNKNOWN. The database system cannot determine that NULL is equal to 9.37—because NULL isn't equal to anything—and yet it also cannot determine that NULL is *not* equal to 9.37—because NULL isn't *not* equal to anything either. It's confusing, certainly, but it's just how standard SQL defines NULL. NULL is not equal to anything, not even another NULL. Any comparison involving NULL evaluates as UNKNOWN. So the result of the evaluation is UNKNOWN.

Don't let this confuse you. NULLs are tricky, but all you have to remember is that *the WHERE clause wants only those conditions which evaluate as TRUE*. Rows for which the WHERE conditions evaluate either FALSE or UNKNOWN are filtered out.

Operators

WHERE clause conditions can utilize many other operators besides equal and not equal. These other operators are mostly straightforward and work just as we would expect them to.

Comparison Operators

When making a comparison between two values, SQL—as well as being able to determine whether the values are equal—can also determine whether a value is greater than the other, or less than the other.

Here's a typical example that compares whether one number (integer or decimal) is less than another:

```
                                          Cart_01_Comparison_operators.sql (excerpt)
SELECT
   name
 , type
FROM
   items
WHERE
   price < 10.00
```

This sample query will return the name and type for any items that have a price less than ten (dollars). An item with a price of 9.37 would be included in the result set by the WHERE clause filtering operation, because 9.37 is less than 10.00.

Inequality operators also work on other data types, too. For example, you can compare two character strings:

```
WHERE name < 'C'
```

This is a perfectly good WHERE condition, which compares the values in the name column with the string 'C' and returns TRUE for all names that start with 'A' or 'B' because those name values are considered *less than* the value 'C.'

For any comparison, a database uses a natural or inherent sequencing for the type of values being compared. With this in mind, comparing which value is less than the other can be seen as determining which of the values *comes first* in the natural sequence. For numbers, it's the standard numeric sequence, (zero, one, two, etc) and for strings, it's the alphabetical, or, more correctly, the *collating sequence*.

Collations

Collations in SQL are determined by very specific rules involving *the sequence of characters in a character set*. We're accustomed to think of the English alphabet as consisting of twenty-six simple letters from A to Z. Actually, there are 52, if you count lower case letters too. But there are also a few other letters, such as the accented é in the word résumé. Obviously, é with an accent is not the same as e without an accent; they are different characters. The question now is: does résumé (a noun meaning summary) come before or after the word resume (a verb meaning to begin again)? It's the collating sequence that decides.

Collations exist to support many languages and character sets. All database systems have default collations, and these are safe to use without you even knowing about them. For more information, consult your manual for information specific to the database system you're using. You can also find general information about collating sequences at Wikipedia.[1]

Besides comparing numbers and strings, we can also compare dates using the equals and not equals operators (= and <>). For example, consider this WHERE clause:

```
WHERE created >= '2009-04-03'
```

For each row, the `created` column value is compared to the date constant value of 2009-04-03, and the row will be filtered out if the WHERE condition is not evaluated as TRUE. In other words, *earlier* dates are filtered out. We saw that the sequence for numbers is numeric (0, 1, 2, etc), and the sequence for strings is alphabetic (as defined by the collation). The sequence for date values is chronological. So 2008-12-30 comes before 2009-02-28, which comes before 2009-03-02.

Notice that the operator used in the example above is *greater than or equal to*. In total, there are six comparison operators in SQL, as shown in Table 4.1.

---

[1] http://en.wikipedia.org/wiki/Collating_sequence

Table 4.1. Comparison operators in SQL

=	equal to
<>	not equal to
<	less than
<=	less than or equal to
>	greater than
>=	greater than or equal to

Remember, these can be applied to numbers, strings, and dates, but in each case, a specific sequence is used.

The LIKE Operator

The LIKE operator implements *pattern matching* in SQL: it allows you to search for a pattern in a string (usually in a column defined as a string column), in which portions of the string value are represented by **wildcard characters**. These are a small set of symbolic characters representing one or more missing characters.

For example, consider the query:

```
                                                    Cart_02_LIKE_and_BETWEEN.sql (excerpt)

SELECT
    name
, type
FROM
    items
WHERE
    name LIKE 'thing%'
```

The results of this query are shown in Figure 4.3.

In standard SQL, LIKE has two wildcards: the percent sign (%), which stands for zero or more characters, and the underscore (_), which stands for exactly one character. Notice how in the query above, name values which satisfied the WHERE condition each start with the characters *thing*, followed by zero or more additional characters. Thus, these values match the pattern specified by the LIKE string, so the condition evaluates as TRUE.

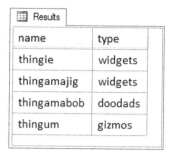

Figure 4.3. Using a wildcard in a query

The BETWEEN Operator

The purpose of the BETWEEN operator is to enable a *range test* to see whether or not a value is between two other values in its sequence of comparison. A typical example is:

```
                                          Cart_02_LIKE_and_BETWEEN.sql (excerpt)
SELECT
    name
, price
FROM
    items
WHERE
    price BETWEEN 5.00 AND 10.00
```

The way BETWEEN works here is fairly obvious. Items are included in the result set if their price is between 5.00 and 10.00, as the result set in Figure 4.4 shows.

Results

name	price
thingie	9.37
gewgaw	5.00
knickknack	10.00
jigger	6.00
gimmick	9.37
dingbat	9.37

Figure 4.4. Using a BETWEEN operator

The BETWEEN range test is actually equivalent to the following *compound condition*, in which two conditions—in this case 5.00 <= price and price <= 10.00—are combined:

```
WHERE
    5.00 <= price AND price <= 10.00
```

There are two important aspects to note here.

▪ The first is the sequence. 5.00 has to be *less than or equal to* price, and price has to be *less than or equal to* 10.00. In other words, the smaller value comes first, and the larger value comes last, with the value being tested coming between them. If the actual value does not lie between the endpoints, the BETWEEN condition evaluates as FALSE.

▪ The second important detail to notice is that the *endpoints are included*.

BETWEEN: It haz a flavr

I haz a flavr!

Here are two examples which will illustrate the *flavor* or correct usage of BETWEEN.[2] In the first example, we want to return all entries posted in the last five days:

```
WHERE
    created BETWEEN CURRENT_DATE AND CURRENT_DATE - INTERVAL 5 DAY
```

---

[2] Illustration by Alex Walker

Here, `CURRENT_DATE` is a special SQL keyword that always corresponds to the current date when the query is run. Furthermore, the `CURRENT_DATE - INTERVAL 5 DAY` expression is the standard SQL way of doing *date arithmetic* (because that's a minus sign rather than a hyphen). Yet this `WHERE` clause fails to return any rows at all, even though we know that there are rows in the table with a `created` value within the last five days. What's going on?

Let's assume that the `CURRENT_DATE` is 2009-03-20, which would mean that `CURRENT_DATE - INTERVAL 5 DAY` is 2009-03-15. The `WHERE` clause is then equivalent to:

```
WHERE
   created BETWEEN '2009-03-20' AND '2009-03-15'
```

This might look okay, but it isn't. *Syntactically*, it's fine, but *semantically*, it's flawed. The flaw can be seen more easily if we rewrite the `BETWEEN` condition using the equivalent compound condition:

```
WHERE
   '2009-03-20' <= created AND created <= '2009-03-15'
```

Now, there may be some rows with a `created` value that is greater than or equal to 2009-03-20. There may also be some rows with a `created` value that is less than or equal to 2009-03-15. However, the same `created` value, on any given row, cannot *simultaneously* satisfy both conditions. Our mistake is to have placed the larger value first. Remember, *with dates, smaller means chronologically earlier*. The original `WHERE` clause should have been written with the earlier date first, like this:

```
WHERE
   created BETWEEN CURRENT_DATE - INTERVAL 5 DAY AND CURRENT_DATE
```

Our second example of correct `BETWEEN` usage concerns the endpoints. Consider the following `WHERE` clause, intended to return all entries for February 2009:

```
WHERE
   created BETWEEN '2009-02-01' AND '2009-03-01'
```

This is fine, except that it includes entries posted on the first of March, which is outside the date range we're aiming for. Immediately, you might think to rewrite this as follows:

```
WHERE
    created BETWEEN '2009-02-01' AND '2009-02-28'
```

This is correct, but inflexible. If we wanted to generalize this so that it returns rows for any given month, we would need to calculate the last day of the month; this can become extremely hairy, as anyone can attest who's coded a general date expression that takes February 29 into consideration. The best-practice approach in these cases, then, is to abandon the BETWEEN construction and code an *open-ended upper end-point* compound condition:

```
WHERE
    '2009-02-01' <= dateposted AND dateposted < '2009-03-01'
```

Notice that the second comparison operator is solely *less than*, not less than or equal. All values of created greater than or equal to 2009-02-01 and up to, but *not* including, 2009-03-01, are returned.

The compound condition is usually written like this, for convenience:

```
WHERE
    created >= '2009-02-01' AND created < '2009-03-01'
```

The only requirement then is to calculate the date of the first day of the following month, rather than try to figure out when the last day of the month in question is.

Compound Conditions with **AND** and **OR**

Compound conditions—multiple conditions that are joined together—in the WHERE clause are common. Here's an example:

Cart_04_ANDs_and_ORs.sql *(excerpt)*

```
SELECT
    id
  , name
  , billaddr
```

```
FROM
  customers
WHERE
  name = 'A. Jones' OR 'B. Smith'
```

It's clear what is meant here—return all rows from the `customers` table that have a name value of 'A.Jones' or 'B.Smith'. Unfortunately, this produces a syntax error, because 'B.Smith', by itself, is not a condition *except in MySQL*. In MySQL the string is interpreted by itself as FALSE, so the compound condition above is equivalent to "name equals 'A.Jones' (which may or may not be true), *or* FALSE."

The correct way to write the compound condition shown above would be:

```
WHERE
  name = 'A.Jones' OR name = 'B.Smith'
```

To Create the Customers Table

The SQL script to create the `customers` table and add data to it is available in the download for the book. The file is called **Cart_04_ANDs_and_ORs.sql**. It's also found in the section called "Shopping Carts" in Appendix C.

Truth Tables

For convenience, Table 4.2 and Table 4.3 illustrate how compound conditions are evaluated.

Table 4.2. AND Truth Table

Combination	Result
TRUE AND TRUE	TRUE
TRUE AND FALSE	FALSE
FALSE AND TRUE	FALSE
FALSE AND FALSE	FALSE

Table 4.3. OR Truth Table

Combination	Result
TRUE OR TRUE	TRUE
TRUE OR FALSE	TRUE
FALSE OR TRUE	TRUE
FALSE OR FALSE	FALSE

Logically, these evaluations work just as you would expect them to. Sequence does not matter, so TRUE AND FALSE evaluates the same as FALSE AND TRUE, and TRUE OR FALSE evaluates the same as FALSE OR TRUE, as you can see. One way to remember them is that AND means *both*, while OR means *either*. With AND, *both* conditions must be TRUE for the compound condition to evaluate as TRUE, while with OR, *either* condition can be TRUE for the compound condition to evaluate as TRUE.

There are actually more complex truth tables than these, which involve the third logical possibility in SQL: UNKNOWN. However UNKNOWN, as mentioned previously, only comes up when NULLs are involved, and for the time being we shall leave them to one side in our exploration. Just keep in mind that UNKNOWN is not TRUE, and that the WHERE clause wants only TRUE to keep a row in the result set—FALSE and UNKNOWN are filtered out.

 Queens and Hearts

Let's step into a real-world application of AND and OR. An ordinary deck of playing cards consists of four suits (Spades, Hearts, Diamonds, and Clubs) of 13 cards each (Ace, 2 through 10, Jack, Queen, and King). There is only one card that is both a Queen AND a Heart. The only card that satisfies these combined conditions is the *Queen of Hearts*.

There are 16 Queens OR Hearts. Not 17. There are four Queens, and there are 13 Hearts, but only 16 Queens and Hearts in total. This is because the combined conditions—be they AND or OR—are evaluated on each card separately. If the connector is OR, then 15 of those cards will evaluate either TRUE OR FALSE or FALSE OR TRUE. Only one will evaluate TRUE AND TRUE, which is still just TRUE, and which doesn't make two cards out of one.

So there are only 16 Queens and Hearts, and we can see now that this use of *and* in the above title "Queens and Hearts" really means OR. And there is only one

Queen of Hearts, because in this term, *of* means AND. After you do it for a while, you can see SQL everywhere.

Combining AND and OR

Here's a typical WHERE clause that combines AND and OR:

```
WHERE
    customers.name = 'A.Jones' OR customers.name = 'B.Smith'
        AND items.name = 'thingum'
```

The intent of this WHERE clause is to return thingums for either A.Jones or B.Smith. However the results of this query will actually return all thingums purchased by B.Smith, and *all items* for A.Jones. It is another example of an SQL statement that is syntactically okay, but semantically flawed. In this case, the reason for the semantic error is that *AND takes precedence over OR* when they are combined.

In other words, the compound condition is evaluated *as though* it had parentheses, like this:

```
WHERE
    customers.name = 'A.Jones'
        OR ( customers.name = 'B.Smith' AND items.name = 'thingum' )
```

Do you see how that works? The AND is evaluated first, and the expression in parentheses will evaluate to TRUE only if both conditions inside the parentheses are TRUE—the customer has to be B.Smith, and the item name has to be 'thingum.' Then the OR is evaluated with the other condition, customers.name = 'A.Jones.' So no matter what the item's name is, if the customer is A.Jones, the row will be returned.

The above example should therefore be rewritten, with explicit parentheses, like this:

```
WHERE
    ( customers.name = 'A.Jones' OR customers.name = 'B.Smith' )
        AND items.name = 'thingum'
```

Use Parentheses When Mixing **AND** and **OR**

The best practice rule for combining **AND** and **OR** is always to use parentheses to ensure your intended combinations of conditions.

WHERE 1=1

You may see in a web application a WHERE clause that includes the condition 1=1 and wonder what in the world is going on. For example consider the following:

```
WHERE
   1=1
      AND type = 'widgets'
      AND price BETWEEN 10.00 AND 20.00
```

You usually find this in queries associated with search forms; it's basically a way to simplify your application code.

If you have a search form where the conditions are optional, you'll need a way of determining if a condition will require an **AND** to create a compound condition. The first condition, of course, won't require an **AND**.

So rather than complicate your application code that creates the query with logic to determine if each condition should include an **AND**, if you always start the WHERE clause with 1=1 (which always evaluates as true), you can safely add **AND** to all conditions.

There's another version of this trick using WHERE 1=0 for compound conditions using **OR**, like so:

```
WHERE
   1=0
      OR name LIKE '%Toledo%'
      OR billaddr LIKE '%Toledo%'
      OR shipaddr LIKE '%Toledo%'
```

Just like the 1=1 trick, you can safely add or remove conditions without worrying if an **OR** is required.

IN Conditions

You'll recall this example from the section on AND and OR:

```
WHERE
  ( customers.name = 'A.Jones' OR customers.name = 'B.Smith' )
    AND items.name = 'thingum'
```

There's another way to write this:

```
WHERE
  customers.name IN ( 'A.Jones' , 'B.Smith' )
    AND items.name = 'thingum'
```

In this version, we've moved the parentheses to be part of the IN condition rather than being used to control the evaluation priority of AND and OR. The IN condition syntax consists of an expression, followed by the keyword IN, followed by a list of values in parentheses. If *any* of the values in the list is *equal* to the expression, then the IN condition evaluates as TRUE. Should you wish to set the condition to check if a value is not in a list of values, you can prefix the IN condition with the NOT keyword:

```
WHERE
  NOT ( customers.name IN ( 'A.Jones', 'B.Smith' ) )
```

You could also write this as:

```
WHERE
  customers.name NOT IN ('A.Jones', 'B.Smith')
```

Note that while the NOT keyword can be used with an IN condition in these two ways, this doesn't always apply to other operators. For example, it's perfectly okay to write:

```
WHERE
  NOT ( customers.name = 'A.Jones' )
```

However, it's *not* okay to write:

```
WHERE
  customers.name NOT = 'A.Jones'
```

Another reason I prefer to place NOT in front of a parenthesized condition is that it's easier to spot it in a busy WHERE clause (that is, one which has many conditions) than a NOT keyword buried inside a condition.

IN with Subqueries

The list of values used in an IN condition may be supplied by a subquery. As we saw in Chapter 3, a subquery simply produces a tabular structure as its result set. A list of values is merely another fine example of a tabular structure, albeit a structure with only one column. Take, for example, a query that uses a subquery to provide the values for the IN condition:

Cart_06_IN_subquery.sql *(excerpt)*

```
SELECT
  name
FROM
  items
WHERE
  id IN (
    SELECT
      cartitems.item_id
    FROM
      carts
        INNER JOIN cartitems
          ON cartitems.cart_id = carts.id
    WHERE
      carts.customer_id = 750
  )
```

The subquery returns only one column, the item_id column from the cartitems table. There's a WHERE clause in the subquery, which filters out all carts that don't belong to customer 750. The values in the item_id column, but only for the filtered cart items, become the list of values for the IN condition; that way the outer or main query will return the names of all items for the selected customer.

This example again illustrates how to understand what a query with a subquery is doing: read the subquery first, to understand what it produces, and then read the outer query, to see how it uses the subquery result set.

Correlated Subqueries

Since this chapter is all about the WHERE clause, this is the appropriate context in which to discuss the concept of **correlation**. In this context, a subquery correlates (co-relates) to its parent query if the subquery refers to—and is therefore dependent on—the parent to be valid.

A **correlated subquery** can't be run by itself, because it makes reference—via a correlation variable— to the outer or main query. To demonstrate, let's work through an example based on the entries table in the Content Management System application that we saw in Chapter 3. This is shown in Figure 4.5.

entries		
category	title	created
angst	What If I Get Sick and Die?	2008-12-30
humor	Uncle Karl and the Gasoline	2009-02-28
advice	Be Nice to Everybody	2009-03-02
humor	Hello Statue	2009-03-17
science	The Size of Our Galaxy	2009-04-03
computers	Windows Media Center Rocks	2009-04-29

Figure 4.5. The CMS entries table

The example will use this table in the outer query, and have a correlated subquery that obtains the latest entry in each category based on the `created` date:

```
                                    CMS_13_Correlated_subquery.sql (excerpt)
SELECT
  category
, title
, created
FROM
  entries AS t
WHERE
  created = (
    SELECT
      MAX(created)
    FROM
      entries
    WHERE
      category = t.category
  )
```

Let's start looking at this by reviewing the subquery first. There are two features to note here:

▪ The subquery has a WHERE condition of `category = t.category`. The "t" is the correlation variable, and it's defined in the outer or main query as a table alias for the `entries` table.

▪ You'll also notice the MAX keyword in the subquery's SELECT clause. We haven't covered aggregate functions yet, of which MAX is one, although we did see another one, COUNT, in Chapter 2. In this case, MAX simply returns the highest value in the named column—the latest `created` date.

 AS Means Alias

> AS is a versatile keyword. It allows you to create an alias for almost any database object you can reference in a SELECT statement. In the example above, it creates an alias for a table. It can also alias a column, a view, and a subquery.

In essence, what this query does can be paraphrased as: "return the category, title, and created date of all entries, but only if the created date for the entry being returned is the latest created date for all the entries in that particular category." Or, in brief, *return the most recent entry in each category.* The correlation ensures that the particular category is taken into consideration to determine the latest date, which is then used to compare to the date on each entry, as shown in Figure 4.6.

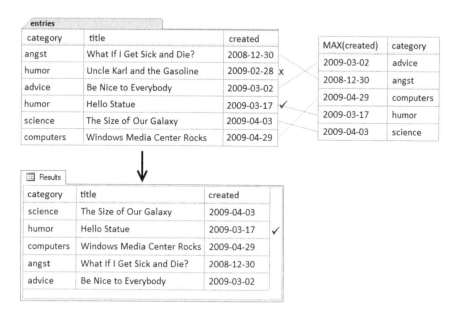

Figure 4.6. How correlation works

In this example, a comparison is made between each entry's `created` value, and the `maximum` `created` value of all rows in that category, as produced by the subquery. If that entry contains the same date for its category as found by the subquery, it's returned in the result set. If it's not the same date, it's discarded.

Because this is a very simple example, only one category actually has more than one entry: *humor*. The subquery determines that "Hello Statue" has the most recently created date, and thus discards "Uncle Karl and the Gasoline."

If Figure 4.6 reminds you of Figure 3.11 (which demonstrated how an inner join worked), remember that the distinguishing characteristic of a correlated subquery is that it's *tied* to an object in the outer or main query, and can't be run on its own. Joins, on the other hand, are part of the main query.

Aside from that, the inner join and the correlated subquery are quite similar. In the join, the rows of the categories and entries tables were joined, based on the comparison of their category columns in the join condition. In the correlated subquery, the rows of the entries table are compared to the rows of the tabular result set produced by the correlated subquery, and if this somehow reminds you of a join, full marks. In fact, correlated subqueries can usually be rewritten as joins.

Here's the equivalent query written using a join instead of a correlated subquery:

CMS_13_Correlated_subquery.sql *(excerpt)*

```
SELECT
   t.category
, t.title
, t.created
FROM
   entries AS t
     INNER JOIN (
       SELECT
         category
       , MAX(created) AS maxdate
       FROM
         entries
       GROUP BY
         category
     ) AS m
     ON m.category = t.category AND m.maxdate = t.created
```

The join version employs a subquery as a derived table, containing a GROUP BY clause. We'll cover the GROUP BY clause in detail in Chapter 5, but for now, please just note that the purpose of the GROUP BY here is to produce one row per category. So the subquery produces a tabular result set consisting of one row per category, and each row will have that category's latest date, which is given the column alias maxdate. Then the derived table, called m, is joined to the entries table, which uses the table alias t. Notice that there are *two* join conditions. You can see both of these conditions in the correlated subquery version, too—one inside the subquery (the category correlation), and the other in the WHERE clause (where maxdate in the subquery should equal the created date in the outer query).

EXISTS Conditions

An EXISTS condition is very similar to an IN condition with a subquery. The difference is that the EXISTS condition's subquery merely needs to return *any* rows, be it a million or just one, in order for the EXISTS condition to evaluate to TRUE. Furthermore, *it does not matter what columns make up those rows*—merely that some rows exist (hence the name).

To demonstrate the use of EXISTS, we'll use the Shopping Cart sample application again, but this time focus on the **customers** and their **carts**. To put these terms in context here, a customer is a person who has registered on the web site, and a cart is the collection of items that the customer has selected for purchase. Let's say we want to find all the customers who have yet to create a cart. The key idea here is the *not* part of the requirement, so we'll use NOT EXISTS in the solution:

Cart_07_NOT_EXISTS_and_NOT_IN.sql *(excerpt)*

```
SELECT
  name
FROM
  customers
WHERE
  NOT EXISTS (
    SELECT
      1
    FROM
      carts
    WHERE
      carts.customer_id = customers.id
  )
```

As you can see, we're using a correlated subquery again within the WHERE clause. This time, the correlation variable is not a table alias, but rather just the name of the table in the outer query. In other words, the subquery will return rows from the carts table where the cart's customer_id column is the same as the id column in the customers table in the outer or main query. If a customer has one or more carts, as returned by the subquery, EXISTS would evaluate to TRUE. However, we're using NOT EXISTS in the main query so a customer's name will only be included in the result set if there are no carts for the customer returned by the subquery, exactly as required.

But what, you may well ask, is SELECT 1 all about? Well, as noted earlier, the EXISTS condition *does not care* which columns are selected, so SELECT 1 simply returns a column containing the numeric constant 1. The subquery could just as easily have selected the customer_id column. EXISTS will evaluate TRUE or FALSE, no matter which columns the subquery selects. We'll cover the SELECT clause in detail in Chapter 7.

NOT IN or NOT EXISTS?

The query above can be rewritten using a NOT IN condition rather than a NOT EXISTS condition, if required. In fact, it can be written in two different ways using NOT IN. The first way is to use an uncorrelated subquery:

Cart_07_NOT_EXISTS_and_NOT_IN.sql *(excerpt)*

```
SELECT
  name
FROM
  customers
WHERE
  NOT (
    id IN (
      SELECT
        customer_id
      FROM
        carts
    )
  )
```

The second way uses a correlated subquery:

Cart_07_NOT_EXISTS_and_NOT_IN.sql *(excerpt)*

```
SELECT
  name
FROM
  customers AS t
WHERE
  NOT (
    id IN (
      SELECT
        customer_id
      FROM
        carts
      WHERE
        customer_id = t.customer_id
    )
  )
```

Which is better? That's the subject of the next section: performance.

A Left Outer Join with an IS NULL Test

Incidentally, the same query can also be rewritten as a LEFT OUTER JOIN with a test for an unmatched row. We saw in the previous chapter that a left outer join will return NULLs in the columns of the right table for unmatched rows. In this case, we want customers without a cart, and the query is:

```
                              Cart_08_LEFT_OUTER_JOIN_with_IS_NULL.sql (excerpt)
SELECT
  customers.name
FROM
  customers
    LEFT OUTER JOIN carts
      ON customers.id = carts.customer_id
WHERE
  carts.customer_id IS NULL
```

Because it's a left outer join, this query returns rows from the left table—in this case, customers—with matching rows, *if any*, from the right table. If there are no matching rows, then the columns in the result set which would have contained values from the right table are set to NULL. So then, if we test for NULL in the right table's join column, this will allow the WHERE clause to filter out all the matched rows, leaving only the unmatched rows. In other words, testing for NULL effectively returns customers without a cart.

Note that the correct syntax to test for NULL is: IS NULL. You cannot use the equals operator (WHERE carts.customer_id = NULL), because NULL is not equal to anything.

WHERE Clause Performance

We've just seen four different ways to write an SQL query to achieve a specific result:

- NOT EXISTS
- NOT IN (uncorrelated)
- NOT IN (correlated)
- LEFT OUTER JOIN with an IS NULL test

In practice, which of these is the best approach to take? Generally, you should let the database system optimize your queries for performance. The database **optimizer**—the part of the database system which parses our SQL, and then figures out how to obtain the data as efficiently as possible—is a lot smarter than many people think. It may realize that it doesn't have to retrieve any carts at all!

Let's consider what the LEFT OUTER JOIN version of the previous example is doing. The query will retrieve all carts for all customers, including customers who have no cart (since it's a LEFT OUTER JOIN); then the WHERE clause *throws away* all rows retrieved, *except* those rows for customers who have no cart. Seems wasteful, doesn't it? And it might well be ... if it were an accurate portrayal. It's unnecessary to actually retrieve any cart rows; what's needed is simply to know which customers don't have one. So the left outer join with an IS NULL test is the same, semantically, as the NOT EXISTS version.

What about the correlated and uncorrelated subqueries using the NOT IN condition? How will they perform? Here's one way to think about what they're doing: the uncorrelated subquery retrieves a list of customer_ids from all carts, and then, in the outer query, checks each customer's id against this list, keeping those customers whose id is not in the list. The correlated subquery retrieves the customer_id from individual cart rows, but only the cart rows for that customer. Yet in the end, the correlated query will actually have retrieved all the cart rows too (like the uncorrelated query did), even though it keeps only those customers who don't have a cart, as well. So it would seem that these queries, too, might wastefully retrieve all carts.

Intuition alone cannot lead us to a happy conclusion here. Our next step might be to test all versions and see how they fare. More often than not, they will all perform the same; ultimately, we'll need to base our analysis on some facts, and for that, we need to do some research. See the section called "Performance Problems and Obtaining Help" in Appendix A for some ideas on how to proceed.

Indexes

Indexing is the number one solution to poor performance.

Indexes are a special way of organizing information about the data in the database tables. In a sense, indexes are additional data, much the same way that the index at the back of a book is additional information about what's in the book. Indexes are used by the database optimizer to find rows quickly. An index is built on a specific table column, and sometimes on more than one column.

A quick search for a topic in the index of a book will tell you which page/s it's on, and then you can simply jump right to those pages. Similarly, if the database optimizer is looking for the cart rows for customer 880, the index can tell the optimizer where those rows are located. The important part about this is that the database optimizer *does not need* to read through all the rows in the table. It just goes directly to the desired rows.

Reading through all the rows in a table is called doing a **table scan**. Generally, this is to be avoided, although it must be done if you actually need to retrieve all the rows in the table. Using an index is known as performing an **indexed retrieval** and is—compared to a table scan—much, much faster (especially if it needs to be repeated many times, such as for every customer).

Where do indexes come from? We have to create them. As this is one of those database administration topics we won't be covering in this book, you should consult the documentation for your particular database system if you'd like to investigate indexes. The important points to note, with regard to WHERE clause performance, are listed below:

- Primary keys already have an index (by definition). There is no need to create an additional index on a primary key. Primary keys will be discussed in Chapter 10.

- Foreign keys need to have an index declared (usually). Foreign keys will be discussed in Chapter 10.

- Columns used in the ON clause of joins are almost invariably either primary or foreign keys; in those instances where they're not, they'll typically benefit from having an index declared.

- Search conditions—conditions in the WHERE clause—will usually benefit from having an index declared.

In time, you'll gain a complete understanding of these concepts, so don't worry if you're feeling a little overwhelmed. Just remember, when you do encounter your first performance problem, to see the section called "Performance Problems and Obtaining Help" in Appendix A.

To tie this back to the recent customer example, you'll recall that we had four different ways to write the SQL to find customers without a cart. Knowing that indexes are used by the database optimizer to improve performance, we can finally see that the cart rows, as hinted, *do not actually need to be retrieved at all*. The optimizer simply needs to know if a particular cart row exists. It can determine which customers have no cart by looking only at the data in the indexes, a much faster way of locating the cart than queries that require a table scan.

Wrapping Up: the WHERE Clause

We covered a lot of ground in this chapter, but the main points that you should take away from it are:

- The WHERE clause acts as a *filter* on the rows of the tabular result set produced by the FROM clause.

- The WHERE clause consists of one or more conditions, which are applied to each row produced by the FROM clause; each condition must evaluate to TRUE in order for that row to be accepted and not filtered out. These conditions can be combined with AND and OR to make compound conditions. Sometimes we need to use NOT to specify the condition that we want to apply to the rows.

- WHERE clause conditions can use comparison operators, IN lists, IN with a subquery, and EXISTS with a subquery.

- Performance depends largely on indexing and not quite so much on the actual syntax of the SQL statement. Queries can often be written in different ways to achieve the same result.

In Chapter 5, we'll look at the GROUP BY clause, which operates on the rows produced by the FROM clause that weren't filtered out by the WHERE clause.

Chapter

5

The **GROUP BY** Clause

In Chapter 3, we learned that the FROM clause creates the intermediate tabular result containing the data for a query. In Chapter 4, we learned that the WHERE clause acts as a filter on the rows produced by the FROM clause. In this chapter, we'll learn what happens when we use the GROUP BY clause, and the effect it has on the data produced by the FROM clause and filtered by the WHERE clause.

The Latin expression *E pluribus unum* is well known to Americans (it's stamped on every American coin), and can be interpreted as representing the "melting pot" concept of creating one nation out of many diverse peoples. Literally, it means: *out of many, one*. In SQL, the GROUP BY clause has a similar role: it groups together data in the tabular structure generated and filtered by a query's FROM and WHERE clauses, and produces a single row in a query's result set for each distinct group. The GROUP BY clause defines how the data should be grouped.

Grouping is More than Sequencing

Grouping is more than simply sequencing data. **Sequencing** simply means sorting the data into a certain order. **Grouping** does involve an aspect of sequencing, but it goes beyond that. To demonstrate, we'll first review the data in our sample Shopping Cart application tables, and then work through several GROUP BY queries to see how grouping affects the results.

Our first goal, therefore, is to write a query that produces a result set that displays a useful set of data from our application, much like the queries we've been writing so far. To make the distinction between the queries we've used up till now and a query involving grouping, we call this type of query a **detail query** because it returns **detail rows**—the columns and rows of data as they are stored in the database tables—ungrouped. The distinction between detail rows and group rows is important and will become clear shortly.

As always, the first item to write is the FROM clause. The sample Shopping Cart application data is spread out over several tables, so we'll need to bring it together with a join query:

Cart_09_Detail_Rows.sql *(excerpt)*

```
FROM
   customers
     INNER JOIN carts
       ON carts.customer_id = customers.id
     INNER JOIN cartitems
       ON cartitems.cart_id = carts.id
     INNER JOIN items
       ON items.id = cartitems.item_id
```

This query joins four tables together. We haven't seen a quadruple join before, so we'll walk through it slowly and examine each join in turn. It may help to look back at the FROM clause as we walk through the joins.

The FROM clause starts with the customers table. Then the carts table is joined to the customers table, based on the customer_id in each row of the carts table matching the corresponding id in the customers table. We're on solid ground here, because all our previous join examples have involved two tables.

Then the `cartitems` table is joined, based on the `cart_id` in each row of the `cartitems` table matching the corresponding `id` in the `carts` table. This is now the third table in the join, and it might help to think of this third table as being joined to the tabular structure produced by the join of the first two tables. Since that tabular structure consists of the matched rows of the first two tables joined or concatenated together (to form a *wider* tabular structure), the join of the third table is, in effect, a join of two tabular structures again: the tabular structure produced by joining the first two tables, to which the third table is joined. You're probably ahead of me here, but I still need to say it: the result of joining the third table is yet another tabular structure.

Finally, the `items` table is joined, based on the `id` in the `items` table matching the corresponding `item_id` in the `cartitems` table. This is the fourth table, and it joins the tabular structure produced by the join of the previous three.

 Testing the FROM Clause

At this point, if we wanted to test the result of our quadruple join we could use what I commonly refer to as "the dreaded and evil *select star*." This is my name for the perfectly valid SQL syntax of **SELECT** *, where the star (or asterisk) is a special keyword that represents all columns. I call it "dreaded and evil" because using it for anything other than testing is rarely a good idea. We'll examine it in more detail in the section called "The Dreaded, Evil Select Star" in Chapter 7, but for now, you just need to know it's used to select all columns like so:

```
SELECT
  *
FROM ...
```

SELECT * is useful when we want to see what the **FROM** clause is producing because it simply outputs all columns. For now, though, be aware that **SELECT** * is completely incompatible with the **GROUP BY** clause, which requires that individual columns are named in the **SELECT** clause before it works.

Retrieving the *entire* tabular result set produced by the four table join is too much detail for our purposes here. There are many extraneous columns that would be in the way of trying to understand the available data, as we prepare to use our first GROUP BY clause. Therefore, we'll specify only a few carefully chosen columns in the SELECT clause:

```
                                          Cart_09_Detail_Rows.sql (excerpt)

SELECT
    customers.name    AS customer
  , carts.id          AS cart
  , items.name        AS item
  , cartitems.qty
  , items.price
  , cartitems.qty
        * items.price AS total
FROM
    ⋮
```

We've yet to cover the SELECT clause in detail (we will in Chapter 7), but we've certainly seen it before; in this particular case, the columns are straightforward, with perhaps the exception of the last line. This expression computes the total price of each item in a cart by multiplying its price by the amount of that item in the cart.

We'll also add an ORDER BY clause:

```
                                          Cart_09_Detail_Rows.sql (excerpt)

    ⋮
ORDER BY
    customers.name
  , carts.id
  , items.name
```

The purpose of the ORDER BY clause here is to sort the result set into the specified sequence: first by customer name, then the cart ID, and then the item name. We'll examine this clause in detail in Chapter 8.

Our completed detail query looks like so:

```
                                    Cart_09_Detail_Rows.sql (excerpt)
SELECT
  customers.name    AS customer
, carts.id          AS cart
, items.name        AS item
, cartitems.qty
, items.price
, cartitems.qty
      * items.price AS total
FROM
  customers
    INNER JOIN carts
      ON carts.customer_id = customers.id
    INNER JOIN cartitems
      ON cartitems.cart_id = carts.id
    INNER JOIN items
      ON items.id = cartitems.item_id
ORDER BY
  customers.name
, carts.id
, items.name
```

Figure 5.1 shows the result set the detail query produces: several customers, the carts that they created, and the items in those carts, together with the quantity of the items purchased, the price of each item, and the total price for that quantity.

 "One-to-Zero-or-Many" Relationships

As a point of interest, there are actually eight customers in the sample application customers table, but only seven of them are included in the result set produced by our detail query. One customer has no cart yet and so isn't included in the results; this is because the join between customers and carts is an INNER JOIN, which requires a match.

We can say that the customers-carts relationship is actually a "one-to-zero-or-many" relationship, because a customer could have no cart. This situation exists when customers register on the web site, before their first cart is created.

customer	cart	item	qty	price	total
A. Jones	2131	gimmick	3	9.37	28.11
A. Jones	2131	thingum	2	22.22	44.44
B. Smith	2921	dingus	3	29.37	88.11
B. Smith	2921	whatsis	2	93.70	187.40
B. Smith	3002	doohickey	1	12.00	12.00
C. Brown	2937	thingum	1	22.22	22.22
C. Brown	3001	thingamabob	3	22.22	66.66
C. Brown	3001	whatsis	2	93.70	187.40
C. Brown	3937	thingum	3	22.22	66.66
D. White	3197	whatchamacallit	1	59.95	59.95
E. Baker	2461	doohickey	2	12.00	24.00
E. Baker	2461	whatnot	3	15.00	45.00
G. Scott	3321	whatchamacallit	3	59.95	179.85
H. Clark	3081	dingus	3	29.37	88.11
H. Clark	3081	thingum	2	22.22	44.44

Figure 5.1. The results of the detail query: all the customers, carts, and items

Notice that the customers are in sequence. Within each customer, the carts are in sequence (if there is more than one per customer), and within each cart, the items are in sequence by name. This sequencing was accomplished by the ORDER BY clause, which was used so we could see the customers-to-carts and carts-to-cartitems relationships in the data more easily (they would be harder to spot if the rows came back in random order, for example).

So to recap what we've seen in the results for the detail query:

- Customers included in the result set have at least one cart, represented by a row in the carts table, with some having more than one cart.
- Each cart has one or more items, represented by a cartitems row.
- Each cart item has a matching row in the items table.

You may well be wondering at this point, "Yes, that's nice, it makes sense, and I can see the query results are sorted nicely, but what has this to do with GROUP BY?"

The reason for looking at the detail data carefully, and in this particular sequence, is to see how the items for a cart are grouped together, and how the carts for a customer are grouped together. However, this is *not* the grouping that the GROUP BY clause produces; it is merely the sequencing that the ORDER BY clause produces. In other words, if we want to see *detailed* row data "grouped" into a certain sequence, we use ORDER BY. GROUP BY has another purpose altogether.

Out of Many, One

The role of the GROUP BY clause is to **aggregate**, meaning to collect together, or unite. Let's look at our first example of a query that uses a GROUP BY clause:

```
                                           Cart_10_Group_rows.sql (excerpt)
SELECT
    customers.name      AS customer
,  carts.id             AS cart
,  COUNT(items.name)    AS items
,  SUM(cartitems.qty
        * items.price)  AS total
FROM
    customers
      INNER JOIN carts
        ON carts.customer_id = customers.id
      INNER JOIN cartitems
        ON cartitems.cart_id = carts.id
      INNER JOIN items
        ON items.id = cartitems.item_id
GROUP BY
    customers.name
,  carts.id
```

This is almost the same as the detail query; it has the same FROM clause, but there are some slight differences in the SELECT clause, and the GROUP BY clause is new.

The SELECT clause now contains two common *aggregate functions*, COUNT and SUM. As you might have guessed, COUNT counts rows, and SUM produces a total. We'll look at these and other aggregate functions in more detail in Chapter 7.

The GROUP BY clause contains the names of two columns: customers.name and carts.id. In doing so, the GROUP BY clause will produce *one row*, a **group row** or **aggregate row**, in the query's result set for every distinct combination of the values in the columns specified. The tabular structure shown in Figure 5.2 is the result set returned by the above query. Instead of detail rows, we now have group rows.

customer	cart	items	total
A. Jones	2131	2	72.55
B. Smith	2921	2	275.51
B. Smith	3002	1	12.00
C. Brown	2937	1	22.22
C. Brown	3001	2	254.06
C. Brown	3937	1	66.66
D. White	3197	1	59.95
E. Baker	2461	2	69.00
G. Scott	3321	1	179.85
H. Clark	3081	2	132.55

Figure 5.2. Results of the GROUP BY query

The items column in this result set is the number of items in each particular cart, while the total column is the sum of the individual line item totals on the cart. Where a customer cart includes more than one item, those multiple item rows have been *aggregated* into one row per cart per customer. There are still multiple rows per customer, but there is now only one row per cart per customer.

The GROUP BY clause has aggregated the rows for each customer cart, producing one out of many, while the COUNT and SUM functions have computed the aggregate quantities—a count and a sum—for all those rows taken together. Hence, the presence of the GROUP BY clause has created group rows from the detail rows of the tabular result set, which was produced from the FROM clause.

Figure 5.3 illustrates the grouping concept by showing the results of the detail query and the results of the above GROUP BY query, side by side. Note that the grouping columns have been highlighted, and some spacing has been inserted, to make it easier to see the grouping.

Detail Rows

Group Rows

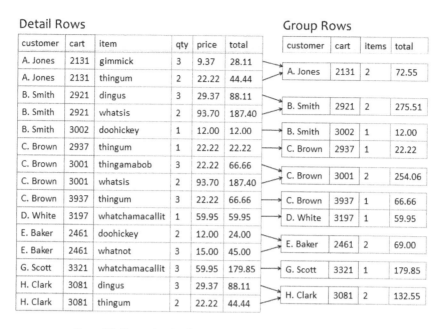

customer	cart	item	qty	price	total
A. Jones	2131	gimmick	3	9.37	28.11
A. Jones	2131	thingum	2	22.22	44.44
B. Smith	2921	dingus	3	29.37	88.11
B. Smith	2921	whatsis	2	93.70	187.40
B. Smith	3002	doohickey	1	12.00	12.00
C. Brown	2937	thingum	1	22.22	22.22
C. Brown	3001	thingamabob	3	22.22	66.66
C. Brown	3001	whatsis	2	93.70	187.40
C. Brown	3937	thingum	3	22.22	66.66
D. White	3197	whatchamacallit	1	59.95	59.95
E. Baker	2461	doohickey	2	12.00	24.00
E. Baker	2461	whatnot	3	15.00	45.00
G. Scott	3321	whatchamacallit	3	59.95	179.85
H. Clark	3081	dingus	3	29.37	88.11
H. Clark	3081	thingum	2	22.22	44.44

customer	cart	items	total
A. Jones	2131	2	72.55
B. Smith	2921	2	275.51
B. Smith	3002	1	12.00
C. Brown	2937	1	22.22
C. Brown	3001	2	254.06
C. Brown	3937	1	66.66
D. White	3197	1	59.95
E. Baker	2461	2	69.00
G. Scott	3321	1	179.85
H. Clark	3081	2	132.55

Figure 5.3. Comparing detail rows to group rows—two column grouping

Let's write another example using the GROUP BY clause:

Cart_10_Group_rows.sql (excerpt)

```
SELECT
  customers.name      AS customer
, COUNT(items.name)   AS items
, SUM(cartitems.qty
      * items.price)  AS total
FROM
  customers
    INNER JOIN carts
      ON carts.customer_id = customers.id
    INNER JOIN cartitems
      ON cartitems.cart_id = carts.id
    INNER JOIN items
      ON items.id = cartitems.item_id
GROUP BY
  customers.name
```

This is practically the same query as before, except that in this case, the GROUP BY clause contains only one column, customers.name. Thus, the GROUP BY clause produces one row for every customer, as shown in Figure 5.4.

Results		
customer	items	total
A. Jones	2	72.55
B. Smith	3	287.51
C. Brown	4	342.94
D. White	1	59.95
E. Baker	2	69.00
G. Scott	1	179.85
H. Clark	2	132.55

Figure 5.4. Results grouped by customer name only

This time, the items column is a count of the number of items in all carts for the customer, while the total column is the sum of the individual line item totals on all carts for the customer. Figure 5.5 shows the side-by-side comparison of the detail data with the results of GROUP BY customers.name:

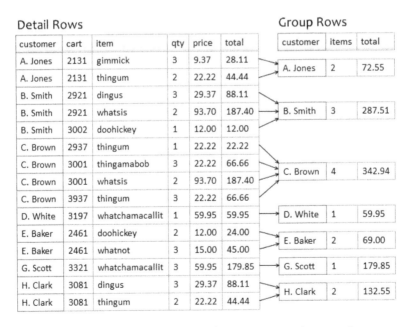

Figure 5.5. Comparing detail and group rows—one column grouping

Let's recap what we've covered so far.

■ First we ran a detail query—that is, a query without a GROUP BY clause—to show the detail rows, using ORDER BY to ensure we could see the data relationships easily.

■ Next we ran the first GROUP BY clause, with two columns, and produced group rows for distinct combinations of customer and cart.

■ Finally, we ran the second GROUP BY clause, with just one column, producing group rows for distinct customers only. This resulted in the counts and totals in the second query being larger.

GROUP BY is easier to understand—if you are meeting it for the first time—when going in steps, from detailed data, to small aggregations, to larger aggregations.

Drill-down SQL

While it's easier to understand grouping by working from more detailed to less detailed breakdowns, going in the other direction—from large numbers to more detailed breakdowns—is a great tactic to use in the analysis of data. Suppose we want to understand customer sales. Since this would be data at the customer level, we would start with:

```
GROUP BY
  customers.name
```

Figure 5.4 shows that the results of this grouping are at the customer level of detail. Perhaps those results need to be more detailed, so we'll drill down another level with:

```
GROUP BY
  customers.name
, carts.id
```

The results in Figure 5.2 reflect the further breakdown.

The more columns in the GROUP BY clause, the deeper down into the data we drill. In other words, grouping by customer, and then grouping by customer and cart, is an *exploratory* process that follows the one-to-many relationships inherent in the joined data.

Many SQL tutorials and books teach the GROUP BY clause in this top-down direction. However, I think it's better to proceed from the bottom up, from detailed data to smaller and then larger aggregations; this is because it mirrors the way the GROUP BY clause works—producing, out of many rows, one row per group.

GROUP BY in Context

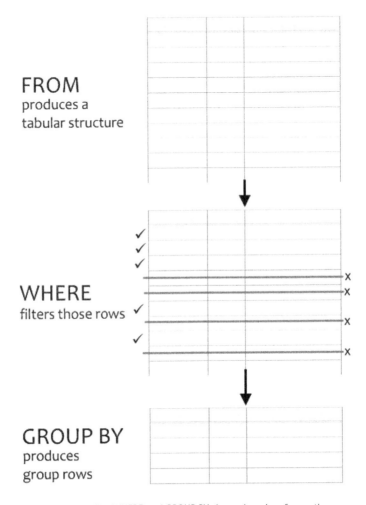

Figure 5.6. FROM, WHERE, and GROUP BY clauses in order of execution

The GROUP BY clause fits into the context of the overall query right after the WHERE clause. Syntactically, a query begins with the SELECT clause which we'll cover in Chapter 7. Then comes the FROM clause, the WHERE clause, and then the GROUP BY clause. More importantly, however, is the sequence in which the query clauses are executed:

- The FROM clause determines the contents of the intermediate tabular result that the query starts with.
- The WHERE clause, if present, filters the rows of that tabular structure.
- The GROUP BY clause, if present, aggregates the remaining rows into groups.

This is illustrated in Figure 5.6.

How GROUP BY Works

When a GROUP BY clause is present in the query, it aggregates many rows into one. After this is done, all the original rows produced by the FROM clause that survived the WHERE filter, *are removed*. The GROUP BY clause produces group rows, which you'll recall from Chapter 2 are new rows created to represent each group of rows found during the aggregation process. The original rows are no longer available to the query. Only group rows come out of the grouping process.

Group Rows

One way to think about the grouping process goes like this:

- The FROM clause produces a temporary result set, held as a *temporary table* within the memory of the database system while the query is being executed.

- If a WHERE clause is present, only some of those rows will be retained. If a row passes the WHERE clause criteria, it is copied to a second temporary table. The second temporary table would still have the same tabular structure as the first one.

- If a GROUP BY clause is present, another temporary table is created for the group rows. This would have a *different tabular structure* from those produced by the FROM or WHERE clauses.

To see this process one more time, let's look at another grouping example. Here again is the query from the previous example, but with an added WHERE condition:

```
                                    Cart_11_GROUP_BY_WITH_WHERE.sql (excerpt)
SELECT
  customers.name          AS customer
, SUM(cartitems.qty)      AS qty
, SUM(cartitems.qty
      * items.price)      AS total
FROM
  customers
    INNER JOIN carts
      ON carts.customer_id = customers.id
    INNER JOIN cartitems
      ON cartitems.cart_id = carts.id
    INNER JOIN items
      ON items.id = cartitems.item_id
WHERE
  items.name = 'thingum'
GROUP BY
  customers.name
```

The purpose of this query is to produce totals for each customer, but only for items called `thingum`. Thus, rather than seeing how many carts each customer has, we're more interested in how many thingums were purchased. Remember the context of GROUP BY in the overall query. The GROUP BY clause operates after the WHERE clause, on the filtered intermediate tabular result, so we know that only thingum rows will be grouped. Notice also that in this query, instead of counting items in the customer carts, the qty result column in the SELECT clause is SUM(`cartitems.qty`), the total quantity of items.

Figure 5.7 shows the results:

customer	qty	total
A. Jones	2	44.44
C. Brown	4	88.88
H. Clark	2	44.44

Figure 5.7. Thingum purchases grouped by customer

Aggregate Functions and GROUP BY

In the various preceding examples, different aggregate functions were used to produce different kinds of totals—number of carts, number of items, total quantity, total cost—while different GROUP BY clauses were used to produce aggregates at different levels.

We'll discuss aggregate functions again in Chapter 7. For now, we need only to be aware that aggregate functions are often used in GROUP BY queries, to produce the kinds of totals—sums, counts, and so on—that we would expect them to from their function names.

Rules for GROUP BY

As we've seen, the GROUP BY clause performs an aggregation on the rows produced by the FROM clause, and this grouping process creates group rows. Group rows are *not the same* as rows from the tabular structure coming out of the FROM clause.

So the first *rule* for using the GROUP BY clause is that the result set can contain only columns specified in the GROUP BY clause, or aggregate functions, or any combinations of these. This rule will show up again when we discuss the SELECT clause in Chapter 7.

Actually, columns in group rows can also include constants, as well as expressions built by combining GROUP BY columns, aggregate functions, and constants. But this nuance is inconsequential to the main point: group rows can contain only columns that are mentioned in the GROUP BY clause or are contained inside aggregate functions (or expressions built from these). The grouping process produces only these two column types.

Columns with Certain Large Data Types

Another point about using GROUP BY is that only some database systems let you specify columns with large data types in a GROUP BY clause. These particular data types, Binary Large Objects (BLOBs), and Character Large Objects (CLOBs), are covered in more detail in Chapter 9. Just quickly though, CLOBs are used to store large amounts of character data, while BLOBs are used to store binary data, such as images, sound, and video.

The restriction depends on the specific database system you're using. However, it's unnecessary to specify a BLOB or CLOB column in the GROUP BY clause in the first place. This is the direct consequence of a strategy I call *pushing down* the GROUP BY clause into a subquery whenever possible. The following example will illustrate this process.

In Chapter 2, we briefly encountered the Content Management System sample application. The CMS application is described in detail in the section called "Content Management System" in Appendix B. The entries table holds the entries that are the basis for our CMS. An entry has a title, date created, and so on. It also may have a large block of actual content. In the model of the CMS application (shown in Figure 5.8—more on these diagrams in the section called "Entity–Relationship Diagrams" in Chapter 10), this content is stored separately in a related row in the contents table. (In Chapter 2, the content column was actually in the entries table.)

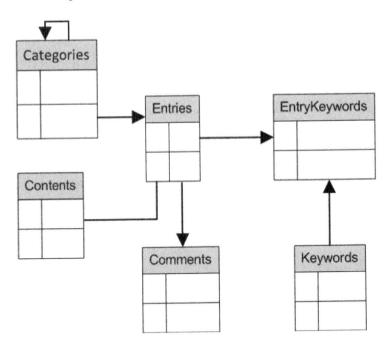

Figure 5.8. The structure of the CMS database

Each row in the entries table has, at most, one row in the contents table, but could have none, because content is optional in our CMS. So, if we were to write a query to return the entries in our CMS, along with the content for each entry (if any), our query would look like this:

```
                                    CMS_14_Content_and_Comment_tables.sql (excerpt)
SELECT
    entries.id
, entries.title
, entries.created
, contents.content
FROM
    entries
      LEFT OUTER JOIN contents
        ON contents.entry_id = entries.id
```

This is a straightforward left outer join; all entries are returned, including their related content, if any. If an entry has no matching contents row, then the row in the result set for that entry will have NULL in the content column.

But we've still to reach where the GROUP BY complexity comes into play. To do so, we need another table to join to—the comments table. Besides having an optional content row, each row in the entries table also has one or more optional rows in the comments table. Multiple comments can be made against each entry. In addition to returning each entry with its optional content, we want also to return a count of the number of comments for that entry.

Here's the first attempt at the query to do this:

```
                                   CMS_14_Content_and_Comment_tables.sql (excerpt)
SELECT
   entries.id
 , entries.title
 , entries.created
 , contents.content
 , COUNT(comments.entry_id) AS comment_count
FROM
   entries
     LEFT OUTER JOIN contents
       ON contents.entry_id = entries.id
     LEFT OUTER JOIN comments
       ON comments.entry_id = entries.id
GROUP BY
   entries.id
 , entries.title
 , entries.created
 , contents.content
```

Let's take a look at the changes. First of all, the SELECT clause contains an aggregate function. The COUNT function will count the number of comments for each entry. However, we need a GROUP BY clause in order to do this, because a GROUP BY clause is what collapses the multiple comments rows into one, so that the COUNT function will work correctly.

Notice that the GROUP BY clause lists exactly the same columns as the columns in the SELECT clause. We want to return those columns in the query results, but in a GROUP BY query, only group row columns may be specified in the SELECT clause outside of aggregate functions. Therefore those columns have to be in the GROUP BY clause.

This would all be wonderful, if it actually ran. Unfortunately, contents.content is a TEXT column, another large data type like CLOB which—as noted earlier—some database systems won't let you have in the GROUP BY clause.

There are two ways to work around this limitation, both involving a subquery.

The first solution is to *push down* the grouping process into a subquery, and then join this subquery into the query as a derived table, in place of the original table:

```
                        CMS_14_Content_and_Comment_tables.sql (excerpt)
SELECT
  entries.id
, entries.title
, entries.created
, contents.content
, c.comment_count
FROM
  entries
    LEFT OUTER JOIN contents
      ON contents.entry_id = entries.id
    LEFT OUTER JOIN (
      SELECT
        entry_id
      ,  COUNT(*) AS comment_count
      FROM
        comments
      GROUP BY
        entry_id
    ) AS c
      ON c.entry_id = entries.id
```

Notice that in the derived table subquery, the GROUP BY clause specifies the entry_id.
If there are multiple rows in the comments table for any entry_id, they are aggregated by the GROUP BY. Thus, the derived table consists of only group rows, which
have only the entry_id and comment_count columns. The derived table therefore,
has only one row per entry_id, and this is the column used to join the derived
table to the entries table. The outer query no longer has a GROUP BY clause; it's
been *pushed down* into a subquery.

The second solution is similar, but instead of a subquery as a derived table in the FROM clause, it uses a correlated subquery in the SELECT clause:

CMS_14_Content_and_Comment_tables.sql *(excerpt)*

```
SELECT
  entries.id
, entries.title
, entries.created
, contents.content
, (
    SELECT
      COUNT(entry_id)
    FROM
      comments
    WHERE
      entry_id = entries.id
  ) AS comment_count
FROM
  entries
    LEFT OUTER JOIN contents
      ON contents.entry_id = entries.id
```

We first discussed correlated subqueries back in the section called "Correlated Subqueries" in Chapter 4. The above solution omits the GROUP BY clause, yet it produces the same result. Once again, we see that there's often more than one way to write an SQL query to achieve the results we want.

In fact, there *is* grouping in the above correlated subquery, but it's implicit. We'll explore this concept in the section called "Aggregate Functions without GROUP BY" in Chapter 7, but for now all you need to know is that when there's only aggregate functions in the SELECT clause, like the COUNT(entry_id) aggregate function above, all of the rows returned by the FROM clause are considered to be one group. The effect of this, in the above query, is that the subquery produces an aggregate count of all correlated rows from the comments table for each id in the entries table from the outer query.

Wrapping Up: the GROUP BY

In this chapter, we learned about the concept of grouping.

▨ The GROUP BY clause is used to aggregate or collapse multiple rows into one row per group. The groups are determined by the distinct values in the column(s) specified in the GROUP BY clause.

▨ During the grouping process, group rows are created. These rows have a different tabular structure than the underlying tabular result produced by the FROM clause.

▨ Only group row columns can be used in the SELECT clause. We'll come back to this point in Chapter 7.

▨ In addition, this chapter introduced a technique to *push down* the GROUP BY clause into a subquery. This technique avoids one minor problem: that columns with certain large data types cannot be specified in the GROUP BY clause.

In Chapter 6, we'll meet the companion to the GROUP BY clause, the HAVING clause.

6

The **HAVING** Clause

In Chapter 5, we learned that the GROUP BY clause produces group rows by aggregating rows of the tabular structure extracted from the database by the FROM clause and then filtered by the WHERE clause. Each distinct value or combination of values in the GROUP BY column(s) forms a separate group row.

In this chapter, we'll look at the HAVING clause. This follows the GROUP BY clause both in syntax (its position in the SELECT statement) and in the sequence of execution. Its purpose is simple once you understand GROUP BY and group rows. HAVING is basically the same as WHERE, with the difference that HAVING works on group rows.

HAVING Filters Group Rows

The purpose of the HAVING clause is to act as a filter for the group rows produced by the GROUP BY clause. Everything we learned about conditions—how conditions are evaluated to TRUE or FALSE, how they're combined with ANDs and ORs—can be applied to the HAVING clause as well. The only difference is that HAVING operates on group rows, instead of on the rows from the original tabular structure (which are now gone since grouping took place).

Figure 6.1 illustrates the execution of the SELECT statement clauses.

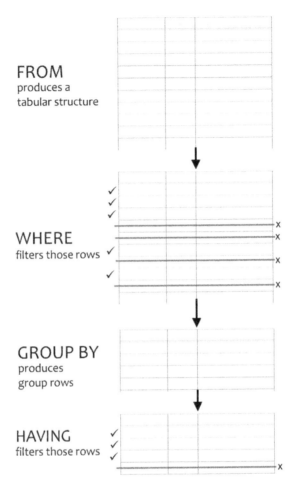

FROM
produces a
tabular structure

WHERE
filters those rows

GROUP BY
produces
group rows

HAVING
filters those rows

Figure 6.1. Where HAVING fits in the sequence of execution

When we say that the HAVING clause acts as a filter on group rows, what does this actually mean? If you recall from Chapter 5, the only possible column types in group rows are:

- columns specified in the GROUP BY clause
- aggregate functions

Expressions can be built from any combination of these two options, and constant values may also be used. As with the GROUP BY clause, the HAVING clause can only use these column types in its conditions.

To demonstrate, let's use one of the GROUP BY queries from Chapter 5 and add a HAVING clause:

```
                                           Cart_12_GROUP_BY_with_HAVING.sql (excerpt)
SELECT
  customers.name        AS customer
, SUM(cartitems.qty)    AS sumqty
, SUM(cartitems.qty
      * items.price)    AS totsales
FROM
  customers
    INNER JOIN carts
      ON carts.customer_id = customers.id
    INNER JOIN cartitems
      ON cartitems.cart_id = carts.id
    INNER JOIN items
      ON items.id = cartitems.item_id
GROUP BY
  customers.name
HAVING
  SUM(cartitems.qty) > 5
```

This is the same query as the one we used for the *thingum* totals, except that the WHERE clause has been removed (because we want all items to be included in this query). Remember, the WHERE clause is optional, so if there isn't one, then all the rows produced by the FROM clause go straight into the GROUP BY clause. This time only group rows where SUM(cartitems.qty)—an aggregate function expression that calculates the total number of cart items—is greater than 5 are retained. All others are removed.

In the above example, the HAVING condition is a single condition: SUM(cartitems.qty) > 5. It's known as a **group condition** because it's a condition applied to group rows. The intent is to return customers with more than five items purchased; Figure 6.2 shows the results.

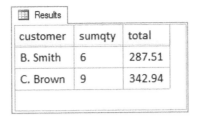

Figure 6.2. The HAVING clause filters out unwanted group rows

 Column Alias or Aggregate Expression

In the SELECT clause the aggregate expression SUM(cartitems.qty) is given the column alias sumqty. You should be able to use the column alias instead of the aggregate function expression in a query's HAVING clause. Thus, HAVING sumqty > 5 and HAVING SUM(cartitems.qty) > 5 are equivalent. Try running one of the grouping queries in the code archive or one of your own, for confirmation. Note that using a column alias was not permitted in early versions of SQL.

If there was no HAVING clause in the query, its results would have been those shown in Figure 6.3; all group rows are returned.

customer	sumqty	total
A. Jones	5	72.55
B. Smith	6	287.51
C. Brown	9	342.94
D. White	1	59.95
E. Baker	5	69.00
G. Scott	3	179.85
H. Clark	5	132.55

Figure 6.3. No HAVING clause means returning all group rows

HAVING without a GROUP BY Clause

No sooner than some people first learn about the HAVING clause, they happen to stumble upon a HAVING clause *without* a GROUP BY clause. Naturally, they're perplexed; if HAVING filters group rows, which are only achieved with a GROUP BY clause, why and how do they work?

When there is no GROUP BY clause, all of the rows in the tabular structure produced by the FROM clause (optionally filtered by the WHERE clause), are considered to be a *single group.*

Threshold Alert

One example of HAVING without GROUP BY is as a **threshold alert**, in which an SQL query produces a result *only* if some aggregate amount exceeds a threshold value.

Let's consider the following scenario. Your boss has sent you the following email:

> Hi Steve,
>
> Just wanted to add one item to the list of features.
>
> My control panel should have an alert. Every time I log in I want to see total sales for the previous day, but don't bother unless it's over $1,000. Thanks, and looking forward to seeing this in your demo next week.
>
> T.

To satisfy this new feature request, a query is needed to return the total sales amount for yesterday, but only if it's over $1,000:

```
SELECT
  SUM(cartitems.qty * items.price) AS totsales
FROM
  carts
    INNER JOIN cartitems
      ON cartitems.cart_id = carts.id
    INNER JOIN items
      ON items.id = cartitems.item_id
WHERE
  carts.cartdate = CURRENT_DATE − INTERVAL 1 DAY
HAVING
  totsales > 1000
```

This query returns either a total sales number over 1,000, or NULL. It's unusual in the combination of clauses used but it's syntactically correct and it works nicely. Indeed, it's quite similar to our first HAVING query example, which filtered out customers with 5 items or less. Of course, our first example query had a GROUP BY clause for the customer, unlike this one. And yet it has a HAVING clause. Which may seem a bit weird at first.

When there is no GROUP BY clause, all of the rows in the tabular structure produced by the FROM clause (optionally filtered by the WHERE clause), are considered to be a *single group*. So in this example, SUM(`cartitems.qty*items.price`) is calculated for the entire single group of rows coming out of the WHERE clause—yesterday's sales. SUM is an aggregate function, so this expression (or its alias) is allowed in the HAVING clause. So the HAVING condition is evaluated on the (single) group row, specifically on the total sales amount for yesterday.

What happens if the total sales amount is *not* over 1,000?

Let's step back just for a second and imagine this query without the HAVING clause. If this were the case, the query would simply return the total sales number, the aggregate sum of the sales of all items sold yesterday. The result set of the query will be one row consisting of one column. There's only one row because, since there's no GROUP BY clause, there's only one group.

With the HAVING clause, however, the query will either return a single row or none at all.

Are Thresholds Database or Application Logic?

Web developers working with a database may already know the importance of distinguishing between tasks more appropriately performed by the database, and tasks that should be done in the application programming language.

This query—"I want to see total sales for the previous day, but don't bother unless it's over $1,000"—is a small example, but it allows us to see the difference. If this query returns NULL, that is, no result set, the application programming code needs to be able to detect this situation, and take the appropriate action not to display the total sales. But many database application developers already routinely detect the "nothing returned from database" situation. They do so in order to raise a user-friendly application error condition when a query *doesn't work*. That's because there's an assumption that there's something wrong if a query returns no rows—and most of the time that's right. This example shows that a NULL result—nothing returned from the query—may be just that, a NULL result, rather than an error.

Remember, the point of the alert was to report the sales, but only if they're over $1,000. An alert that says "Yesterday's sales were $937" fails this requirement. On the other hand, an alert that says "Yesterday's sales were NULL" would be alarming, as it would almost certainly be misinterpreted as "Yesterday, there were no sales." This is why application developers like to trigger the alert within the application, and I agree with them. Instead, I'd write the query without the HAVING clause, using an if test in the application.

Performance virtually is the same when the HAVING clause restricts the results, too. The query has to retrieve and aggregate all those detail rows into one group anyway, and this is 99.9% of the effort. Whether there is then one row or no row in the result set will not affect overall performance. There are many tasks better accomplished in the database than in the application side, but presentation logic like this should be implemented in the application.

 ## The Use of Column Aliases in the HAVING Clause

You may see the HAVING clause used to get around the fact that you can't use a column alias in the WHERE clause. For example, consider this hypothetical query in which a WHERE clause has been changed to a HAVING clause just so the author could make use of the column alias calc:

```
SELECT
    columnA
  , columnB
  , (some horribly complicated expression) AS calc
FROM
  tableA
HAVING
  calc > 9 OR
      (columnC = 0 AND calc > 37)
```

The query would not have worked with the HAVING clause as a WHERE clause; it would have failed with an error message, such as "Unknown column 'calc' in WHERE clause." This particular approach is not standard SQL behaviour, but it works in some database systems, notably MySQL.

Rather than rely on non-standard SQL, we can use a subquery to produce the same results instead:

```
SELECT
  *
FROM
  (
    SELECT
      columnA
    , columnB
    , ( some horribly complicated expression ) AS calc
    FROM
      tableA
  ) AS dt
WHERE
  calc > 9
      OR ( columnC = 5 AND calc > 37 )
```

The query has been *pushed down* into a subquery, and because that is executed before the WHERE clause, the alias is now available to the WHERE clause.

Wrapping Up: the HAVING Clause

In this chapter, we learned how the HAVING clause works with the GROUP BY clause to filter group rows; this works in the same way the WHERE clause filters the rows of the tabular result set returned by the FROM clause. HAVING can specify conditions involving only GROUP BY columns, aggregate functions (and expressions built from these), and constants.

The next chapter finally tackles the SELECT clause.

The **SELECT** Clause

The SELECT clause has been used in every sample SQL SELECT statement we've seen so far. This is not surprising, because the SELECT clause is mandatory; it's the first clause in any SELECT statement. I've tried to avoid describing the SELECT clause in too much detail along the way, in order not to detract from the other clauses being discussed, but now it's time for us to get to know the SELECT clause a little better.

We've taken a different route to arrive here than most SQL tutorials or books, which usually begin with the SELECT clause. Instead, we looked at the other clauses of the SELECT statement first, and there's a very good reason why we do this: it's the order in which they're executed.

In the preceding chapters, we reviewed the clauses of the SELECT statement in the following sequence:

1. FROM retrieves data from one or more database tables
2. WHERE filters the detail rows of the FROM clause's tabular result
3. GROUP BY produces group rows from filtered detail rows
4. HAVING filters group rows

We are now—finally—ready to examine the SELECT clause. As we first learned in Chapter 2, the SELECT statement's single purpose is to retrieve data from our database and return it in a tabular structure. The purpose of the SELECT clause is to define the columns that will be returned in the final, tabular result set.

SELECT in the Sequence of Execution

Understanding the sequence of execution of clauses in a SELECT statement is important: the presence—or absence—of the GROUP BY clause in the SELECT statement determines which columns we can have in our SELECT clause.

The SELECT clause is executed after the FROM clause, and any optional WHERE, GROUP BY, and HAVING clauses, if present. We've already learned in the section called "All Columns Are Available after a Join" in Chapter 3 that the execution of the FROM clause builds an intermediate tabular result set from which the SELECT clause ultimately selects the data to be returned. However, the presence of a GROUP BY clause changes the structure of this intermediate table, thus changing the data available to the SELECT clause when it's finally executed.

If no GROUP BY clause is present, the SELECT clause can include any column from any table mentioned in the FROM clause. If a GROUP BY clause is present, the SELECT clause can include only grouping columns.

This distinction applies only to the columns that can appear in the SELECT clause. In Chapter 5, we saw aggregate functions used in the SELECT clause in addition to grouping columns. As you'll recall, the syntax of the SELECT statement specifies that the SELECT clause consists of expressions that involve keywords, identifiers, and constants:

```
SELECT expression(s) involving keywords, identifiers, and constants
FROM tabular structure(s)
[WHERE clause]
[GROUP BY clause]
[HAVING clause]
[ORDER BY clause]
```

Keywords used in the SELECT clause are mostly functions. A small number of other special keywords can be used, and we'll see some of the more useful ones in this chapter. Identifiers used in the SELECT clause are column names. They may be qualified by their table names or table aliases. Constants are fixed values, but they provide a means of making useful expressions when combined with the keywords and identifiers.

We'll start our detailed analysis with columns.

Which Columns Can Be Selected?

The columns that are allowed in the SELECT clause are entirely determined by the presence or absence of the GROUP BY clause. If it seems like I'm really hammering away at this point, there's good reason. I've seen many people get into trouble writing SELECT statements without an appreciation of the distinction between detail rows and group rows.

Detail Rows

When there's no GROUP BY clause, the SELECT clause can include any column from any table mentioned in the FROM clause.

If there's more than one table in the FROM clause, then the rows of all the tables involved are joined together to form the intermediate result set, as depicted in Figure 7.1. This is the same figure we saw in the section called "All Columns Are Available after a Join" in Chapter 3. At the time, I mentioned that the entries table actually had several additional columns that were not shown: id, updated, and content. These columns are also available, but they've been omitted from the diagram to keep it simple.

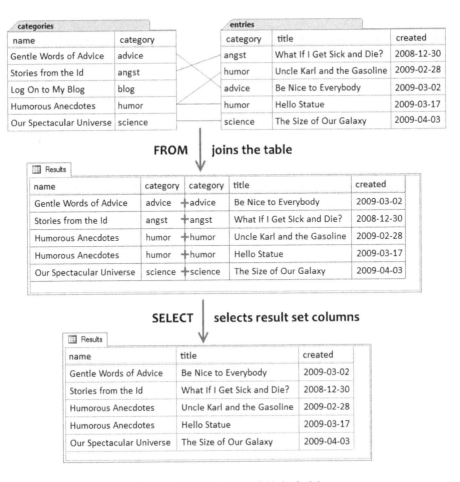

Figure 7.1. All columns are available in the join

When the query includes a GROUP BY clause, however, then the columns that can be specified in the SELECT clause change dramatically.

Group Rows

Planning and designing an SQL SELECT query must take into account these two major considerations:

1. deciding which tables contain the data we need, and specifying how to join them
2. determining whether grouping is required

If grouping is required, then, as a rule, the only columns allowed in the SELECT clause are the grouping columns: the columns listed in the GROUP BY clause. All sample GROUP BY queries that we've seen in previous chapters have followed this rule.

This may seem limiting, until we realize that when grouping is performed, many useful aggregate functions are permitted. For example, let's look again at the following grouping query from Chapter 5:

```
                                        Cart_10_Grouped_rows.sql (excerpt)
SELECT
  customers.name       AS customer
, COUNT(items.name)   AS items
, SUM(cartitems.qty
      * items.price)  AS total
FROM
  customers
    INNER JOIN carts
      ON carts.customer_id = customers.id
    INNER JOIN cartitems
      ON cartitems.cart_id = carts.id
    INNER JOIN items
      ON items.id = cartitems.item_id
GROUP BY
  customers.name
```

The only column we can select in the SELECT clause is the customers.name column, since that's the only column in the GROUP BY clause—the only grouping column. However, we also have two aggregate functions in the SELECT clause—we first met these functions back in Chapter 5—that refer to columns that are not grouping columns: COUNT(items.name) and SUM(cartitems.qty * items.price).

Inside aggregate functions, the use of columns that aren't grouping columns is perfectly okay. During the grouping process, the aggregate functions compute an aggregate or total from each group's set of detail rows. While there are multiple rows in each group, only a single calculated value appears in the group row as a result of the aggregate function.

SUM and COUNT, of course, do just what we expect them to—they produce the aggregate sums and counts for the group rows. There's nothing special about what they do, but circumstances dictate that they can only be used in grouping queries, and the grouping columns determine their **granularity**—how many detail row values are aggregated into the group row value. In this case, there's one group row for each customer.

COUNT(items.name) produces a count of the number of items in all carts for every customer. The grouping column, customers.name, determines the scope for the COUNT aggregate function: there is one count produced for each customer.

Being an expression in the SELECT clause, COUNT(items.name) also produces one of the columns in the query's final result set. This expression is given a column alias, items, which is the name used for that column in the result set. The other aggregate function in the above query is SUM(cartitems.qty * items.price). This expression is also given a column alias, total, which becomes the column name used for that column in the query's result set shown. Figure 7.2 displays the results of our SELECT clause

customer	items	total
A. Jones	2	72.55
B. Smith	3	287.51
C. Brown	4	342.94
D. White	1	59.95
E. Baker	2	69.00
G. Scott	1	179.85
H. Clark	2	132.55

Figure 7.2. Aggregate totals for each customer

Aggregate functions are the primary reason we write grouping queries in the first place, and we'll look at the more useful ones in a moment. First, though, I'd like to introduce yet another sample application, Discussion Forums.

The Discussion Forum Application

In the section called "Discussion Forums" in Appendix B, you'll find a detailed description of the database for the Discussion Forums application, which allows registered members to make posts about various topics that are organized into threads within forums.

The `forums` Table

Our sample data has three forums as you can see in Figure 7.3.

forums	
id	name
10001	Search Engines
10002	Databases
10003	Applications

Figure 7.3. The `forums` table

Of course, in the real world, a forum application might have many more columns—for example, a column for a forum's description—but we'll keep it simple.

The `members` Table

Figure 7.4 shows that the sample data includes five members in the `members` table.

members	
id	name
9	noo13
37	r937
42	DeepThought
99	BarbFeldon
187	RJNeedham

Figure 7.4. The `members` table

As anyone who is a member of SitePoint's forums[1] knows, a *real world* forum application has many more columns—such as avatar, signature, and so on—but again, simplicity is our goal in these samples.

The `threads` Table

Each thread belongs to a specific forum, and is started by a particular member. See if you can visualize the relationships of the threads table, shown in Figure 7.5, to the forums and members tables.

---

[1] http://sitepoint.com/forums/

threads			
id	name	forum_id	starter
15	Difficulty with join query	10002	187
25	How do I get listed in Yahoo?	10001	9
35	People who bought ... also bought ...	10002	99
45	WHERE clause doesn't work	10002	187

Figure 7.5. The threads table

The relationship of forums to threads can be categorized as *one-to-zero-or-many*; a forum can have any number of threads, even zero. The Databases forum has three threads, the Search Engines forum has one thread, and the Applications forum has none. Similarly, the relationship of members to threads is also one-to-zero-or-many.

The posts Table

Finally, the posts table is depicted in Figure 7.6.

posts					
id	name	thread_id	reply_to	posted_by	post
201	Difficulty with join query	15		187	I'm having a lot of trouble joining my tables. What's a fore
215	How do I get listed in Yahoo?	25		9	I've figured out how to submit my URL to Google, but I can
216		25	215	42	Try http://search.yahoo.com/info/submit.html
218	That's it!	25	216	9	That's it! How did you find it?
219		25	218	42	There's a link at the bottom of the homepage called "Sugg
222	People who bought ... also bought ...	35		99	For each item in the user's cart, I want to show other item
230	WHERE clause doesn't work	45		187	My query has WHERE startdate > 2009-01-01 but I get 0 re

Figure 7.6. The posts table

The relationship of threads to posts is categorized as *one-to-one-or-many*. Each thread can have any number of posts but must have at least one: the post that starts the thread. Notice that the reply_to column relates one post to another, but that each post is also related to the thread it belongs to. The starting post in each thread has no reply_to value.

Now let's go back to discussing the SELECT clause, and the expressions that you may use. We'll begin where we left off, with aggregate functions.

Functions

Functions in SQL are considered either aggregate or scalar, depending on the scope of the data values that they operate on. **Aggregate functions** are allowed only in grouping queries and produce an aggregate result for a group of rows, while **scalar functions** can be used in both detail queries and grouping queries, and produce values based upon the input of single values.

Standard SQL includes many functions, and the developers of the various database systems (like the five mentioned in Appendix A) have added a few more of their own. All of the following functions are Standard SQL unless otherwise noted.

Aggregate Functions

The distinguishing feature of aggregate functions is that they operate on groups of column values. This makes sense when we consider the grouping operation performed by the GROUP BY clause: multiple detail rows are collapsed or aggregated into one group row, and aggregate functions are used to do the heavy lifting—providing additional meaningful data for those group rows.

Table 7.1 displays the main aggregate functions that you'll probably need as a web developer:

Table 7.1. Common Aggregate Functions

Aggregate Function	Purpose
COUNT	Counts the number of values in a group
SUM	Calculates the sum of a group of values
MIN	Finds the minimum (lowest) value from a group of values
MAX	Finds the maximum (highest) value from a group of values
AVG	Calculates the average value of a group of values

The SUM and AVG aggregate functions operate only on numeric columns. The COUNT, MIN, and MAX aggregate functions can operate on any type of column. We'll learn more about data types in Chapter 9.

Most database systems have additional, non-standard aggregate functions, such as STDEV[2] for standard deviation and VAR[3] for variance. Consult your SQL reference manual to see what's available to you.

---

[2] http://msdn.microsoft.com/en-us/library/ms190474.aspx
[3] http://msdn.microsoft.com/en-us/library/ms186290.aspx

Aggregate Functions without GROUP BY

When there's no GROUP BY clause, all of the rows in the tabular structure produced by the FROM clause—and optionally filtered by the WHERE clause—are considered to be a single group.

Thus, aggregate functions are allowed without a GROUP BY clause, but only if they're the sole expressions in the SELECT clause (along with certain keywords and constants). If the database system parses the SELECT statement to find that there's no GROUP BY clause and only aggregate functions in the SELECT clause, it knows that it must aggregate all the detail rows. If aggregate functions appear alongside column names within the SELECT clause in a SELECT statement that has no GROUP BY clause, then a syntax error occurs.

The first example of an aggregate function that we'll look at (involving our Discussion Forums application) also has no GROUP BY clause, as we shall see.

To set the stage for this example, we will again start with a non-grouping (detail) query. The following query uses LEFT OUTER JOINs to join the forums, threads, and posts tables, so that we can get a close look at the related data:

```
                                 Forums_02_Aggregate_functions.sql (excerpt)

SELECT
    forums.id    AS f_id
  , forums.name  AS forum
  , threads.id   AS t_id
  , threads.name AS thread
  , posts.id     AS p_id
  , posts.name   AS post
FROM
    forums
      LEFT OUTER JOIN threads
        ON threads.forum_id = forums.id
      LEFT OUTER JOIN posts
        ON posts.thread_id = threads.id
```

Nothing too complicated in this query, except that we've qualified the columns—we've used dot notation, because the same column name is used in more than one table—and assigned column aliases to distinguish the columns in the final result set. We use LEFT OUTER JOINs because there can be forums without threads.

The results of this query are shown in Figure 7.7.

f_id	forum	t_id	thread	p_id	post
10001	Search Engines	25	How do I get listed in Yahoo?	215	How do I get listed in Yahoo?
10001	Search Engines	25	How do I get listed in Yahoo?	216	
10001	Search Engines	25	How do I get listed in Yahoo?	218	That's it!
10001	Search Engines	25	How do I get listed in Yahoo?	219	
10002	Databases	15	Difficulty with join query	201	Difficulty with join query
10002	Databases	35	People who bought ... also bought ...	222	People who bought ... also bought ...
10002	Databases	45	WHERE clause doesn't work	230	WHERE clause doesn't work
10003	Applications				

Figure 7.7. Results: forums, threads, and posts

Each forum is included, even if it's without threads.

The reason for showing the results of this detail query is so you can visualize this as the intermediate table produced by the FROM clause, prior to the grouping operation. Now let's do a grouping query on this data, using the COUNT aggregate function:

```
                                          Forums_02_Aggregate_functions.sql (excerpt)
SELECT
   COUNT(forums.id)  AS forums
 , COUNT(threads.id) AS threads
 , COUNT(posts.id)   AS posts
FROM
   forums
     LEFT OUTER JOIN threads
        ON threads.forum_id = forums.id
     LEFT OUTER JOIN posts
        ON posts.thread_id = threads.id
```

Notice that there's no GROUP BY clause, so the entire intermediate table produced by the FROM clause is considered a single group. Therefore, the results of this query (see Figure 7.8) are, as expected, a single group row.

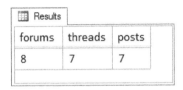

Figure 7.8. COUNT Function Results

Are you surprised by the values of the counts? They certainly do need an explanation, because—for example—we know there are only three forums!

Aggregate Functions Ignore NULLs

Firstly, why are there **8** forum values, and only **7** thread and post values? One of the most important features of aggregate functions is that they ignore any NULLs in the set of values that they operate on.

This is indeed what happened in the query above. The COUNT function has counted occurrences of values, and has ignored the NULLs in the last row of the intermediate tabular result produced by the FROM clause: the row for the Applications forum. Aggregate functions ignore NULLs by design; COUNT counts only values, SUM only sums values, and so on.

However, we know that there are only three forums. Is there a way to correct this misinformation? The answer is, yes.

COUNT(DISTINCT)

One option available within aggregate functions is the use of the keyword DISTINCT. This keyword tells the database system to aggregate only the distinct, or unique, values within the scope of the aggregate function.

Let's try it on our counting query:

```
                                    Forums_02_Aggregate_functions.sql (excerpt)
SELECT
  COUNT(DISTINCT forums.id)  AS forums
, COUNT(DISTINCT threads.id) AS threads
, COUNT(DISTINCT posts.id)   AS posts
FROM
  forums
    LEFT OUTER JOIN threads
      ON threads.forum_id = forums.id
    LEFT OUTER JOIN posts
      ON posts.thread_id = threads.id
```

Figure 7.9 shows the results returned with DISTINCT used inside each aggregate function.

forums	threads	posts
3	4	7

Figure 7.9. Results using DISTINCT

This certainly makes a lot more sense, doesn't it? However, the usefulness of COUNT(DISTINCT) comes at a hefty price. The database system will require additional processing overhead to determine the distinct values in the intermediate table produced by the FROM clause. Only after it has built up a separate, temporary table of distinct values somewhere in its memory, during execution of the query, can the database system count these distinct values. Obviously, we'll want to use COUNT(DISTINCT) sparingly.

In the query above, notice that the count produced by COUNT(DISTINCT posts.id) is 7, and this is the same value returned by the preceding query, which used COUNT(posts.id). This makes sense, when we consider all post_id values are distinct. In this case, the use of DISTINCT is a waste of resources.

Thus, to make our grouping queries slightly more efficient,[4] we should only use DISTINCT in aggregate functions for values that we know will repeat in the intermediate table produced by the FROM clause—but leave it out if they won't.

COUNT(*)

This special version of the COUNT function is used to count rows, not values. In this case all rows are counted, regardless of NULLs in any of the columns. The archetypal COUNT(*) query, the one in all the SQL tutorials, is the query that returns the number of rows in a table:

Forums_03_COUNT.sql (excerpt)

```
SELECT
  COUNT(*) AS rows
FROM
  members
```

So why is it so special, compared to other uses of the COUNT function? It turns out that COUNT(*) is extremely fast in comparison to the COUNT aggregate function used on a particular column. The reason has to do with the fact that the database system doesn't have to examine any values looking for NULLs when it calculates COUNT(*).

Always use COUNT(*) if you are interested in the number of rows, not the number of values.

To illustrate the difference, consider this detail query—which produces only the forums and threads—again using LEFT OUTER JOIN because some forums may not have threads:

Forums_03_COUNT.sql (excerpt)

```
SELECT
  forums.id    AS f_id
, forums.name  AS forum
, threads.id   AS t_id
, threads.name AS thread
FROM
```

---

[4] The bulk of the processing load is in retrieving the rows from the database tables on disk.

```
forums
   LEFT OUTER JOIN threads
      ON threads.forum_id = forums.id
```

The results of this query, which we'll again use to visualize the intermediate table produced by the FROM clause in the subsequent count queries, is shown in Figure 7.10.

f_id	forum	t_id	thread
10001	Search Engines	25	How do I get listed in Yahoo?
10002	Databases	15	Difficulty with join query
10002	Databases	35	People who bought ... also ...
10002	Databases	45	WHERE clause doesn't work
10003	Applications		

Figure 7.10. forums and threads detail query results

Our task is to retrieve data from our database that indicates how many threads exist in each forum. The first query we'll try, uses COUNT(*):

```
                                              Forums_03_COUNT.sql (excerpt)
SELECT
   forums.id     AS f_id
, forums.name    AS forum
, COUNT(*)       AS rows
FROM
   forums
     LEFT OUTER JOIN threads
        ON threads.forum_id = forums.id
GROUP BY
   forums.id
, forums.name
```

Notice that we've had to add a GROUP BY clause, because we want counts for each forum. Figure 7.11 shows the results of the above query.

Results

f_id	forum	rows
10001	Search Engines	1
10002	Databases	3
10003	Applications	1

Figure 7.11. A row count for each forum

Can you spot the problem with these results? The Applications forum has no threads, but the total returned is `1`. This result is an example of one of the more frequent problems encountered by people using `COUNT(*)`. What has happened is that the database engine has counted the rows in the intermediate table produced by the `FROM` clause. Since the Applications forum was included—on purpose, because it's a `LEFT OUTER JOIN`—there's a row for it in the intermediate result, and therefore the count is `1`.

What we actually want our query to do is to count the threads:

Forums_03_COUNT.sql *(excerpt)*

```
SELECT
  forums.id    AS f_id
, forums.name  AS forum
, COUNT(threads.id) AS threads
FROM
  forums
    LEFT OUTER JOIN threads
      ON threads.forum_id = forums.id
GROUP BY
  forums.id
, forums.name
```

Now the results, shown in Figure 7.12, make sense.

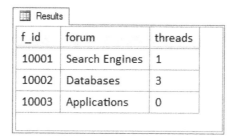

Figure 7.12. A thread count for each forum

 Avoid Using COUNT(*) in LEFT OUTER JOINs

If you're aggregating something in the right table of a LEFT OUTER JOIN, remember that LEFT OUTER JOINs (like all outer joins) produce NULLs.

Usually this will mean that you don't want to use COUNT(*). Instead, apply COUNT to non-NULL columns of the right-hand table.

Note that COUNT is the only function that allows the *all rows* asterisk. You cannot say SUM(*), for example.

Scalar Functions

Scalar functions, like aggregate functions, produce a single value as their result. However, while aggregate functions return a result based upon the aggregation of a group of column values, scalar functions return a result based on the input of single values (with a few exceptions).

Here are some of the Standard SQL scalar functions that are commonly available in all database systems.[5]

The SUBSTRING Function

The syntax of the SUBSTRING function is as follows:

```
SUBSTRING(string FROM position FOR length)
```

---

[5] Your database system may use different function names or syntax. Check your SQL reference manual to find the specifics for your system.

Anyone who has done any programming will immediately recognize this function and what it does. The result of the SUBSTRING function is a string that has been extracted from the given string specified as the first parameter of the function, beginning at character position *position*, for a length of *length* characters. For example, SUBSTRING('Samuel' FROM 1 FOR 3) would return the string 'Sam'.

Here's an example of the SUBSTRING function used in a query:

Forums_04_Scalar_functions.sql (excerpt)

```
SELECT
  threads.id AS t_id
, threads.name AS thread
, posts.id AS p_id
, SUBSTRING(posts.post FROM 1 FOR 21) AS excerpt
FROM
  threads
    LEFT OUTER JOIN posts
      ON posts.thread_id = threads.id
```

The results can be seen in Figure 7.13. Notice that the excerpt column contains only the first 21 characters of the actual post column; this is the result of the SUBSTRING function.

t_id	thread	p_id	excerpt
15	Difficulty with join query	201	I'm having a lot of t
25	How do I get listed in Yahoo?	215	I've figured out how
25	How do I get listed in Yahoo?	216	Try http://search.yah
25	How do I get listed in Yahoo?	218	That's it! How did yo
25	How do I get listed in Yahoo?	219	There's a link at the
35	People who bought … also bought …	222	For each item in the
45	WHERE clause doesn't work	230	My query has WHERE st

Figure 7.13. Using SUBSTRING

LEFT

Many database systems have a LEFT scalar function, which assumes that the FROM position parameter is 1. In database systems that support the LEFT function, the query above could have used LEFT(`posts.post`,21) instead.

The COALESCE Function

COALESCE is a very useful function that returns the first non-NULL value in a list of values.

Consider the example of concatenation. The standard SQL concatenation operator is the *double pipes* symbol: || (we'll discuss operators later on in this chapter). This is how we write the query:

```
SELECT lastname || ', ' || firstname AS fullname
```

Here we're returning the last name, then a string constant consisting of a comma and a space, and then the first name, all concatenated together into a single string. Now let's assume that we've anticipated the need to handle people who only submit one name, by using `firstname` for those cases, and setting `lastname` to NULL. But NULLs behave in a special way: they propagate, so we may have a problem.

NULLs Propagate in Expressions

When writing expressions that involve more than one value, be aware that NULLs propagate; concatenating anything with NULL produces NULL, and adding any numeric value with NULL again produces NULL. We'll cover numeric addition later in this chapter.

To make the concatenation work successfully, we have to deal with the possibility of a NULL in `lastname`, and this is where we use COALESCE. First, concatenate `last-name` and the comma and space together:

```
lastname || ', '
```

Now use this expression as the first parameter of the COALESCE function, and an empty string (' ') as the second:

```
COALESCE(lastname || ', ', '')
```

If `lastname` is NULL, then the first parameter is NULL. Now, COALESCE is looking for the first non-NULL parameter, so it goes to the next parameter along: the empty string. Since the empty string is not NULL, COALESCE will return it. So either "`lastname` plus comma and space," when it's not NULL, or the empty string, will be concatenated with `firstname`. Thus, the NULL value never propagates to `firstname`.

The CASE Function

This function returns a value, or NULL, based on a series of conditional evaluations using the keywords WHEN, THEN, ELSE, and END. It works the same way as the extremely common if/then programming construct, which some of you may be familiar with.

The WHEN keyword indicates the expression to evaluate. The THEN keyword indicates the value to return should the WHEN expression be evaluated as true. CASE can take multiple WHEN expressions with matching THEN values. Finally, if none of the expressions evaluate as true, then the ELSE keyword indicates the value to return.

For example, consider the following:

```
CASE WHEN lastname = ''
   THEN ''
   ELSE lastname || ', '
END || firstname AS fullname
```

You can translate the above code like this: in the CASE WHEN the `lastname` column value is an empty string THEN return an empty string, ELSE return the `lastname` value concatenated with a space and a comma, the END. This is finally concatenated with the value of the `firstname` column.

CASE does not look like a normal function as it's missing the usual parameters enclosed in parentheses. The CASE keyword begins the expression, and the END keyword ends it. It produces a single value, so it's a scalar function.

While COALESCE is neater than CASE, COALESCE checks only for NULL. CASE can be used to check for anything and return anything; it's the Swiss Army Knife of scalar functions.

EXTRACT

EXTRACT is used to extract portions of a DATE or DATETIME value. For example, this expression will extract the year and month from the date stored in the posts.created column as a number:

```
EXTRACT(year_month FROM posts.created)
```

Temporal functions vary greatly between different database systems. See your SQL reference manual, typically under Date Functions.

CHAR_LENGTH

CHAR_LENGTH is used to determine the character length of a value. We'd use the following to return the length of each post:

```
CHAR_LENGTH(posts.post)
```

The CAST Function

The CAST function is used to change the data type of a value. This operation is also known as **casting**. The following changes the data type of the members.id column as VARCHAR:

```
CAST(members.id AS VARCHAR)
```

Casting becomes important when importing data from external sources, or preparing data to be exported. All too often, the external source is another application in the same organization, with a different data structure. Casting is also used often in UNION queries to ensure that corresponding columns in the subselects all have the same data type. We discussed UNION queries back in the section called "UNION Queries" in Chapter 3.

The NULLIF Function

NULLIF is tricky. This function returns NULL if the values of the two parameters are equal. How might this be useful? Just as we *wrapped* an expression with COALESCE to protect against a possible NULL, we use NULLIF to produce a NULL if the two parameters are equal.

For example if we wanted to display only post names that are different from their thread names, we could use the following to detect when the value in the posts.name column is equal to the value in the threads.name column:

```
NULLIF(threads.name,posts.name)
```

Operators

Operators can be used within SELECT clause expressions, and we'll briefly review them here.

Numeric Operators

These include the usual suspects: addition, subtraction, multiplication, and division, represented by the expected symbols: +, -, *, and /. We've already seen the multiplication operator used in a SELECT clause expression, in the example in the section called "Group Rows":

```
SELECT cartitems.qty * items.price AS total
```

Note that this is not that same as the star we saw in COUNT(*) previously.

The special unary operators + and - are used to specify signed (negative or positive) values. Sometimes a modulus operator (returns the remainder of a division expression) is available, but often it's a function like MOD instead. Additional arithmetic operations are accomplished with functions, and there is a large variety available in every database system. Consult your database system's documentation for details.

The Concatenation Operator

The concatenation operator is the only character operator and is used to concatenate strings. The standard SQL concatenation operator is the *double pipes* symbol: ||. For an example of concatenation, consider the code snippet that we saw previously:

```
SELECT lastname || ', ' || firstname AS fullname
```

Here, the lastname and firstname column values are concatenated together with a comma and a space.

In MySQL Use the CONCAT Function Instead

In MySQL, concatenation is performed with an actual function. The MySQL code equivalent to the concatenation example above is:

```
SELECT CONCAT(lastname, ', ', firstname) AS fullname
```

Additional string manipulations are handled by character functions, such as SUBSTRING and others like it.

SUBSTRING_INDEX in MySQL

The SUBSTRING_INDEX function is surprisingly useful at deconstructing a string into multiple substrings based on the number of occurrences of a specified character, either from the left or the right.

If you use MySQL, make sure to look it up.

Temporal Operators

Date and time arithmetic uses intervals. For example, "tomorrow" is equivalent to "today *plus* one day" and in this context, the *plus* is a temporal calculation. This is how we would write such an expression in the SELECT clause:

```
SELECT CURRENT_DATE + INTERVAL 1 DAY AS tomorrow
```

CURRENT_DATE returns the current date on the server, which we then add to an expression we define as INTERVAL 1 DAY, meaning—obviously—1 day. This is very similar to the interval calculation we saw in the section called "BETWEEN: It haz a flavr" in Chapter 4.

All database systems have robust date and time handling capabilities, implemented in most cases by proprietary, or non-standard, functions. This is primarily because the need for date calculations was anticipated by every database system, and implemented as date functions, long before the standard was agreed to.

For example, here are 3 different ways to implement the same calculation:

```
ADDDATE(CURDATE(),1)
SYSDATE + 1
CURRENT DATE + 1 DAY
```

The first is for MySQL, the second for Oracle, and the third for IBM DB2. As always, please check your database system's documentation.

The Dreaded, Evil *Select Star*

We first met SELECT * back in Chapter 5, where I mentioned that I call it "dreaded and evil" because using it is rarely a good idea. SELECT * is a short form for specifying all columns. Here's a reminder of what it looks like in an SQL query:

```
SELECT * FROM entries
```

This query would return all columns—and all rows because there are no other clauses—from the entries table.

Using SELECT * can be useful, though. When building up a query from scratch, the first step is, of course, writing the FROM clause. This is actually a good time to use the dreaded, evil *select star* because we want to concentrate first on making our joins work. The advantage of using SELECT * at this point is that we can examine the results carefully and confirm that the rows have been joined properly, that is, on the correct columns.

The disadvantage is that SELECT * usually produces far too many columns to see important data relationships easily.

Of course, once you're sure your SQL query is working, it's important to remove the asterisk and only select the data that you really need.

There are three main reasons why the dreaded, evil "select star" should be avoided in production systems:

Performance

Whether there is just one table in the query, or a number of tables involved in joins, SELECT * returns all columns of all tables. A cardinal rule is to only return the data that you will use. Otherwise you are simply wasting resources.

Stability

When changes take place which result in adding columns to tables, or removing columns from tables, application code which uses SELECT * queries will be at risk of failing.

Clarity

In line with good coding practice, specifying only the columns you want in the SELECT clause can be useful for documentation purposes.

SELECT DISTINCT

DISTINCT is an optional keyword (which comes right after the SELECT keyword) to indicate that duplicate rows in the result set are to be removed, leaving only one instance of each. We could use it to build a list of all item types from the Shopping Cart application. Figure 7.14 shows the contents of the items table. To produce a list of only the three existing items types, our query would look like this:

```
SELECT DISTINCT type FROM items;
```

Remove the keyword DISTINCT and the query will return all 18 instances.

DISTINCT is actually one of two optional keywords that can come after the SELECT keyword. The other is ALL, which is the default (so hardly anyone ever actually specifies it). ALL simply means return all rows; do not remove duplicates. The use of ALL or DISTINCT is valid in a few other places in SQL; we've already seen it within the COUNT function.

items		
name	type	price
thingie	widgets	9.37
gadget	doodads	19.37
dingus	gizmos	29.37
gewgaw	widgets	5.00
knickknack	doodads	10.00
whatnot	gizmos	15.00
bric-a-brac	widgets	2.00
folderol	doodads	4.00
jigger	gizmos	6.00
doohickey	widgets	12.00
gimmick	doodads	9.37
dingbat	gizmos	9.37
thingamajig	widgets	
thingamabob	doodads	
thingum	gizmos	
contraption	widgets	49.95
whatchamacallit	doodads	59.95
whatsis	gizmos	

Figure 7.14. The items table

Another way to think of DISTINCT is as a quick way of writing a grouping query without any aggregate functions. Consider the following hypothetical DISTINCT query:

```
SELECT DISTINCT
  column1
, column2
, column3
, column4
FROM
  table
```

This DISTINCT query produces rows where all combinations of values in the specified columns are distinct. Sound familiar? This is exactly like grouping; in fact, it *is* grouping! The same results are produced by this query:

```
SELECT
  column1
, column2
, column3
, column4
FROM
  table
GROUP BY
  column1
, column2
, column3
, column4
```

If you're deciding which approach to take, DISTINCT merely collapses all duplicate rows into one, but has the benefit of simplicity. The advantage of using a GROUP BY clause is that you can use aggregate functions.

Finally, make sure you remember that DISTINCT applies to all columns in the SELECT clause.

Wrapping Up: the SELECT Clause

In this chapter, we learned that the SELECT clause is processed much later in the sequence of execution of the clauses of the SELECT statement—after FROM, WHERE, GROUP BY, and HAVING. Of most importance is the presence (or absence) of the GROUP BY clause, which determines the scope of the columns and expressions that the SE-LECT clause may include.

In addition, we made a very brief survey of aggregate and scalar functions, as well as SQL operators, with a smattering of examples and just a hint of the many permutations that SELECT expressions might allow.

The dreaded, evil *select star* was explained, and we touched on the use of SELECT DISTINCT.

In the next chapter, we'll complete our exploration of the SELECT statement with a discussion of the ORDER BY clause.

The **ORDER BY** Clause

In this chapter, we'll look at the ORDER BY clause, the last of the clauses of the SELECT SQL statement.[1] Not only is ORDER BY the last clause in the syntax, it's also the last clause in the execution sequence. Fortunately, ORDER BY is a really simple clause, so let's jump right in.

The purpose of the ORDER BY clause is to ensure that the result set produced by the query is returned in the specified sequence. Simply, ORDER BY sorts the results. (Personally, I think SORT BY might have been a better keyword, but it's ORDER BY and we just have to live with it.)

---

[1] Actually, **ORDER BY** is not part of the **SELECT** statement in the SQL standard; there, **ORDER BY** is defined in the context of cursors, which enable query results to be returned to application programs one row at a time. The distinction is probably moot, since all database systems support **ORDER BY** used as the last clause of the **SELECT** statement.

ORDER BY Syntax

Like the SELECT clause, the ORDER BY clause has very simple syntax:

```
ORDER BY
    column [ASC | DESC]
[, column [ASC | DESC]]
 : further columns if required…
```

Following the ORDER BY keywords is at least one column with an optional ASC (ascending) or DESC (descending) keyword; if neither is specified, ascending is the default.

There are some restrictions on which columns may be referenced, and we'll cover the scope of the ORDER BY clause a bit later on in this chapter. First, let's examine how ORDER BY works.

How ORDER BY Works

The function of the ORDER BY clause is to ensure that the result set produced by the query is returned in the sequence specified by the list of columns. Sorting a query's result set is pretty much the same here as sorting rows or records in other areas of computer technology—specifically, sorting may be performed on one or more fields, resulting in major-to-minor sequencing.

When the ORDER BY clause specifies multiple columns, the query will return rows in major-to-minor sequence by evaluating those columns in the order that they're listed—left to right, first to last, major to minor.

Let's start with a familiar example. In Chapter 5, we discussed the difference between sequencing and grouping, using the Shopping Cart sample application. To understand how grouping works, we first looked at sequenced detail data.

I needed to use an ORDER BY clause in the detail query to present the detail rows in the sequence necessary to make the GROUP BY concept easier to visualize:

```
                                                    Cart_09_Detailed_Rows.sql (excerpt)
SELECT
  customers.name     AS customer
, carts.id           AS cart
, items.name         AS item
, cartitems.qty
, items.price
, cartitems.qty
      * items.price AS total
FROM
  customers
    INNER JOIN carts
      ON carts.customer_id = customers.id
    INNER JOIN cartitems
      ON cartitems.cart_id = carts.id
    INNER JOIN items
      ON items.id = cartitems.item_id
ORDER BY
  customers.name
, carts.id, items.name
```

Now, we can finally look at this ORDER BY clause more closely. The results of the query are returned in the sequence shown in Figure 8.1.

We can confirm quickly that the results are in sequence by customer name, given that customer name here is a single value that begins with an initial.[2]

So customers.name, the first column listed in the ORDER BY clause, is the major sort field. Looking more closely, we can see that within each customer, rows are in sequence by cart, and within each cart, rows are in sequence by item. So subsequent columns listed after the first one, in this case carts.id and items.name, are progressively minor sort fields.

---

[2] Remember, this is just sample data. In a real application, it's more likely that we'd have separate customer first and last name columns.

Figure 8.1. Shopping Cart details in order

When we inspect the sorted results, we see groupings of rows in sequences, and these groupings correspond exactly to the columns listed in the ORDER BY clause.

ASC and DESC

The sequence of values for each column in the ORDER BY clause is either ascending or descending, with ascending being the default.

In the Shopping Carts example above, the ORDER BY clause sorted the details by customer (ascending), cart (ascending), and item (ascending). Let's change the ORDER BY clause to:

Cart_13_ORDER_BY_qty_DESC.sql (excerpt)

```
ORDER BY
  cartitems.qty DESC
, items.name
```

This new ORDER BY clause produces the results shown in Figure 8.2.

customer	cart	item	qty	price	total
B. Smith	2921	dingus	3	29.37	88.11
H. Clark	3081	dingus	3	29.37	88.11
A. Jones	2131	gimmick	3	9.37	28.11
C. Brown	3001	thingamabob	3	22.22	66.66
C. Brown	3937	thingum	3	22.22	66.66
G. Scott	3321	whatcham...	3	59.95	179.85
E. Baker	2461	whatnot	3	15.00	45.00
E. Baker	2461	doohickey	2	12.00	24.00
A. Jones	2131	thingum	2	22.22	44.44
H. Clark	3081	thingum	2	22.22	44.44
C. Brown	3001	whatsis	2	93.70	187.40
B. Smith	2921	whatsis	2	93.70	187.40
B. Smith	3002	doohickey	1	12.00	12.00
C. Brown	2937	thingum	1	22.22	22.22
D. White	3197	whatcham...	1	59.95	59.95

Figure 8.2. Shopping Cart details in order of quantity and item names

Notice that cart items with a quantity of 3 are listed first, then those with a quantity of 2, and finally 1. The ORDER BY clause specifies cartitems.qty as the first column, so that's the major sort key, and the direction is descending (DESC), so we see the 3s first, then the 2s, then the 1s.

Within each of these major groupings, cart items are listed in ascending sequence by name. As a point of interest, we see that dinguses are quite popular, since three of them were purchased on two different occasions.

Detecting ORDER BY Groupings in Applications

When ORDER BY has multiple columns, groupings of major-to-minor column values are produced as a natural consequence of sorting on multiple fields. The rows of the result set are returned in the ORDER BY sequence, and we can *see* the groupings.

Application logic can also *see* these groupings, by detecting control breaks while processing the result set returned by the query.

In an application, the rows of the result set are processed one at a time, sequentially. Typically this is done with looping code. As each row in the sorted results is processed, a comparison is made with a control field that contains the value from the previous row. This is sometimes referred to as **current/previous logic**. If the current row's control field value is different from that of the previous row, a **control break** has been detected.

In our original ORDER BY example the customer name was the first column specified in the ORDER BY clause. When the application code is processing the first row for B. Smith, a control break is detected on the customer name, a change from the previous name which was A. Jones. Before the data for B. Smith is printed out, the application logic can do things like print subtotals for the previous customer, A. Jones.

Current/previous logic can be extremely useful in displaying results on your web page. The SQL is kept simple, which means that database processing efficiency is optimal, and yet the processed results can include subtotals, even at multiple levels. A detailed explanation belongs in a book about programming, not SQL, but it's still worth mentioning.

To recap, the grouping performed by the ORDER BY clause is different to the grouping performed by the GROUP BY clause. The same groups of rows are involved in both cases, but the GROUP BY clause aggregates or collapses each group of multiple rows into one group row, whereas the ORDER BY clause just sequences the rows. Groupings in the sorted result set commonly appear when multiple ORDER BY expressions are specified.

ORDER BY Clause Performance

How does the ORDER BY clause actually achieve its sequencing of result rows? Most often, it does this simply by sorting the result set. Just as in other computer applications, sorting is a relatively taxing process in executing SQL queries.

If the rows to be sorted are few in number then the performance overhead required by the ORDER BY clause will be negligible. If the sort can be performed in the server's memory, it's extremely fast. Of course that depends on several factors, such as how much server memory is available to the database system and how busy it is.

However, if there are more than a few rows, the database system may need to place the rows of the result set into a temporary table, and then sort that table. Writing rows to a temporary table, and then reading them back (often in several passes) to sort them, requires extra, expensive processing cycles.

If you're thinking of presenting the results of a query in a particular sequence, the only alternatives are:

- use an ORDER BY clause
- sort the result set in the application, without using an ORDER BY clause
- forego sorting altogether

Using an ORDER BY clause is the simplest approach, because it's dead easy to specify the sequence you want. Furthermore, it's self-documenting, meaning your intentions are obvious to other programmers: these columns, from these tables, filtered by these conditions, in this sequence.

Sorting query results in the application also makes sense. For example, you may have seen web pages where tabular data is presented, with clickable column headers, so that the web page visitor can sort the data into different sequences by those columns. This can even be accomplished using JavaScript,[3] which can sort the data in the browser, independent of the server.

Finally, forgoing sorting also makes sense in certain situations. For example, if the query's purpose is to extract data which is to be exported somewhere, such as in a backup file or a file sent to another application, sorting is unnecessary.

---

[3] The SitePoint book *The Art & Science of JavaScript* has a chapter on implementing table sorting with JavaScript. See http://www.sitepoint.com/books/jsdesign1/

Be aware that ORDER BY often has a relatively big performance cost. Use it only when it's required.

When ORDER BY Seems Unnecessary

Sometimes the results of a query appear to be in sequence even though an ORDER BY clause has not been specified. Two common situations may tempt you into omitting the ORDER BY clause.

Query results are often returned in a first-in-first-out sequence when an autonumbering column is involved. Auto-numbering columns will be explained in detail in Chapter 10 but, in short, an auto-numbering column has its incrementing numbers assigned as new rows are inserted into the table. When a simple query involving an auto-numbering column produces a result set, the result set rows are often in sequence by this column. Adding an ORDER BY clause for this column would seem to be unnecessary.

The other situation involves the use of an indexed column. Indexes, first mentioned in the section called "WHERE Clause Performance" in Chapter 4, allow for efficient resolution of WHERE conditions. A query using an indexed column in the WHERE clause will almost always produce its results in sequence by that column, without an ORDER BY clause having been specified.

Since ORDER BY has a relatively high overhead, is it safe to omit it in these situations? The answer is yes and no. The only way to guarantee a sequence is to specify that sequence with the ORDER BY clause. You can omit the ORDER BY clause provided that you don't mind if the results are in a slightly difference sequence.

Also, a database system will know if the ORDER BY clause sequence is already satisfied by indexed retrieval; it will avoid the overhead of sorting them. So even when ORDER BY is specified, sorting may not actually be performed.

The Sequence of Values

We discussed the sequence of values in the section called "Comparison Operators" in Chapter 4. For example, the *less than* (<) operator makes its TRUE or FALSE determination based on the sequence of the values it compares.

The sequence used to compare values is of course also used to sort them. The data type of the values determines the nature of the sequence:

- Numeric data sorts numerically, from smaller to larger, with negative values being smaller than zero.
- String data sorts alphabetically, as defined by the collating sequence.
- Temporal data sorts chronologically, from earlier to later dates and times.

Thus ORDER BY customers.name sorts alphabetically, while ORDER BY cartitems.qty DESC sorts numerically, descending.

Dealing with ORDER BY Problems

Problems can occur when a column with an inappropriate data type is used in an ORDER BY clause. For example, when the month *name* is used in the ORDER BY clause instead of the month *number*, the results are returned in the following sequence:

```
Apr, Aug, Dec, Feb, …
```

Another common problem is when numbers are being sorted as string values alphabetically, as is the case with this sequence:

```
1, 10, 11, 12, 2, 3, …
```

The results of both sequences are exactly as specified, but are probably undesirable. (It's that old *syntax versus semantics* issue again.)

However, if you're stuck with a database design you can't change (for example, a column containing numbers was defined as a character data type), use the standard SQL CAST function in the SELECT clause; you can convert strings containing numbers into actual numeric values, assign a column alias to the result of the CAST, and use the alias in the ORDER BY clause. We met the CAST function in the section called "Scalar Functions" in Chapter 7.

NULLs Usually Sort First

When query result rows are sequenced with the ORDER BY clause, NULL values in the ORDER BY expressions are usually sorted first. I'll explain the *usually* part in a moment.

Back in Chapter 4, we initially loaded our items table with sample items, but some of those items had NULL in the price column, as you can see in Figure 8.3.

items		
name	type	price
thingie	widgets	9.37
gadget	doodads	19.37
dingus	gizmos	29.37
gewgaw	widgets	5.00
knickknack	doodads	10.00
whatnot	gizmos	15.00
bric-a-brac	widgets	2.00
folderol	doodads	4.00
jigger	gizmos	6.00
doohickey	widgets	12.00
gimmick	doodads	9.37
dingbat	gizmos	9.37
thingamajig	widgets	
thingamabob	doodads	
thingum	gizmos	
contraption	widgets	49.95
whatchamacallit	doodads	59.95
whatsis	gizmos	

Figure 8.3. The items table

To demonstrate what happens with NULL values in an ORDER BY query, let's run this query:

```
SELECT
  name
, price
FROM
  items
ORDER BY
  price
```

Figure 8.4 displays the results you'll get in most database systems.

name	price
thingamajig	
thingamabob	
thingum	
whatsis	
bric-a-brac	2.00
folderol	4.00
gewgaw	5.00
jigger	6.00
thingie	9.37
gimmick	9.37
dingbat	9.37
knickknack	10.00
doohickey	12.00
whatnot	15.00
gadget	19.37
dingus	29.37
contraption	49.95
whatchamacallit	59.95

Figure 8.4. The result of ordering NULL values

In point of fact, standard SQL allows you to specify whether NULLs sort first or last. Many database systems will sequence NULLs first, while a few, like Oracle, will sequence them last. This was the reason I said that NULLs *usually* sort first. It depends on your database system, and of course you can determine exactly what your particular database system does simply by trying the above query.

If we use the DESC option, then the situation is reversed. NULLs will sort last—or first, again depending on your database system:

```
SELECT
   name
, price
FROM
   items
ORDER BY
   price DESC
```

The results of the query using descending price ordering can be seen in Figure 8.5.

name	price
whatchamacallit	59.95
contraption	49.95
dingus	29.37
gadget	19.37
whatnot	15.00
doohickey	12.00
knickknack	10.00
thingie	9.37
gimmick	9.37
dingbat	9.37
jigger	6.00
gewgaw	5.00
folderol	4.00
bric-a-brac	2.00
whatsis	
thingamajig	
thingamabob	
thingum	

Figure 8.5. The result of ordering NULL values

What should we do if our database system sorts NULLs first, but we want NULLs to sort last in ascending sequence? We can do this easily using an expression. But before we look at an example, we need to discuss the scope of the ORDER BY clause.

The Scope of ORDER BY

At the beginning of this chapter, the first ORDER BY clause we discussed was from the familiar customer-cart-items query we first saw in Chapter 5:

```
ORDER BY
    customers.name
, carts.id
, items.name
```

This example of the ORDER BY clause allowed us to explore the major-to-minor sequencing produced when you specify multiple columns.

So the ORDER BY clause can specify table columns, but here's the neat part—those columns don't necessarily have to be mentioned in the SELECT clause. For example, we could do this:

```
SELECT
    name
FROM
    items
ORDER BY
    price DESC
```

This query returns item names only, in order of item price with higher prices first.

The ORDER BY clause also allows column aliases to be used. Let's use the customer-carts query again, but change the ORDER BY clause as follows:

```
SELECT
  customers.name     AS customer
, carts.id           AS cart
, items.name         AS item
, cartitems.qty
, items.price
, cartitems.qty
     * items.price AS total
FROM
  customers
    INNER JOIN carts
      ON carts.customer_id = customers.id
    INNER JOIN cartitems
      ON cartitems.cart_id = carts.id
    INNER JOIN items
      ON items.id = cartitems.item_id
ORDER BY
  total DESC
```

This time, there's only one column in the ORDER BY clause, but it's not a table column, it's a column alias assigned to an expression in the SELECT clause: the expression cartitems.qty * items.price. The results are shown in Figure 8.6.

The last column of the query results—total—is our ORDER BY column. This means we can sort query results not just by simple table columns, but also by more complex expressions.

customer	cart	item	qty	price	total
B. Smith	2921	whatsis	2	93.70	187.40
C. Brown	3001	whatsis	2	93.70	187.40
G. Scott	3321	whatcham...	3	59.95	179.85
H. Clark	3081	dingus	3	29.37	88.11
B. Smith	2921	dingus	3	29.37	88.11
C. Brown	3001	thingamabob	3	22.22	66.66
C. Brown	3937	thingum	3	22.22	66.66
D. White	3197	whatcham...	1	59.95	59.95
E. Baker	2461	whatnot	3	15.00	45.00
A. Jones	2131	thingum	2	22.22	44.44
H. Clark	3081	thingum	2	22.22	44.44
A. Jones	2131	gimmick	3	9.37	28.11
E. Baker	2461	doohickey	2	12.00	24.00
C. Brown	2937	thingum	1	22.22	22.22
B. Smith	3002	doohickey	1	12.00	12.00

Figure 8.6. Shopping carts ordered by cart totals

Using ORDER BY with GROUP BY

As we learned in previous chapters, when a GROUP BY clause is present in the query, the SELECT clause may include only the GROUP BY columns, aggregate functions, and constants (and expressions formed by combining any of these).

This same restriction applies to the ORDER BY clause when a GROUP BY clause is present. According to standard SQL, each column used in the ORDER BY clause must be either a grouping column or a column alias in the SELECT clause for any other expressions.

As you begin to feel comfortable writing GROUP BY queries, you may notice that, in your particular database system, the results often seem to be returned in the GROUP BY sequence. In other words, it appears as though the GROUP BY clause somehow *pre-sorts* the detail rows, before collapsing them into group rows. It's as though an ORDER BY clause were present with the same columns as the GROUP BY clause.

The reason for this is simple: one easy way for the database system to perform the grouping function is to first sort the rows. Leaving out the ORDER BY clause would then appear to be reasonable, given that it's an additional overhead. However, as with the scenarios discussed earlier in this chapter, there's no guarantee that the result rows will actually be returned in the GROUP BY sequence.

Once again, the guideline is clear: the only way to guarantee a sequence is to specify that sequence with the ORDER BY clause.

ORDER BY Expressions

Standard SQL allows only columns in the ORDER BY clause, however, most database systems have relaxed this requirement. What this means is that we could have written the ORDER BY clause of our previous detail query like this:

```
ORDER BY
   cartitems.qty * items.price DESC
```

By coding an expression into the ORDER BY clause, we can avoid having to include the expression in the SELECT clause and assigning it an alias. However, in this specific example, the sequence of the results would be more apparent if the total column was included in the result set. Sometimes, though, we'll want the results of a query to be sequenced by a column or expression that we don't necessarily need in the SELECT clause. This is feasible, and allowed by most database systems, provided that the scope is respected if a GROUP BY clause is present.

Special Sequencing

Here's a slightly more complex example of where the use of expressions in the ORDER BY clause is useful: special sequencing. **Special sequencing** is when you use an expression in the ORDER BY clause to specify a sequence for data without relying on the natural sequence for that data type. For an example of special sequencing, we'll use the situation mentioned earlier in this chapter: ensuring that NULLs sort last, when they'd normally sort first.

We'll use the same query as before, to return items and their prices, except this time we'll modify the ORDER BY clause, using the CASE function we learned about in the section called "Scalar Functions" in Chapter 7, so that NULL prices appear last in the sequence:

```
                          Cart_15_ORDER_BY_with_NULLs_last.sql (excerpt)
SELECT
   name
, price
FROM
   items
ORDER BY
   CASE WHEN price IS NULL
      THEN 2
      ELSE 1
   END
, price
```

The results, shown in Figure 8.7, are sequenced first by an expression, and second by the `price` column. As you can see above, the first expression does not appear in the SELECT clause.

The CASE expression evaluates the price on each row, and produces a value of either 1 or 2 depending on whether or not the price is NULL. Thus, rows with a NULL price get assigned a value of 2, and this group of rows will sort after the group of rows with real prices, which have a value of 1 for the CASE expression.

Within each of these two groups, rows are sequenced by price, which is the second ORDER BY column. Of course, this produces the desired result for actual prices, while rows with NULL prices are also sorted within their group, except that they all have the same value—actually, an absence of a value—so the sequence of these rows within that second group is indeterminate. Whew!

It's as if this first expression in the ORDER BY clause creates a *pseudo-column* which is appended to each row, so that the rows can be sorted into major-to-minor sequence (that is, 2s then 1s), just as if we'd declared the CASE expression in the SELECT clause and assigned it a column alias. When the sorted results are ready to be returned to the application which executed the query, the pseudo-column is not included.

name	price
bric-a-brac	2.00
folderol	4.00
gewgaw	5.00
jigger	6.00
thingie	9.37
gimmick	9.37
dingbat	9.37
knickknack	10.00
doohickey	12.00
whatnot	15.00
gadget	19.37
dingus	29.37
contraption	49.95
whatchamacallit	59.95
whatsis	
thingamajig	
thingamabob	
thingum	

Figure 8.7. The result of special sequencing—so that NULLs appear last

ORDER BY with UNION Queries

As you know from Chapter 3, a UNION query combines the results of several SELECT queries—more properly referred to as subselects—into a single query.

When a UNION query's results are to be sorted, there's only one ORDER BY clause permitted, and it must go at the end. The general form of the query is:

```
SELECT …
UNION
SELECT …
UNION
SELECT …
ORDER BY …
```

In standard SQL, the UNION query must be given a table alias, but the above general form—where the ORDER BY clause is simply *tacked on* after the last subselect in the UNION—is supported by most database systems.

The example we'll explore for sorting the results of a UNION involves returning both detail and group rows in the same result set. Let's first have a look at the query:

```
                                    Cart_16_Details_and_Totals.sql (excerpt)
SELECT
  *
FROM (
  SELECT
    customers.name      AS customer
  , carts.id            AS cart
  , items.name          AS item
  , cartitems.qty
  , items.price
  , cartitems.qty
        * items.price AS total
  FROM
    customers
      INNER JOIN carts
        ON carts.customer_id = customers.id
      INNER JOIN cartitems
        ON cartitems.cart_id = carts.id
      INNER JOIN items
        ON items.id = cartitems.item_id

  UNION ALL

  SELECT
    customers.name                    AS customer
  , NULL                              AS cart
  , CAST(COUNT(items.name) AS CHAR)   AS item
  , NULL                              AS qty
  , NULL                              AS price
  , SUM(cartitems.qty
        * items.price)                AS total
  FROM
    customers
      INNER JOIN carts
        ON carts.customer_id = customers.id
      INNER JOIN cartitems
```

```
        ON cartitems.cart_id = carts.id
      INNER JOIN items
        ON items.id = cartitems.item_id
    GROUP BY
      customers.name
  ) AS dt
ORDER BY
  customer
, cart
, item
```

Notice that the UNION query (in this case UNION ALL) has been *pushed down* into the FROM clause, making it a derived table, with dt as the imaginatively chosen table alias. SELECT * star has been used in the outer query, but that's okay, because it's clear exactly which columns are in the result set—the ones specified in the derived table.

Look at each of the two subselects in the UNION. The first, by now, should be easily recognized as our detail query. The second, because it has a GROUP BY clause, is a grouping query, which produces aggregates for each customer. In the SELECT clause of the second subselect, we see the same total expression as in the first subselect, but within a SUM aggregate function, as well as an additional aggregate, COUNT(items.name). This is the count of cart items for each customer, and it is *shoe-horned* into the same column occupied by the item name in the first subselect, using the CAST function to turn it into a string. This is because the matching columns in each subselect of a UNION query must have the same data type.

Clearly, as Figure 8.8 shows, the detail and total (grouped) rows have been *inter-leaved* in the result set. Notice furthermore that the totals row for each customer precedes the detail rows for that customer. This is accomplished by the simple fact that NULLs sort first, and the value of the cart column, the second column in the ORDER BY clause, is NULL on total rows.

customer	cart	item	qty	price	total
A. Jones		2			72.55
A. Jones	2131	gimmick	3	9.37	28.11
A. Jones	2131	thingum	2	22.22	44.44
B. Smith		3			287.51
B. Smith	2921	dingus	3	29.37	88.11
B. Smith	2921	whatsis	2	93.70	187.40
B. Smith	3002	doohickey	1	12.00	12.00
C. Brown		4			342.94
C. Brown	2937	thingum	1	22.22	22.22
C. Brown	3001	thingamabob	3	22.22	66.66
C. Brown	3001	whatsis	2	93.70	187.40
C. Brown	3937	thingum	3	22.22	66.66
D. White		1			59.95
D. White	3197	whatchamacallit	1	59.95	59.95
E. Baker		2			69.00
E. Baker	2461	doohickey	2	12.00	24.00
E. Baker	2461	whatnot	3	15.00	45.00
G. Scott		1			179.85
G. Scott	3321	whatchamacallit	3	59.95	179.85
H. Clark		2			132.55
H. Clark	3081	dingus	3	29.37	88.11
H. Clark	3081	thingum	2	22.22	44.44

Figure 8.8. The results of using ORDER BY with a UNION query

If you are an experienced programmer, you can see an immediate benefit in having the total row ahead of the detail rows for each customer if you need to use this data in your application. Printing totals before details is normally quite complicated if the result set contains only detail rows. Refer to Detecting ORDER BY Groupings in Applications earlier in this chapter for comparison. The UNION query that produces totals as well as details, and then interleaves them, is more complex than the simple detail query, but nowhere near as complex as the application programming required to achieve the same effect.

Wrapping Up: the **ORDER BY** Clause

In this chapter, we learned how the ORDER BY clause works to return sequenced query results.

The ORDER BY clause is used to ensure that the query results are returned in the specified sequence, even though a sort may not always be involved. Multiple ORDER BY columns may be specified, and they act as major-to-minor sort keys. The nature of the sequence—alphabetical, numerical, or chronological—is determined by the data type of the column.

Sequencing of each ORDER BY column can be ascending or descending. NULLs usually sort first, except in some database systems where they sort last. The scope of the ORDER BY clause is the same scope as the SELECT clause, and the columns that can be referenced in the ORDER BY clause depend on the presence or absence of the GROUP BY clause.

This concludes our detailed examination of the SELECT SQL statement. In summary, we learned that the clauses are executed in the following sequence:

1. FROM retrieves data and creates a tabular structure
2. WHERE filters the rows of this tabular structure
3. GROUP BY aggregates or collapses detail rows into group rows
4. HAVING filters group rows
5. SELECT specifies expressions to be returned as columns in the result set of the query
6. ORDER BY sequences the results

We'll now move on to the next part of the book, which is all about database design, and learn more about creating effective tables for our applications.

SQL Data Types

Not everything that counts can be counted, and not everything that can be counted counts.

—Albert Einstein

Welcome to the first of three chapters in this book about database design. If you've followed along faithfully until now, well done. Several chapters were needed to cover the SELECT statement in detail, so that we could gain an appreciation for how tabular data is extracted from the database, filtered, summarized, presented, and sequenced. Now it's time to turn our attention to the challenges of creating database tables.

Creating tables is straightforward, with only a few tricky aspects to watch out for. These are encountered primarily when deciding how tables should be related to each other, and we'll cover table relationships in Chapter 10. In this chapter, we'll examine table columns in isolation, and discuss the options available to define them.

In our sample applications, we've seen several examples of the CREATE TABLE statement. When we create a table, we must give it one or more columns, and once the table has been defined, we can go ahead and insert rows of data into it, and then use it in our SELECT queries.

This chapter looks at how to choose a column's data type. A data type must be assigned to each column, and we'll cover the choices available. We'll also discuss briefly some of the constraints that we may employ to tailor the columns more to our requirements.

An Overview of Data Types

When we create a column, we must give it a data type. The data type will correspond to one of these basic categories of data:

1. numeric
2. character
3. temporal (date and time)

Each of these data type categories allows for a wide range of possible values, and each of them is, by its very nature, different from the others. Numeric data type columns are used to store amounts, prices, counts, ratings, temperatures, measurements, latitudes and longitudes, shoe sizes, scores, salaries, identifier numbers, and so on. Character data type columns are used to store names, descriptions, text, strings, words, source code, symbols, identifier codes, and so on. Temporal data type columns are used to store a date, a time, or a timestamp (which has both date and time components). Although the concept is easy, temporal data types are often the most troublesome for novices.

The process of choosing an appropriate data type begins with an analysis of the data values that we wish to store in the column. Because the categories of data types are so inherently different from each other, this is often a trivially easy step. Perhaps the only difficulty arises in a few *edge cases*, where it may look like numeric data but should actually be defined with a character data type. There's an example later in the chapter.

So let's start discussing the data types in detail.

Numeric Data Types

Numeric data types can be divided into in two types: exact and approximate. Before you begin to wonder how a number can be approximate, let me reassure you that most of the numeric data types we use in web development are exact.

Exact numbers are those like 42 and 9.37. When you store a numeric value in an exact numeric column, you'll always be able to retrieve exactly the same value in a SELECT query. This is not the case with approximate numbers, where the value you retrieve might be a different number, although it would be very, very close.

Let's start with the exact numeric data types, which are either integers or decimals.

Integers

Integers are the whole numbers that we have been accustomed to from the earliest days of our childhood: 1, 2, 3, and so on. In standard SQL, there are three integer data types. INTEGER and SMALLINT have been standard all along, and BIGINT appears to have been added in either the SQL-1999 or SQL-2003 standard.[1]

INTEGER

INTEGER columns can hold both positive and negative numbers (and zero, of course). The range of numbers that can be supported is usually from -2,147,483,648 to 2,147,483,647. This is the range of numbers that can be implemented in binary notation using 32 bits (4 bytes). Curiously, the SQL standard does not actually specify a range for INTEGER, but all database systems uniformly use 32 bits.

SMALLINT

SMALLINT columns will support—you guessed it—a smaller range of integers than INTEGER. As with INTEGER, standard SQL does not specify the range, merely stipulating that the range be smaller. SMALLINT is usually implemented in 16 bits (2 bytes), leading to a range of -32,768 to 32,767.

---

[1] The various versions of the SQL standard, as I mentioned before, are not freely available and must be purchased. What matters much more than minutiae like this, of course, is whether your particular database system has implemented a given feature. MySQL, PostgreSQL, SQL Server, and DB2 all support BIGINT.

BIGINT

BIGINT columns support a much larger range of integers than INTEGER. Database systems that support BIGINT usually use 64 bits (8 bytes), resulting in a range of numbers from -9,223,372,036,854,775,808 to 9,223,372,036,854,775,807. That's over nine quintillion. Hence, it's extremely unlikely that you'll need to use BIGINT. We'll see BIGINT again in the section on autonumbers in Chapter 10.

 ## Pros and Cons of Non-standard Data Types

Some database systems have implemented additional, non-standard integer data types.

MySQL has added MEDIUMINT, implemented in 24 bits (3 bytes), giving a range of −8,388,608 to 8,388,607. This slots MEDIUMINT in between SMALLINT and INTEGER.

MySQL and SQL Server also support TINYINT, although they have different implementations. Both are based on 8 bits (1 byte). MySQL's range is −128 to 127 or 0 to 255, while SQL Server disallows negative TINYINT values and so has a range of 0 to 255.

If your database system supports TINYINT, using it can seem irresistible. Why declare a numeric column with the 2-byte SMALLINT data type, when you know that there will be only a few small values, comfortable fitting within the 1-byte TINYINT range of -128 to 127 or 0 to 255?

One benefit of using TINYINT over SMALLINT or INTEGER comes from the reduced disk space requirements. Of course, our table will need to have many millions of rows in order for the saved space to amount to more than a few megabytes, and we'll also need to take the total space requirements of all other columns into consideration to determine if the overall savings are meaningful.

One disadvantage is that we'll need to change the data type if we have to port our tables to a database system that doesn't support TINYINT. This is mitigated by the fact that changing the data type is easily accomplished; for example, we could use a text editor on the source DDL, changing all occurrences of TINYINT to SMALLINT in one command.

So while the best practice strategy is to use either SMALLINT or INTEGER because these are portable to all database systems, many SQL developers will use TINYINT anyway, if it's available, even though the space saved is rarely considerable. Perhaps we're just being neat and tidy.

Decimals

Decimal numbers have two parts: the total number of digits, and the number of digits to the right of the decimal point; the decimal point isn't actually stored. For example, the number 9.37 has three total digits, of which two are to the right of the decimal point.

There are two, almost identical, kinds of decimal data type: NUMERIC and DECIMAL. Both data types have the same format:

```
NUMERIC(p[,s])
DECIMAL(p[,s])
```

The mandatory parameter *p* above, represents the **precision**: the total number of digits allowed. The optional parameter *s* (which defaults to 0 if omitted) represents the **scale**: the total number of digits to the right of the decimal point.

Standard SQL says that the difference between NUMERIC and DECIMAL is *implementation dependent*. NUMERIC columns must have the exact precision specified, but DECIMAL columns might have a larger precision than specified if this is more efficient or convenient for the database system. In practice, they behave identically. My personal preference is DECIMAL.

NUMERIC and DECIMAL data types each allow both positive and negative values, and have the same range of possible values. However, the size of this range varies from one database system to another. PostgreSQL, for example, allows a precision of 1,000 digits. In practice, you'll rarely approach the limits of the range, whatever they are.

Use DECIMAL but Consult Your SQL Reference Manual

Check your manual for details about the DECIMAL data types available to you. The maximum precision (total number of digits) and maximum scale (number of digits to the right of the decimal point) can vary from one database system to another.

DECIMAL data types are almost always preferred over floating-point data types (discussed further on), simply because decimals are exact and floating-point numbers are approximate.

DECIMAL data types are also preferred over non-standard ones such as SQL Server's MONEY data type, which is **deprecated**. (Deprecated means that you shouldn't use it because it will be removed in a future release of this SQL standard or product, even though you can at present.)

Let's look at a few quick examples of DECIMAL data types.

To define a column which will hold a value such as 9.37, we could employ DECIMAL(3,2) as the data type. The precision and scale of 3 and 2 mean that:

1. 3 digits in total are allowed

2. 2 of those digits are to the right of the decimal point

Note that DECIMAL(3,2) is inadequate for holding a value such as 12.34, because 12.34 has two digits to the left of the decimal point, and we allowed for only one. Attempting to insert this value usually results in an error message about "arithmetic overflow."

Nor can DECIMAL(3,2) properly hold a value such as 0.567, because even though there are only three significant digits in total, the column can hold only two positions to the right of the decimal point. Attempting to insert this value, however, does proceed, with the value being rounded to 0.57 to fit into the column. The column can hold the value, but with an accuracy of only two decimal digits. As to what your particular database system will do, in the case where you attempt to insert a value that does not conform to the column data type, you'll just have to test it to make sure.

Test Your Database System

Depending on your database system, attempting to insert the value above might be allowed *silently*. To confirm how your database system handles this situation, you might like to run a test query like the following. In this query we create a table called `test_decimals`, add a column called `d`, and try to insert various decimal values into it:

```
                                          test_02_DECIMAL.sql (excerpt)
CREATE TABLE test_decimals
(
   d    DECIMAL(3,2)   NOT NULL PRIMARY KEY
);

INSERT INTO test_decimals (d) VALUES (    9.37  );
INSERT INTO test_decimals (d) VALUES (    0.567 );
INSERT INTO test_decimals (d) VALUES (   12.34  );
INSERT INTO test_decimals (d) VALUES (  888.88  );

SELECT
   d
FROM
   test_decimals
;
```

The two emphasized `INSERT` statements above will fail when run on SQL Server with the error "`arithmetic overflow error converting numeric to data type numeric`", but MySQL will allow them. Interestingly, when running the `SELECT` query, MySQL will return:

```
 0.57
 9.37
12.34
99.99
```

In answer to the question, *why*, I'll leave it as an exercise for you.

When using decimal data types, always choose a precision that comfortably holds the maximum range of data that the column is expected to contain. Make the scale adequate for your needs, too, considering that rounding will take place, especially where arithmetic calculations are performed.

For financial amounts, some people like to specify four decimal places instead of two for greater decimal accuracy, for example, interest calculations. Accuracy here refers to the decimal portion of the number; 12.0625 is more accurate than 12.06 if the number being represented is twelve and one sixteenth.

 PS: Precision, scale, and accuracy

It's easy to confuse the words *accuracy* and *precision* in this context, because in everyday language they are synonyms. The syntax of the decimal and numeric data type keywords is often written as:

```
DECIMAL(p,s)
NUMERIC(p,s)
```

A more accurate decimal number has more digits to the right of the decimal point, but precision (the first parameter above: *p*) means the total number of significant digits. A more accurate decimal number has a larger scale, but since scale digits are counted within the total number of precision digits, a more accurate number means a larger precision as well.

Scale (the second parameter above: *s*) can also be misunderstood as the range of values describing how large or small the number can be; in everyday language, to scale something up means to allow for it to enlarge. In decimal numbers, to allow for a larger range, we need to increase the number of digits to the left of the decimal point, which is equal to *p* minus *s*. So to increase the range also means increasing the total number of significant digits, the *p* in DECIMAL(p,s).

PS: An easy way to remember which words to use is with the mnemonic, *PS*.

Example: Latitude and Longitude

Latitude and longitude (see Figure 9.1) are often expressed as decimals. Suppose we wanted to keep 6 positions to the right of the decimal point. The values we're planning to store look like 43.697677 and -79.371643. Maybe that's too accurate, because specifying 6 digits to the right of the decimal point corresponds to pinpointing a location on earth with a level of accuracy as refined as to the size of a grapefruit. To locate buildings, a scale of 4 (4 digits to the right of the decimal point) is sufficient.

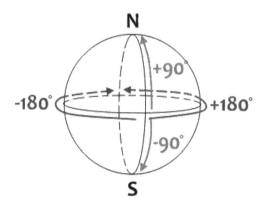

Figure 9.1. Latitude and longitude

We could use DECIMAL(6,4) for latitude, which has values that range from −90° to +90°, but we'd need DECIMAL(7,4) for longitude, which has values that range from −180° to +180°.

Having seen the exact numeric data types—integer and decimal—let's move on to the approximate numeric data types.

Floating-point Numbers

Approximate numbers are implemented as **floating-point numbers**, and are usually either very, very large, or very, very small. Floating-point numbers are often used for scientific data, where absolute accuracy is neither required nor assumed.

Consider this example of a very large number: a glass of water has approximately 7,900,000,000,000,000,000,000,000 water molecules. This number is much larger than a BIGINT column will allow. A decimal specification to hold this number would be DECIMAL(25,0) and that's quite a large precision value—each digit will require extra storage space, but only two of the 25 digits are significant.

A floating-point number is compatible with scientific notation. That humongous number of water molecules can also be written as 7.9×10^{24}, where 7.9 is called the **mantissa** and 24 is called the **exponent**. Scientific notation is useful because it separates the accuracy of the number from its largeness or smallness. Floating-point numbers also have a precision, but it applies to the mantissa only. Thus, 7.91×10^{24} is more accurate than 7.9×10^{24}.

Why are floating-point numbers called approximate? Simply because of rounding errors, which depend in part on the underlying hardware architecture of the computer. A more detailed explanation is beyond the scope of this book; see Wikipedia's page on IEEE Standard 754.[2]

FLOAT, REAL, and DOUBLE PRECISION

As with the decimal data types DECIMAL and NUMERIC, Standard SQL has several kinds of floating-point data types: FLOAT, REAL, and DOUBLE PRECISION. As with DECIMAL and NUMERIC, the differences are minor and *implementation defined*. In practice, they all behave the same. It's common for database systems to use either 4 or 8 bytes to store a floating-point number. DOUBLE PRECISION, as you might have guessed, has greater precision than FLOAT or REAL. Check your SQL reference manual for the full details of floating-point numbers in your database system.

Imagine a table called test_floats with a FLOAT column called f; when storing numbers into a floating-point column, we can specify the value of the number like so:

```
                                                    test_03_FLOAT.sql (excerpt)

INSERT INTO test_floats
  ( f )
VALUES
  ( 7900000000000000000000000 )
```

We can also do the same using *exponent* notation:

```
                                                    test_03_FLOAT.sql (excerpt)

INSERT INTO test_floats
  ( f )
VALUES
  ( 7.9E24 )
```

Exponent notation uses the letter E between the decimal mantissa and integer exponent. The mantissa can be signed, giving a positive or negative number, while the exponent can also be signed, giving a very large or very small number.

---

[2] http://en.wikipedia.org/wiki/IEEE_754

When to Use Floating-point Data Types

Use a floating-point data type to store only very large or very small numbers.

As well, you may also use floating-point when accuracy is not crucial. In the earlier example of latitudes and longitudes, floating-point numbers could be used because the location specified by the latitude and the longitude numbers is only approximate anyway. Think of it like this: with a large enough precision, you can specify a location accurate to within the size of a grapefruit, while the rounding errors due to using an approximate data type are equivalent to the width of the grapefruit peel.

Conversions in Numeric Calculations

Whenever we perform a numeric calculation, data type conversion may occur depending on the calculation. A numeric calculation performed in an SQL statement will have a resulting value that's typically given a data type large enough to accommodate it.

For example, the numbers 123,456,789 and 555 are perfectly good integers on their own, but if we multiply them together, the result is 68,518,517,895. This is also an integer, but will exceed an INTEGER column. If this multiplication is done in the SELECT clause of a query, the result is simply returned as a BIGINT data type. If we try to insert the result into an INTEGER column, we'll receive an error message, as the value is too big.

As another example, suppose we multiply the two perfectly ordinary DECIMAL(3,2) numbers—1.23 and 4.56—together. The answer is 5.6088, and we know this value will be rounded if it's stored into another DECIMAL(3,2) column. (An error would occur if the multiplication result is larger than 9.99.) If we simply return the calculation in a SELECT clause, the expression will have a data type of DECIMAL(5,4) or DECIMAL(6,4).

Numeric Functions

Now that we've learned how and when to assign the various numeric data types, let's have a quick look at the functions that are available to work with them.

In the section called "Numeric Operators" in Chapter 7, we saw the basic arithmetic operators, +, -, *, and / (for addition, subtraction, multiplication, and division) used to combine numeric values when creating expressions in the SELECT clause. There are, in all database systems, a large number of additional numeric functions that can be used. Here are a few:

Table 9.1. Commonly available numeric functions

Numeric Function	Purpose
ABS	returns the absolute value of a number
CEILING	returns the smallest integer greater than or equal to the number specified
FLOOR	returns the largest integer less than or equal to the number specified
MOD	returns the modulus (the remainder) of a division expression
RAND	returns a random number
ROUND	rounds a number to a specified precision

Database systems will vary according to which functions they offer. Some will have many more, including algebraic functions, geometric functions, and so on. Check your SQL reference manual for details.

Now let's move on to the second of the three major data type categories: character.

Character Data Types

Character data types should be very familiar to anyone who has worked with computers. Character data types are used to store any values containing letters, symbols, punctuation marks, and so on. Digits are permitted too, of course, and therein lies one of the few pitfalls that you might encounter in selecting an appropriate data type. We'll discuss this issue in a moment.

CHAR

The first of the three character data types is CHAR, also called CHARACTER, which is used to define a fixed-width character column. When specifying a CHAR column, we must give a width. Thus, CHAR(1) and CHAR(21) are examples of character data types resulting in columns which can hold character strings that are 1 and 21 characters long, respectively.

Again, the terminology here might be confusing. We speak of strings that have a length of so many characters, but we speak of character columns as being so many characters wide. This is mere convention, and both words should convey the same concept in this context.

If a character string value is inserted into a CHAR column with fewer characters than the column allows, it's positioned at the left and padded with spaces on the right until it fills the column. Fortunately, we don't have to specify those spaces when evaluating column values. Consider this condition:

```
WHERE country = 'Cuba'
```

If country is a CHAR(50) column, then the condition will evaluate as TRUE even though the value stored in the column consists of the letters Cuba followed by 46 spaces. Trailing spaces are ignored. All values in the column are 50 characters long.

If a character string value is inserted into a CHAR column with more characters than the column allows, excess characters are truncated from the right until it fits.

VARCHAR

VARCHAR, also called VARYING CHARACTER, requires a width too, but in this case it's the maximum width of the values allowed in the column. The actual width of the column value in each row depends on the value.

Thus, the value Cuba stored in a VARCHAR(50) column will require only 4 characters. This can make the rows substantially shorter. There is a very small amount of overhead required for VARCHAR columns—an additional number is required to indicate how long each value is. This number is typically a one byte binary number, which is why many database implementations allow VARCHAR widths only up to 255.

In Figure 9.2, the lengths for the VARCHAR values are actually stored in the row, whereas the lengths for the CHAR values are not.

VARCHAR(50)

```
 4 | Cuba|
13 | Liechtenstein|
32 | Saint Vincent and the Grenadines |
```

CHAR(50)

```
50 | Cuba                               |
50 | Liechtenstein                      |
50 | Saint Vincent and the Grenadines   |
```

Figure 9.2. How CHAR(50) and VARCHAR(50) are stored in the database

Check your SQL reference manual for the maximum column width allowed for both CHAR and VARCHAR columns.

The additional resource overhead for VARCHAR is typically more than offset by the fact that the rows are, in general, shorter. Thus, more rows can fit onto a single block of disk space, meaning that overall input and output operations performed by the database system will be faster for the same number of rows.

If there is variation in the lengths of a column's values, my own preference is to use CHAR for widths up to 4, and VARCHAR for widths from 5 up, but that's just a hunch as to where the *break even* point might be. The difference in row lengths with CHAR(4) versus VARCHAR(4) would be marginal, and I've yet to tested the differences in performance.

Of course, you can also have large CHAR columns if they're appropriate. If all the values you wish to store are always the same length, then it only makes sense to use CHAR with a fixed width. Fixed length standard codes, like the EAN number used on product bar codes, are good candidates.

Numeric or Character?

One of the few problems in deciding on the data type to use for a column is an *edge case* in which there's a choice between numeric and character. Obviously, this choice is possible only when the values consist of digits and no other characters; as soon as any letter or symbol is involved, a numeric data type is out of the question.

The classic examples are phone numbers and American ZIP codes (postal codes). Neither contains any characters other than digits, so both appear to be good candidates for a numeric data type, especially given that:

1. numeric data types often require fewer bytes of storage than the equivalent number of digits in a character column

2. numeric values are more efficient when used in indexes for searching

These properties are often attractive to novices. Nevertheless, to paraphrase Einstein, not everything that can fit into a numeric column should be numeric. One good rule of thumb is: "if you're not going to do arithmetic with it, leave it as a character data type." Since finding an average phone number or the sum of all ZIP codes is a ridiculous proposition, numeric properties are not needed for these columns. The disadvantages of using numeric data types include formatting issues and sorting problems.

When formatting is required, a character data type is better. The phone number 9375551212 is a valid `BIGINT` value, but we'd rather see it formatted as (937) 555-1212. Doing this in every `SELECT` statement where we want to display the phone number becomes tedious. With a character data type, the formatting can be imposed upon data entry, storing the parentheses and dashes right in the value. Sorting the formatted values works too, since they would all have the same parentheses and dashes in the same positions.

If we store ZIP codes as a numeric data type, applying sorting would be disastrous. For ZIP codes, the presence of the optional last 4 digits—indicating a more specific segment within a delivery area—is problematic, since 5-digit and 9-digit codes would be in separate parts of the sorted results. Table 9.2 shows us that while sorting ZIP codes numerically is accurate for numbers, what we'd really prefer is alphabetical sorting.

Table 9.2. ZIP codes sorted numerically and alphabetically

Sorted Numerically	Sorted Alphabetically
12345	12345
12346	12345-0112
12347	12345-0114
long list of values...	12345-0116
99901	12346
99902	12347
123450112	*long list of values...*
123450114	99901
123450116	99902

As always, if you're careful to analyse the needs of your application, you'll be guided in your decision about which data type to use.

NCHAR and NVARCHAR

The SQL standard also provides for NATIONAL CHARACTER and NATIONAL CHARACTER VARYING data types. The NCHAR and NVARCHAR data types are just like CHAR and VARCHAR, but use a larger character set, most often one of the Unicode character sets such as UTF-8.[3] You'd need this for internationalization purposes, for example, if you store characters from foreign languages.

These data types behave just like CHAR and VARCHAR, except the NCHAR and NVARCHAR columns require 2 bytes to store every character, rather than the 1 byte we're used to with character sets like ASCII.

Consult your SQL reference manual for specifics about the character sets supported.

CLOB and BLOB

When the contents of a character column are expected to be relatively large, larger than can fit into the maximum CHAR or VARCHAR data type, a large-object character data type is required. In web development, this type of column is used to store things like the source text of an article entry (perhaps in plain text, perhaps with

---

[3] http://en.wikipedia.org/wiki/UTF-8

HTML or XML tags), the full description of a shopping cart item (as opposed to its shorter name or description), the content of a forum posting, and so on.

In standard SQL, the two data types CHARACTER LARGE OBJECT and BINARY LARGE OBJECT, also affectionately known as CLOB and BLOB, are provided for large column values. CLOBs are used to store character data (using character sets), while BLOBs are used to store binary data, such as images, sound, and video. Only some database systems implement both CLOBs and BLOBs, and these can vary in the way they're implemented across systems; MySQL, for instance, implements TEXT instead of CLOB. Typical space limitations, if any, are in the megabyte range or even larger.

Both of these data types have restrictions in database systems that implement them. For example, CLOBs and BLOBs can't be indexed or sorted—but then, doing so hardly makes sense.[4] Imagine all the novels ever written stored in a large database; why would you want to list them sorted by their text content?

There are also some limitations with character functions and operators working with CLOBs or BLOBs. Speaking of which, it's time for a quick review of character functions, more commonly known as string functions.

String Functions

In Chapter 7, we saw two basic string functions, SUBSTRING and the concatenation operator (| |), used to extract portions of, or combine character values when creating expressions in the SELECT clause. There are, in all database systems, a large number of additional string functions that can be used. Table 9.3 lists just a few.

---

[4] This refers to normal performance-oriented indexes. Several database systems support full text indexes for large text objects.

Table 9.3. Some common string functions

String Function	Purpose
LEFT	returns a substring from the left of the string value
RIGHT	returns a substring from the right of the string value
CHAR_LENGTH	returns the length of the string in bytes
REVERSE	reverses the characters of the string
TRIM	removes characters from the string
REPLACE	replaces characters in the string with specified characters
LOWER, UPPER	change the characters to lower or upper case

It will vary amongst database systems who has what function, or even whether they use the same function name. There are many other useful string functions, particularly regular expressions, supported by some database systems, which allow for very sophisticated pattern matching. You know the drill by now: check your SQL reference manual for details of the string functions available to you.

Now let's move on to the third major data type category: temporal.

Temporal Data Types

Temporal data types are dates, times, and timestamps (which consist of both date and time components). These are intuitive data types that we can all understand, but working with them causes new SQL developers more trouble than other data types. The situation is not helped by the fact that temporal data types can have vastly different implementations from one database system to another.

On the surface, dates and times are dead simple. The DATE data type is used to store dates, and the TIME data type is used to store times. It gets progressively more complicated after that, so let's take things one step at a time (no pun intended).

DATE

The DATE data type is used to store date values from the **Common Era** calendar, which is the standard, 365-day Gregorian calendar. A date value has three components: year, month, and day. An example of a date constant can be seen in the following query:

```
SELECT
  customer_id
FROM
  carts
WHERE
  cartdate = DATE '2008-09-21'
```

The important point to note here is that, in the above query (and in the SQL standard), the keyword DATE is actually part of the date constant value. However, because most database systems were developed before dates and times were standardized in SQL, standard SQL doesn't always work. For example, the above query works fine in MySQL, but fails in SQL Server until the DATE keyword is removed:

```
SELECT
  customer_id
FROM
  carts
WHERE
  cartdate = '2008-09-21'
```

This form of the date constant looks like a simple character string value, and will work in all database systems, so I recommend using it.

The next issue with dates is even more problematic for novices.

Input Format, Storage Format, and Display Format

Each database system has its own specific rules for how to specify a date value. Checking these rules in your SQL reference manual is a must. We specify input date values when inserting new values into a column, whether with an INSERT or an UPDATE statement, and when writing WHERE conditions such as the one in the previous example.

The allowable date formats for input vary considerably from one database system to another.

All of the following are valid input date value formats in at least one database system:

```
DATE '2008-09-21'
'2008-09-21'
'20080921'
20080921
'09-21-2008'
'21-SEP-2008'
'2008/09/21'
'2008$09$21'
```

Specify Input Date Values Using the YYYY-MM-DD Format

The YYYY-MM-DD format is recognized by all database systems: 4 digits for the year, 2 for the month, and 2 for the day. It's compatible with ISO-8601,[5] which is the international standard for date and time formats.

Note that the dashes are optional, so, for example, we can specify either '2008-09-21' or '20080921' for the 21st of September, 2008.

One of the biggest surprises regarding date and time values in database systems is that they're not stored the way they're entered.

Usually, dates are stored as integers. The integer for a given date is calculated as the number of days since a base or *zero* date. So if January 1, 1900 is the base date—day 1, then January 2, 1900 would be day 2, and December 31, 1900 would be day 365, not 366, since 1900 was not a leap year. (Date handling in database systems is fully aware of the Gregorian leap year rules.) January 1, 1901 would then be day 366, and we can count the days like this all the way from January 1, 1900 to today, and on into the future for as long as we like. If the database system uses an INTEGER internally for this day count, the day numbers can go for almost 12 million years before the size of the INTEGER counter becomes inadequate.

So when we insert a date value, we must specify it using an allowed date constant format, and realize that it will be converted upon entry into an internal storage format. We never see the actual storage format, however, because every time we SELECT a date value, it comes out in a display format. The database system performs a conversion both on input and on output.

---

[5] http://en.wikipedia.org/wiki/ISO_8601

This is where many people stumble. They enter a date as 09/21/2008 (assuming this format is allowed), and are surprised when it comes out as 2008-09-21 in a SELECT query. I've seen people change the data type from DATE to VARCHAR just so they can retrieve exactly the same format they put in! But I'd caution against this; if you value the possibility of doing date calculations, or returning dates in a proper chronological sequence, you'll always store dates in a proper temporal data type and not a character data type.

There are three options for dealing with display formats:

1. only use the default display format of your database system (or find a way to change the default)

2. use whatever formatting functions are provided by your database system to achieve the format you want

3. format the date in your application

The first option is, of course, the easiest. Fortunately, the default format is usually YYYY-MM-DD anyway, which, in my opinion, is the easiest to understand. If formatting is required, the third option is best practice because web application languages (like PHP or ASP) have formatting functions built in. The second option may be appropriate if you're writing the SELECT query to extract data that will be sent elsewhere, like in an XML file.

TIME

Time values are similar to date values, in that there are differences between input format, storage format, and display format. An input time format might look like TIME '09:37' and a display format might look like 9:37 AM. Internally, time values are often stored as another integer, representing the number of clock ticks after midnight. (A clock tick might be a millisecond, or three milliseconds, or some similar value.)

Times, however, have another aspect that makes them a bit trickier. That's because adding dates together is pure folly, yet adding times can make sense.

Times as Duration

TIME values are assumed to be points in time on a time scale, but what if we need to store durations—measures of elapsed time. Suppose we want to have a web site for displaying triathlon race results. We'll need a type of column to record different times like these:

```
swim 20:35
bike 1:49:59
run 1:28:32
```

These times will then be added, and the total needs to come out as 3:39:06.

When dealing with durations like these, there are several choices for the data type to use:

1. We could use TIME, but few database systems allow times to be added. Similarly, DATE values are considered points on a calendric scale, not durations.

2. We could store three separate TINYINT values, for hours, minutes, and seconds, but this requires complex expressions to calculate totals.

3. We could store the equivalent total seconds—instead of hours, minutes, and seconds—in a single SMALLINT; this makes calculating the total easy, but we'd still need to convert it back into hours, minutes, and seconds formatting.

Right about here, those of us from a programming background will start thinking of complex ways to implement the second and third option in our chosen web application languages. And it's right about here that the lazy programmers among us will look for a way to make the first option work. We look for a time function, provided by the database system, to convert times to seconds. We also make sure there's another one for converting back. If we're lucky, we find them both, and the problem of adding times becomes very, very simple:

test_04_SUM_times.sql *(excerpt)*

```
SELECT
  SEC_TO_TIME( SUM( TIME_TO_SEC(splittime) ) ) AS total_time
FROM
  raceresults
```

This example shows the TIME_TO_SEC function is used to convert individual TIME values in the splittime column to seconds. These seconds are then added up by the SUM aggregate function. The result of the SUM is then converted back to a TIME value using the SEC_TO_TIME function.

TIME_TO_SEC and SEC_TO_TIME are MySQL functions, but the same approach can be used in database systems that have different functions. All it takes is a couple of expressions to perform the same calculations. Converting a time to seconds will require use of the EXTRACT function, to pull out the hours, minutes, and seconds separately, with some familiar multiplication (hours multiplied by 3600 and minutes multiplied by 60), as well as addition. Converting seconds to time can be accomplished easily by using the TIMEADD or DATEADD function—which every database system has—to add those seconds to a base time of 00:00:00 (midnight).

The point of this example was to demonstrate, step by step, the thinking process that leads to simplifying an application; because there are no functions to develop in your application programming language, we can do the calculations with SQL instead.

Times as Points in Time

Also known as clock time, this is used for single points in time, independent of any date.

For example, a bricks-and-mortar store would have an opening time and a closing time. These might vary by day of the week, but one feature of a clock time value is that it often recurs. So for this particular store, an opening time of 8:30 AM is the same on every day to which it applies.

TIMESTAMP

Timestamps are data types that contain both a date and a time component. What we've learned about dates and times separately applies equally to dates and times combined in timestamps: be careful with input formats, and reformat for display in the application if necessary.

When to Use DATE, TIME, or TIMESTAMP

Use DATE when the event or activity has a date only, and the time is irrelevant. For example, in most database applications where people's birth dates are stored, the time of birth is not applicable.

Use TIME for recurring clock times and for durations as required. Remember that duration calculations may require conversion.

Use TIMESTAMP when an event has a specific date and time. Tables which store system logins and similar events should use the greatest timestamp precision available.

You should refrain from using separate DATE and TIME columns for the same event. For example, avoid organizing columns like this:

```
event_date    DATE
event_start   TIME
event_end     TIME
```

This may appear to be worthwhile because it avoids repeating the date, but it can cause serious headaches to calculate intervals from one event to another. Instead organize your columns like this:

```
event_start   TIMESTAMP
event_end     TIMESTAMP
```

Calculating intervals is discussed in the next section, where you'll see how using separate DATE and TIME columns make that task much too difficult.

Intervals

Intervals are like the time duration examples we saw earlier in the athletic race: swim 20:35, bike 1:49:59, and run 1:28:32. Naturally, there are date intervals as well. The interval including January 1st through to March 1st is either 59 or 60 days, depending on the year.

In standard SQL, intervals have their own special syntax. However, few database systems have adopted the standard interval syntax, primarily because—as stated previously—the need for date calculations was anticipated by every database system, and implemented as date functions, long before the standard was agreed to.

We saw one example of an interval calculation back in the section called "BETWEEN: It haz a flavr" in Chapter 4:

```
CURRENT_DATE - INTERVAL 5 DAY
```

This is an expression in standard SQL that calculates the date that is 5 days earlier than the current date. If it fails to work in your particular database system, there'll be equivalent date functions for the same purpose. As we mentioned back in the section called "Temporal Operators" in Chapter 7, you'll have to read the documentation for your system.

Date Functions

Database system implementations have a rich variety of date functions. We call them date functions, but they also include time functions, and timestamp functions. Standard SQL has few date functions, EXTRACT being the main one, in addition to functions that perform interval calculations. Standard SQL also has the three functions, CURRENT_DATE, CURRENT_TIME, and CURRENT_TIMESTAMP, designed expressly to return the corresponding date and time value from the computer that database system is running on.

Each database system also has a number of other non-standard date functions. Some, such as WEEKDAY, are decidedly useful in real world applications. Table 9.4 lists some of the date functions available in one database system or another.

Table 9.4. Some common date functions

Date Function	Purpose
DATEADD or ADDDATE	adjusts a date by a specified interval
DATEDIFF	returns the interval between two dates
YEAR, MONTH, DAY	performs the same function as EXTRACT but more intuitively named
WEEKDAY	returns the day of the week of a specified date as a number from 1 through 7
DAYNAME	returns the name of the day of a specified date, for example Sunday, Monday, and so on

Date functions are, in general, very comprehensive, but it's important to use them correctly. Refer to your SQL reference manual for more details.

Column Constraints

Column constraints enable us to specify additional data integrity criteria for columns than what is permitted by their data type.

For example, a SMALLINT column can hold values between -32,768 and 32,767, but we might want to restrict this to a range that is meaningful. We might, for example, have a rule that the maximum purchase of any particular item in a single shopping cart, is 10. This can be implemented with a CHECK constraint, as we'll see in a moment.

NULL or NOT NULL

The first constraint that we should think about for any column, is whether the column should allow NULLs. Any attempt to insert a row in which a value is missing for a column designated as NOT NULL will fail, and the database system will return an error message.

How do we decide if a column should be NULL or NOT NULL? Simply, if we need to have a value in every possible instance. For example, it's impossible to have an item on a customer cart without a selected quantity:

```
                                        Cart_04_ANDs_and_ORs.sql (excerpt)

CREATE TABLE cartitems
(
   cart_id  INTEGER  NOT NULL
,  item_id  INTEGER  NOT NULL
,  qty      SMALLINT NOT NULL
);
```

The qty column is NOT NULL because it's senseless to have a customer cart for a *null* quantity of an item. Key columns, like cart_id and item_id, must also be NOT NULL, but we'll cover them in Chapter 10.

DEFAULT

The DEFAULT constraint allows us to specify a default value for a column. This default value will be used in those instances where a NULL is about to be inserted. Let's adjust the cartitems table so that the default qty value for any item is 1:

Cart_04_ANDs_and_ORs.sql *(excerpt)*

```
CREATE TABLE cartitems
(
  cart_id  INTEGER  NOT NULL
, item_id  INTEGER  NOT NULL
, qty      SMALLINT NOT NULL  DEFAULT 1
);
```

We've also used a DEFAULT constraint in our customers table for the shipping address:

Cart_04_ANDs_and_ORs.sql *(excerpt)*

```
CREATE TABLE customers
(
  id        INTEGER     NOT NULL PRIMARY KEY
, name      VARCHAR(99)  NOT NULL
, billaddr  VARCHAR(255) NOT NULL
, shipaddr  VARCHAR(255) NOT NULL DEFAULT 'See billing address.'
);
```

The default for the shipping address is the constant 'See billing address', and this string would be inserted into the shipaddr column when a customer is added to the table without specifying a shipping address.

CHECK Constraints

CHECK constraints are even more useful, because they can be as complex as needed by the application. A CHECK constraint consists of the keyword CHECK followed by a parenthesized condition. The neat part is that this condition can be a compound condition, involving AND and OR, just like in the WHERE clause.

Lets adjust the CREATE query for the cartitems table so that the maximum qty value for any item is 10:

```
                                          Cart_04_ANDs_and_ORs.sql (excerpt)

CREATE TABLE cartitems
(
  cart_id  INTEGER  NOT NULL
, item_id  INTEGER  NOT NULL
, qty      SMALLINT NOT NULL  DEFAULT 1  CHECK ( qty <= 10 )
);
```

In our forums application, the CHECK constraint was used to ensure the TIMESTAMP value in the revised column was always after (chronologically speaking) the value in the created column:

```
                                          Forums_01_Setup.sql (excerpt)

  created  TIMESTAMP  NOT NULL  DEFAULT CURRENT_TIMESTAMP
, revised  TIMESTAMP  NULL      CHECK ( revised >= created )
```

Wrapping Up: SQL Data Types

In this chapter, we learned about numeric, character, and temporal data types. We also learned when—and in some cases when not—to use them. We did a very quick tour of the functions that are available when working with the different types of data. Selecting an appropriate data type for each column in the tables we're designing is fairly straightforward. Implementing appropriate constraints can ensure the integrity of the data in our database.

In the next chapter, we'll tackle the more difficult task of selecting which columns to combine into which tables, and how to relate the tables properly.

Chapter 10

Relational Integrity

What's in a name? that which we call a rose

By any other name would smell as sweet;

—Juliet

In the previous chapter, we saw the various data types that can be used when defining table columns in our database. Most of the concepts there are simple and straightforward, and should've been familiar if you've had any exposure to programming at all.

By contrast, this chapter will introduce some topics that are the source of much befuddlement for many people new to databases. This chapter is about relational integrity, the real heart and soul of effective database design. We'll start our journey into relational integrity with a simple notion—the concept of identity.

Identity

> ` I yam what I yam
>
>   —Popeye the Sailor Man

What makes someone or something unique? How do we identify him or her or it from other instances of the same kind of thing? Other than simply pointing to it, one way is to assign a different name or label to each instance—but naming is imperfect. Here lies both the essence of the problem, and at the same time, its solution.

The problem is that names and labels are often duplicated. For example, many people share the same name. People's names can change, for example, by marriage or deed poll. However, regardless of name, you are always you. This naming problem exists in all computer applications, and is solved by assigning an identifier to everything.

An identifier is very much like a name or a label; it can even be a name or a label. Often, it's a code, or a number. Throughout this book, you've seen examples of SQL queries with table name and column name identifiers such as `team_id`, `customer_id`, and `forum_id`. Using numeric identifiers is common, but there are other options.

As long as each identifier value unambiguously defines a unique instance of the person or object, it's a good identifier. It's an even better identifier if it's stable, and its value rarely changes. The challenge, therefore, is to find the right identifier for each situation.

Before we develop these ideas further, we need to take a brief tour of the related topic of data modelling, the starting point of good database design. Identity plays a role in data modelling, as we'll soon see.

Data Modelling

Data modelling is a technique used in the early stages of application development. It focuses attention on the items of interest about which we wish to store information in the database—their attributes, and the relationships between items—within the scope of the application.

Data modelling commences with a simple analysis of the application's entities and attributes.

Entities and Attributes

Entities and attributes can be described as follows:

1. **Entities** are persons, objects, places, events, actions, or other items, about which we want to store information in the database; the *nouns* of the data model.

2. **Attributes** are the properties of an entity; the *adjectives* of the data model.

For example, the entities involved in a shopping cart application might be the customers, the purchased items, and the shopping carts. A customer can have multiple attributes, such as name, billing address, and so on. An item has a name, price, and perhaps other attributes, such as size or color.

Entity-attribute modelling is the first step in data modelling. We must discover and catalog all the entities and their attributes that we think will be involved in the database. We do this by an analysis of the application's requirements, by an understanding of the subject matter, by exploring any available information, or by whatever means necessary, including invention—which involves creating the information from scratch, based on the entities and attributes that we think will be required to support the application.

If we compare the finished database design to a blueprint for constructing a house, then the entity-attribute model is the preliminary spec sheet—three bedrooms, two bathrooms, a garden, a garage. This part of the data modelling process is the easiest.

Example: Forums, Threads, Posts, and Members

Let's walk through a simple entity–attribute model, using the Discussion Forums sample application.

The purpose of this application is to have forums in which members can create threads and make posts within threads. With a little bit of analysis, we can conclude that there are four different entities involved, and we can quickly list some of the attributes that we'd like each entity to have.

The following list will be our initial entity–attribute model:

1. Each member will have a member name, password, email address, and so on.
2. Each forum will have a name.
3. Each thread will have a name.
4. Each post can have an optional name, but must have some content (the body of the post), and the date when it was posted.

Did you notice how sparse this list of attributes is? What's missing are the relationships.

Entities and Relationships

Modelling entity relationships is probably the most engaging part of the design process for many database designers. After all, it's where all the action is. Listing the attributes of each entity is pretty straightforward; the relationships are more challenging.

Entity–Relationship Diagrams

The results of entity–relationship modelling are often shown using an **entity–relationship diagram** (or **ER diagram**), and also informally called ER model.

For example, in the Content Management System (CMS) application, two entities of interest are the content entries themselves, and the categories that classify them. These entities are shown in an ER diagram like the one in Figure 10.1. Note that this diagramming convention—using an arrow—is my own diagramming convention, and you probably won't find it in any textbook on data modelling. More on the arrow in a moment.

In the early stages of application development, we use data modelling to initiate the design, which eventually determines which tables the database will contain. Typically, each entity will be implemented in the database as a separate table. Thus, in the CMS application, there'll be a categories table and an entries table.

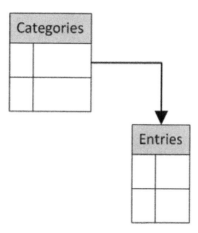

Figure 10.1. The relationship between categories and entries

The ER model also allows us to identify and study the relationships between entities. The arrow between entities in an ER diagram represents a relationship. We can see from Figure 10.1 that there's a relationship between the categories and entries tables. The most important quality of any relationship between entities is the **cardinality** of the relationship: how many instances of each entity are involved on either side of the relationship. The type of arrow linking the entities indicates the cardinality.

In Figure 10.1, the arrow further indicates that it's a **one-to-many** relationship, by pointing from the *one* entity to the *many* entity. We say the categories entity is related to the entries entity in a one-to-many relationship because each category has multiple entries.

If we look at the relationship arrow in the opposite direction, as it were, the relationship can be expressed by saying that each entry belongs to only one category. It's still a one-category-to-many-entries relationship, but from the point of view of the entries, it's a **many-to-one** relationship, in which the important fact is that each entry belongs to only one category.

I prefer using an arrow for the relationship because it's easy to draw. Preliminary ER diagrams are best done with paper and pencil—and an eraser. However, there are several alternatives to the plain arrow to indicate a many-to-one relationship. Data model diagrams using a *crow's foot* are very common, and sometimes you may see a circle in place of the arrow; both of these styles are shown in Figure 10.2. The key point to remember is that the *one* end of the one-to-many relationship is the end of the line with no embellishment.

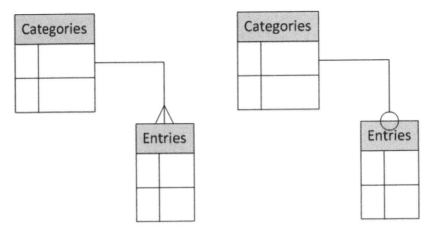

Figure 10.2. The *crow's foot* and circle styles

Two additional ER diagramming conventions exist. An arrow without an arrow-head—a simple unembellished line—is used to indicate a **one-to-one** relationship, while an arrow with an arrowhead at both ends represents a **many-to-many** relationship. Both of these are shown in Figure 10.3.[1]

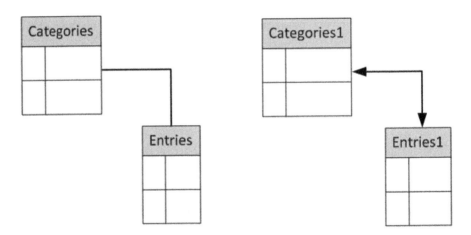

Figure 10.3. One-to-one and many-to-many relationships

As you might expect, there's a lot more to ER diagrams than this very humble introduction. Most of it is beyond the scope of this book. The diagram itself, though, is quite indispensable to your design efforts, so you should always perform this step. The ER diagram, with relationships showing cardinalities—one-to-one, one-to-many,

---

[1] This is not implying that categories and entries share the relationships depicted; those entities were merely used for convenience.

or many-to-many—is most assuredly worth a thousand words. (Okay, several hundred.) Just by looking at an ER diagram, you gain an immediate sense of what kind of data is in the application, and how it's related. If we compare the finished database design to a blueprint for constructing a house, then the ER diagram is the architect's concept sketch.

Let's create the ER diagram for the Discussion Forums application. We'll start by taking the bare bones entity–attribute model we created in the last section and augment it with information about the relationships between entities:

1. Each member will have a member name, password, email address, and so on. Each member can start one or more threads, and make one or more posts in any thread.

2. Each forum will have a name, and each forum may have one or more threads.

3. Each thread will have a name, and, in addition, a thread starter (the member who started the thread). Each thread will belong to only one forum, and can have one or more posts.

4. Each post can have an optional name, but must have some content, and the date when it was posted. Each post will belong to only one thread, have a poster (the member who posted it), and may be a reply to a previous post in the same thread.

In real world applications, the distinction between an attribute and a relationship may be unclear. For example, a thread has a name and a thread starter (the member who started the thread). It isn't initially obvious that the thread starter is actually relationship information and not simply an attribute of the thread.

By using the diagramming technique we introduced above, we can whittle away the verbiage and end up with the diagram shown in Figure 10.4.

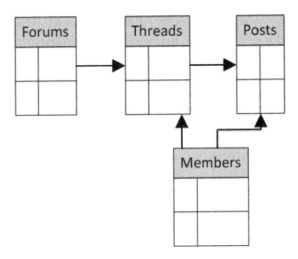

Figure 10.4. The Discussion Forums application ER diagram

The arrows in this diagram can be elucidated in both directions, as follows:

1. Each forum has one or more threads. Each thread belongs to only one forum.
2. Each thread has one or more posts. Each post belongs to only one thread.
3. Each thread is started by only one member. Each member can start one or more threads.
4. Each post is made by only one member. Each member can make one or more posts.

Clarifying all the relationships may seem tedious, but every once in a while, just saying how many of *this* are related to how many of *that* will uncover an issue that needs to be investigated further. Most experienced modellers actually jump straight to the ER diagram, and *flesh out* the entities by listing their attributes afterwards.

ER modelling is not difficult. Mostly, it requires a simple transformation of words and ideas into entities and their relationships, but it can take some time before the process becomes familiar. Review the ER diagrams in Appendix B, and try creating a few of your own if you already have applications containing database tables.

ER Modelling Tools

If your database system is expected to be larger than, say, five or six entities, you might want to look into using an ER modelling tool. They range in price from free to many thousands of dollars per individual license.

There are three main features to look for when evaluating ER modelling tools:

1. graphical ease of use—how easy it is to click, drag, drop, and use various tools to add entities, attributes, and relationships to the ER diagram
2. reverse engineering—the ability to read the catalog information in an actual database and generate the diagram from the tables it contains
3. forward engineering—the ability to generate the DDL to create a database from the entities and relationships in the diagram

My advice is to consider only those tools that have all three features. The reverse and forward engineering capabilities, of course, have to work on your particular database system; there's not much point in using a slick graphical tool that can only generate MySQL DDL if you're using Oracle.

Primary Keys

The purpose of data modelling is to describe clearly the entities that will be represented in the application's database tables, as well as the relationships between those entities. In order for this to work, one very important task must be done. For each entity, a primary key must be selected.

A key is simply the terminology we use in databases to mean an identifier, in the same sense as we discussed earlier in this chapter: a means to identify, unambiguously and uniquely, a particular instance of an entity. When we store or retrieve data in a database table that contains entities, each instance must be uniquely distinguished from every other instance of the same type of entity. This can only be done with a key that has unique values for all instances.

For example, we've seen SQL queries with identifiers such as `customer_id` and `forum_id`. These identifiers are valid keys because every instance, every value, represents a different entity. All the values are unique. It's unlikely we'd ever think of assigning the same `customer_id` value to two different customers, nor the same `forum_id` value to two different forums. Is this too obvious? It seems like only common sense, and, yes, it really is that simple.

So these examples of identifiers are unique keys. Then what is a primary key? A **primary key** is simply any one of the keys that an entity may have. The reason we need to pick one of these keys, and designate it as the primary key, is so that foreign keys or related entities will have a designated key that they can relate to. We'll see how this works in a moment.

Take you, for example: what is it about you that identifies you? As we discussed before, your name is not a good key, because others may share the same name. Some possible keys that would be unique might be a representation of your fingerprints, or your retinal pattern, or even your DNA sequence. Let's leave aside for the moment some obvious questions of practicality—such as whether these identifiers could be forged, whether they're accurate enough, or even what to do about identical twins—and concentrate only on their uniqueness. Assuming for the sake of argument that we accept these identifiers as being capable of uniquely identifying every person in our application, we now have three unique keys to choose from. We pick one of them—even if we plan to store all three—and call it the primary key.

Another important point about primary keys is that they must never allow a NULL. This, too, seems obvious. If the primary key value is NULL, it's unable to be used to identify a particular entity. This makes no sense, and so primary keys quite logically must have a non-NULL value. If we have everybody's fingerprints and retinal patterns, but lack the DNA sequences for everybody, then it's pointless to use the DNA sequence as the primary key—even though all the values of the DNA sequence that we do have are unique. Thus, each entity must have a primary key, which always has unique, non-NULL values.

Turning an ER model into a functioning database involves implementing each entity as a database table (sometimes more than one table, but in most cases as just one table). So there's a nice correspondence between entities and tables. Attributes usually correspond with columns too. The primary key columns that we identify in ER modelling are declared with the keyword PRIMARY KEY in the DDL that creates the database tables. So declared, a database table's primary key column is both unique and NOT NULL by definition.

The DDL for the creation of the forums table provides an example of a primary key column declaration:

```
                                          Forums_01_Setup.sql (excerpt)

CREATE TABLE forums
(
   id      INTEGER        NOT NULL  PRIMARY KEY
, name   VARCHAR(37)   NOT NULL
);
```

It's also possible to use more than one column for the primary key, and this is known as a **composite key**. This means that both columns must be used to uniquely identify each row. The syntax for a composite primary key is shown below:

```
CREATE TABLE table_name
(
   ⋮ column declarations...
, PRIMARY KEY (column1, column2)
);
```

UNIQUE Constraints

In a real world discussion forum application, member names are usually unique. It would be horribly confusing if two different members actually had the same member name, since the application typically displays member names on threads and posts. This is also true of our sample Discussion Forums application that we examined in Chapter 7. The member table from the application can be seen in Figure 10.5.

members	
id	name
9	noo13
37	r937
42	DeepThought
99	BarbFeldon
187	RJNeedham

Figure 10.5. The members table

In our application we want member names to be unique, and this means that the name column would actually be a good key. However, since we're using a numeric id as the primary key, we declare the name column in the members table with a

UNIQUE constraint. Thus, the database will ensure that member names are always unique. Here's how it's done in the DDL that creates the table:

Forums_01_Setup.sql *(excerpt)*

```
CREATE TABLE members
(
  id          INTEGER     NOT NULL  PRIMARY KEY
, name        VARCHAR(37) NOT NULL
, CONSTRAINT name_uk UNIQUE ( name )
);
```

The CONSTRAINT keyword declares that a table constraint condition is to be added, we give it an alias, name_uk, and then define the constraint with UNIQUE (name); that is, the name column value must be unique. If we attempt to insert or update a row that would create a duplicate name, the database system will return an error. We give the constraint an alias, so that in the future, in any DDL that modifies or removes the constraint, we can refer to it by its alias.

It's also possible to declare a composite unique constraint where a combination of values from more than one column must be unique within each row. For example, in our threads table we want to ensure that each thread is uniquely named within each forum (not precluding the possibility of identically named threads in multiple forums). Multiple columns are specified separated by a comma:

Forums_01_Setup.sql *(excerpt)*

```
CREATE TABLE threads
(
  id          INTEGER     NOT NULL  PRIMARY KEY
, name        VARCHAR(99) NOT NULL
, forum_id    INTEGER     NOT NULL
, starter     INTEGER     NOT NULL
, CONSTRAINT thread_name_uk UNIQUE ( id, name )
);
```

Dealing with Keys in Application Code

Knowing that a column is a key is extremely useful, as it helps you avoid unnecessary application code.

The Discussion Forums application needs to provide a means for new members to be added. This would likely be done with a registration form. The application programming logic that accepts the form submission will need to ensure the new member's name is unique. It's common for application developers to write code which first checks the member name with a SELECT query like this:

```
SELECT
  name
FROM
  members
WHERE
  name = 'Todd'
```

This query will return a row if the name Todd already exists. The application then typically displays a message such as "Member name already exists." However, if the query returns no row, then the member name doesn't exist, so the application code then executes the necessary INSERT statement to add the new member.

This two-step process is unnecessary. Just execute the INSERT statement. If the member name already exists, the database will not add a duplicate. Instead, it will return an error code; in this case, a code indicating that the UNIQUE constraint was violated. The application will detect this return code and display the same "Member name already exists" message.

This is one of those great win-win situations in databases (there are many others). We know that the name is unique, and that the database will enforce this. Therefore, there is less application code to write, and it's more efficient.

Foreign Keys

Let's return to the Discussion Forums application and examine a couple of its relationships in more detail, specifically those in the portion of the ER model shown in Figure 10.6.

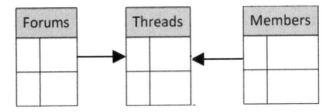

Figure 10.6. The relationships between forums, threads, and members

In our examination of foreign keys we're going to use the same sample data that we saw in Chapter 7 for the Discussion Forums application. Firstly, there were three forums; Figure 10.7 shows the forums table. The id column is the primary key in this table.

forums	
id	name
10001	Search Engines
10002	Databases
10003	Applications

Figure 10.7. The forums table

Next, there were five members in the members table as Figure 10.8 shows. The id column is the primary key in this table as well.

members	
id	name
9	noo13
37	r937
42	DeepThought
99	BarbFeldon
187	RJNeedham

Figure 10.8. The members table

Finally, we have thread data stored in the `threads` table, shown in Figure 10.9. Again, the `id` column is the primary key. Whether thread names need to be unique is debatable; we might want to allow the same thread name to be used in more than one forum, for example, a thread called *Rules for this forum*. The last two columns, `forum_id` and `starter`, as we shall soon see, are **foreign keys**; they relate the data in this table to the primary keys in the other tables.

threads			
id	name	forum_id	starter
15	Difficulty with join query	10002	187
25	How do I get listed in Yahoo?	10001	9
35	People who bought ... also bought ...	10002	99
45	WHERE clause doesn't work	10002	187

Figure 10.9. The `threads` table

How Foreign Keys Work

When we first saw this data in Chapter 7, we had yet to introduce the term *foreign key*. Hopefully, what these columns were doing was obvious, and you were able to visualize the relationships. Now, we can explore their nature and purpose as foreign keys.

First, let's take another look at the portion of the ER model for our application, shown in Figure 10.10, and take notice of which way the arrows point. The forums-to-threads relationship is one-to-many, and the members-to-threads relationship is also one-to-many.

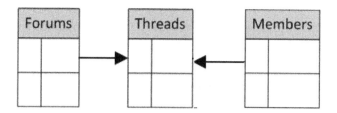

Figure 10.10. The relationships between forums, threads, and members

Relationships defined in the ER diagram are implemented in database tables using foreign keys. For one-to-many relationships, the foreign key resides in the *many* table. The foreign key columns are implemented with the `FOREIGN KEY` clause in the DDL that creates the database tables. We'll see an example in a moment.

How do these foreign keys actually work? It's as simple as it looks.

Each thread has a `forum_id` column value that corresponds to the value of the primary key of the particular entry in the `forums` table, the forum that the thread belongs to. Foreign keys implement the one-to-many relationships, with the *many* instance always relating back to the *one* instance it belongs to. Thus, each thread relates back to the forum it belongs to; we can see that three threads belong to the Databases forum, and one thread to the Search Engines forum.[2]

Similarly, the `starter` column values in the `threads` table correspond to the primary key values in the `members` table. Each thread is related to the member who started that thread.

Using Foreign Keys

There are several rules and properties about foreign keys that are important to know.

The Foreign Key Goes in the *Many* Table

One such rule has already been mentioned in the previous section: the foreign key goes in the table on the *many* side of the relationship. It can hardly be the other way around. The Databases forum has three threads in the `threads` table, and if this information were to be kept in the `forums` table, this would mean somehow storing the thread `id` values: 15, 35, and 45. You may be tempted into thinking you could have an additional column, perhaps called `forum_threads`, which contains a comma-separated list of thread `id` values. But that approach will only lead to frustration.

What about relationships other than one-to-many? Many-to-many relationships occur frequently in ER models, but are always implemented as two one-to-many relationships with an intervening *relationship* table. We examine this type of relationship in the section called "Implementing a Many-to-many Relationship: Keywords" in Chapter 11. In our sample CMS application, `entries` and `keywords` are related through the `entrykeywords` table. Multiple entries can have the same keyword and each entry can have multiple keywords. The ER diagram for this relationship is shown in Figure 10.11.

---

[2] If you're able to visualize this by looking back at the sample data for the forums, it's because you've done a mental inner join. The join's `ON` condition matches `threads.forum_id` with `forums.id`.

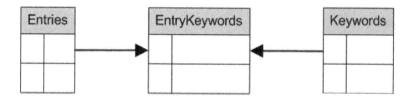

Figure 10.11. The relationships between entries and keywords

The only other possible relationship is one-to-one, in which case it helps to think of one of the entities involved in the one-to-one relationship either as optional or on the *many* side of a one-to-many relationship. In the CMS sample application, there's a one-to-one relationship between entities and content. This is shown in the ER model as an arrow without the arrowhead, depicted in Figure 10.12.

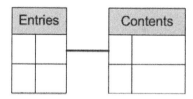

Figure 10.12. The relationship between entries and content

An entry may, optionally, have a row in the `contents` table. An entry can exist without having a content row, but a content row can't exist by itself without an entry to belong to. Thus, the foreign key goes in the `contents` table. Potentially, you could also have multiple rows in the `contents` table for each entry, if, for example, content for each entry was stored in multiple languages.

The Foreign Key Must Reference a Key

The next rule is that foreign keys must reference a key. In actual implementation, this means either a primary key or a key column with a `UNIQUE` constraint. Both work, because both are unique. In practice, a foreign key almost always references a primary key.

The term *referencing* is used because in order to declare a foreign key, we must identify the key it relates to, and the DDL syntax used for this is the `REFERENCES` clause within the `FOREIGN KEY` declaration. This is where the term **referential integ-**

rity comes from. The foreign key must reference a key, either a `PRIMARY KEY` or a `UNIQUE` key.

The benefit of referential integrity is that the database ensures that a foreign key always has a value that can be found in the key column it references. No other values for the foreign key are allowed (except `NULL`, which we'll talk about in a moment).

Another name for referential integrity is **relational integrity**, the subject of this chapter. Just as with the example of the `UNIQUE` constraint enforcing unique member names, where the database ensures that duplication of values is impossible—with foreign keys the database ensures that it's impossible for a foreign key to refer to a non-existent primary key.

Here's an example. Let's change the `threads` table so that the `forum_id` column references the `forums` table's `id` column (the primary key of the forums table):

```
                                      Forums_05_Foreign_keys.sql (excerpt)

ALTER TABLE threads
ADD CONSTRAINT
  forum_fk
    FOREIGN KEY (forum_id)
      REFERENCES forums (id)
```

Using the keywords `ADD CONSTRAINT`, we first declare an alias for this constraint: `forum_fk`. To declare a foreign key, you must specify which column(s) make up the foreign key, within parentheses after the keywords, `FOREIGN KEY`. In the code above, the `forum_id` column is declared as a foreign key column using `FOREIGN KEY (forum_id)`. Note that the foreign key column(s) are rarely primary or unique keys in their table (the referencing table), since foreign keys implement the *many* side of a one-to-many relationship.

After the foreign key declaration, we must specify which key the foreign key column is referencing; this is achieved with the mandatory keyword `REFERENCES`, followed by the name of the table being referenced (and optionally, the specific key column(s) of that table, again within parentheses). If the column names are omitted, the primary key column of the referenced table is used. If the primary key we're referencing is a composite key consisting of two columns, we must declare a foreign key constraint in which two columns from the referencing table match both columns of the composite key.

With the constraint in place, the database will only allow us to insert a thread with a valid `forum_id`. Here *valid* means that the forum exists. Yes, the key that `forum_id` references, namely the `id` column in the `forums` table, is an integer—but guaranteeing full integrity goes beyond just ensuring that `forum_id` is numeric.

 MySQL Requires an Index First

In MySQL, applying a foreign key constraint is a two-step process; you first have to add an index to the foreign key column like so:

```
ALTER TABLE threads
ADD INDEX
   forum_ix (forum_id)
```

Similarly, there's another foreign key that needs to be declared for the `threads` table. We want relational integrity to ensure that it's impossible for the database to allow us to insert a thread with an invalid `starter`. Here, `starter` is the foreign key, referencing the `id` column in the `members` table. Here's the DDL statement to add this constraint:

Forums_05_Foreign_keys.sql (excerpt)

```
ALTER TABLE threads
ADD CONSTRAINT
   starter_fk
     FOREIGN KEY (starter)
       REFERENCES members (id)
```

In the same way that the use of a column constraint means you can avoid the need for application code to ensure that duplicate member names are impossible, foreign keys implement relationships in such a way that only valid relationships are possible. Relational integrity is the *sine qua non* of databases.

Do You Need to Declare a Foreign Key to Use One?

Foreign keys are a concept, and one can quite happily program a database application using the concept of foreign keys without actually declaring foreign keys in the database. This is what so many MySQL developers had to do in the early days of MySQL before foreign keys were actually supported, and many developers still do. (Some database formats even lack support for foreign key constraints like the MyISAM format in MySQL;[3] you can declare them but they are ignored!) Your application logic can insert values into columns which conceptually link tables together, without an explicit foreign key constraint.

To me, it's fair to call these conceptual links *foreign keys*, because that's exactly how they're used—even if the database is not involved in enforcing integrity. Others might disagree, and say that they aren't foreign keys unless they're actually declared and enforced by the database. I think this is merely splitting a semantic hair.

Foreign Keys May Be NULL

Relationships are sometimes optional. This is handled quite simply by allowing the foreign key to be NULL. Naturally, it will only be NULL in some instances—just for those instances where that particular row has no relationship.

For example, in our Shopping Cart data model the relationship between the vendors table and the items table is one-to-many, but it's quite possible that items may not belong to a vendor. What does optionality mean here? Well, it might be that most of the items in our online store are supplied by a vendor, but a few are supplied by the shopping cart provider. For example, we might have items called Gift Wrapping and Discount Coupon, which have a standard price, and which can be selected by the customer in any cart—but are without a vendor. For these types of items, the vendor_id—the foreign key—would be set to NULL. You can always determine if a relationship is optional by seeing whether the foreign key is defined as NULL or NOT NULL.

---

[3] http://dev.mysql.com/doc/refman/5.0/en/myisam-storage-engine.html

ON DELETE and ON UPDATE

Finally, foreign keys can be declared with two additional, very useful properties, which govern what happens to related rows when a change occurs to the primary key.

In the Discussion Forums sample application, consider what would happen if we were to delete the Search Engines forum:

```
DELETE
FROM
  forums
WHERE
  id = 10001
```

What should happen to the threads in a forum, if the forum itself is gone? Obviously, relational integrity might be violated. In our example, there's only one thread, named "How do I get listed in Yahoo?", in the Search Engines forum, but there could be many more when the forum is deleted. There are several choices:

1. prevent the forum from being deleted because it has at least one thread
2. delete the forum's threads as well
3. keep the threads but set its `forum_id` foreign key to NULL

Each of these three choices can be selected as an option in the `ON DELETE` clause of the `FOREIGN KEY` declaration. The corresponding options are:

1. `ON DELETE RESTRICT`
2. `ON DELETE CASCADE`
3. `ON DELETE SET NULL`

Check your SQL reference manual for the exact options available in your particular database system.

Sometimes, an instance of a primary key must change its value. (This hardly ever happens with a numeric primary key, as we'll see shortly.) In those situations, the options specified in the `ON UPDATE` clause of the `FOREIGN KEY` declaration work in a similar fashion to the `ON DELETE` options above. The change can be prevented (`RESTRICT`), or the change can also be made to the foreign key values (`CASCADE`), or the foreign key values can be set to `NULL`—although this last option would be unusual.

In our Forums application we've elected to use the `CASCADE` option:

```
                                        Forums_05_Foreign_keys.sql (excerpt)

ALTER TABLE threads
ADD CONSTRAINT
  forum_fk
    FOREIGN KEY (forum_id)
      REFERENCES forums (id)
        ON DELETE CASCADE
        ON UPDATE CASCADE
```

The main point to remember about the `ON DELETE` and `ON UPDATE` options is that they allow us to fine-tune the relationships; they govern how the foreign keys are affected by deletions of—or updates to—primary key values.

Natural versus Surrogate Keys

Now we come to an important part of the discussion about keys, the issue of whether to use a surrogate key. There have been numerous examples so far in this book of tables that have a numeric id column as their primary key. As you encountered these cases, you may perhaps have noticed that these numeric id primary keys are, in a way, artificial. For example, there's nothing intrinsic about the thread named "Difficulty with join query" that would warrant using the number 15 as its identifier, as opposed to any other number. It seems that this number is not a natural property of the thread, but rather, it's a number that is assigned to the thread.

At the beginning of this chapter, we discussed identity, and how identity is enforced with primary keys. Where did the notion of using a number as the primary key come from? These numbers used as identifiers are called **surrogate keys**. A surrogate key is a key that is used instead of a natural key. A **natural key** is one of the attributes that an entity has, which could be used as the primary key.

In the *members* entity, we wanted to ensure that the member name was unique. The member name would have made a great natural primary key—because it's unique, and because it would never be `NULL`. However, since we're using the numeric id column as the primary key, we gave the name a `UNIQUE` constraint instead. The id column value is a surrogate key.

There's really only one reason for using a surrogate key instead of a natural key: the natural key is unwieldy, mostly because the natural key is too long. To demonstrate this, consider the forums table without the id column. It would have a name column only, meaning the name would have to be the primary key. That's good, because we want all our forums to have unique names.

However, since threads are related to forums, the threads table's foreign key would have to use the name of the forum. Figure 10.13 shows what the threads table looks like in our application with the foreign key referencing the surrogate key of the forums table. Figure 10.14 shows what the threads table would look like if the foreign key was the natural key, the name of the forum. Using a numeric surrogate key saves substantial space, and is also considerably more efficient in queries in which a forum needs to be selected.

id	name	forum_id	starter
15	Difficulty with join query	10002	187
25	How do I get listed in Yahoo?	10001	9
35	People who bought ... also bought ...	10002	99
45	WHERE clause doesn't work	10002	187

Figure 10.13. The relationships between threads and forums using a surrogate key

id	name	forum_id	starter
15	Difficulty with join query	Databases	187
25	How do I get listed in Yahoo?	Search Engines	9
35	People who bought ... also bought ...	Databases	99
45	WHERE clause doesn't work	Databases	187

Figure 10.14. The relationships between threads and forums using a natural key

Myth: Surrogate Keys Reduce Redundancy

When thinking about the database design of the example just outlined—where the `forums` table's primary key is the name of the forum, and also the `threads` table's foreign key—many developers instantly choose to use a surrogate numeric key instead. They reason that doing so will eliminate the *redundancy* of having the same forum name appear in every thread that belongs to that forum.

This notion of eliminating redundancy, is a fallacy; using a numeric surrogate key has just as much redundancy as using a natural key. It just seems neater, that's all. The real benefits of surrogate keys are space and efficiency, as we've already discussed.

Use Suitable Natural Keys When Possible

Using a surrogate key is inappropriate when a suitable natural key exists. For example, consider that in many countries, standard codes exist for the states or provinces within the country: `ON` is Ontario in Canada, `NY` is New York in the United States of America, and `QLD` is Queensland in Australia. If we needed to keep information about states or provinces in a separate table, it would be silly to invent an additional numeric identifier for each state. Just use the code—it's a perfect natural key.

Autonumbers

A specific type of surrogate key is the **autonumber**, which is what it sounds like: an automatically inserted incrementing number. Although it's not part of the SQL standard, it's such a commonly used feature that every database system has a proprietary method for declaring such a number. In MySQL, you can declare a column to be `AUTO_INCREMENT`, In DB2 and SQL Server they're known as `identity` columns, and in PostgreSQL and Oracle they're known as serial numbers. Check your SQL reference manual for specific details on working with these numbers.

When declaring an autonumber, use `INTEGER`. This will allow a range of numbers up to 2 billion (approximately). If you anticipate that you'll exceed this number of rows, the next step up is `BIGINT`. However, very few real world applications need `BIGINT`.

As a hypothetical example, let's assume that our online Shopping Carts application sees a new customer cart created every second. This would be a phenomenally busy application, but let's carry through with the exercise. Each cart is assigned a new `cart_id`, which is defined as `INTEGER`, and let's say it's an autonumber. At the rate of one new number per second, we assign 86,400 new numbers every day, but we'd be safely covered for nearly the next 70 years. You can well imagine that we might have other problems, such as running out of disk space for our two billion orders, long before then. So `BIGINT` would be overkill at the outset, and `INTEGER` will do just fine for the first few years.

 Always Try to Declare a `UNIQUE` Constraint

When using surrogate keys, always try to declare a unique constraint on one of the other columns in the table. The reason for doing so is self-preservation; failure to do so means that you risk having duplicates in your data.

In the `members` table, the `name` was declared unique. Let's imagine that we forgot to specify this unique constraint, and used just the numeric surrogate id.

Nothing will prevent the entry of a duplicate member name with a different numeric id (other than doing the `SELECT` before the `INSERT`, which we know is extra and inefficient processing). The numeric primary key will allow any number of rows with the same name, unless the name is constrained to be unique.

In the `threads` table, we specifically wanted to allow multiple threads with the same name. The example was the "Rules for this forum" thread name, which we wanted to allow in every forum. The unique key in this table would therefore be the composite key consisting of the thread `name` and the `forum_id` foreign key. This prevents the same thread name from occurring more than once in each forum.

Always try to declare a unique constraint. Look carefully for one, even if it has to be composite. Every instance of an entity has a natural key—some column, or combination of columns—that should be declared unique.

Wrapping Up: Relational Integrity

In this chapter, we learned about relational integrity, and how it's one of the cornerstones of databases. Relational integrity depends on the concept of identity, and requires that each instance of an entity be uniquely identified. Primary keys are the keys chosen for this purpose, from among the possible unique keys that an entity may have. Foreign keys are used to implement relationships, and must be defined to reference either a primary or unique key.

In the next chapter, we'll conclude our exploration of database design, with a look at some more complex structures.

Special Structures

> Classifications are theories about the basis of natural order, not dull catalogs compiled only to avoid chaos.
>
> —Stephen Jay Gould

In this final chapter about database design, we'll see a number of special structures. These special structures are illustrated using the same sample applications we've discussed throughout the book.

The special structures in this chapter are just some of the ones you'll encounter; we could fill a second book discussing all of the possible structures, but these are simply the more common ones that you might need. Each will teach you either an SQL technique or a table design strategy—or both, since the SQL and the design are often, of course, interdependent.

Let's begin with an example that requires joining to a table twice.

Joining to a Table Twice

Figure 11.1 depicts a portion of the data model diagram for the Teams and Games application, where the teams table is related to the games table twice. Why would we want to do this? The answer: each game involves two different teams. In every game, one of the teams is the home team, and another team is the away team. Thus, two relationships are needed.

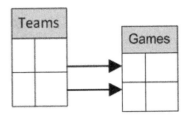

Figure 11.1. The teams table is related to the games table twice

Using the diagramming convention introduced in Chapter 10, the arrows indicates the cardinality of the one-to-many relationship. This data model shows that:

1. a team can participate in many games as the home team
2. a team can participate in many games as the away team

Following the arrows in the data model diagram from the games entity to the teams entity—in the many-to-one direction—we can see that each game can have only one home team, and one away team. The details of the relationship are unspecified in the diagram in Figure 11.1, with no mention of home and away teams; obviously you would annotate the diagram properly, though, if you produce diagrams for your own use or in a professional team environment.

Figure 11.2 shows the data in the games table. The first detail you may notice is that the hometeam and awayteam columns are numbers, not names. These columns are foreign keys that correspond to values of the primary key id column in the teams table. The SQL for the creation of the games table can be found in the section called "The games Table" in Appendix C.

games			
gamedate	location	hometeam	awayteam
2008-09-06	McKenzie	9	24
2008-09-13	Applewood	15	9

Figure 11.2. The games table

So the design of this special structure is fairly straightforward, but to produce a report or display that's useful, we'll need to use team names instead of the foreign key values. We'll need to perform two lookups, to *translate* the foreign keys into names. The SQL that's needed to display team names seems to give many developers trouble.

This is where joining to a table twice comes in. To retrieve the team names, we need to join the games table to the teams table, but we need to use both of the foreign key columns. This, in turn, requires that we use two joins:

Teams_07_Games.sql (excerpt)

```
SELECT
   games.gamedate
 , games.location
 , home.name AS hometeam
 , away.name AS awayteam
FROM
   games
     INNER JOIN teams AS home
       ON home.id = games.hometeam
     INNER JOIN teams AS away
       ON away.id = games.awayteam
```

Each of the inner joins in this query joins the same row of the games table to a different row of the teams table—one being the home team, and the other being the away team. Figure 11.3 illustrates what's happening in the joins.

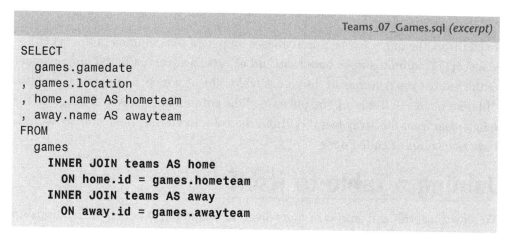

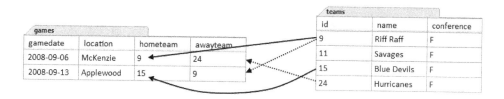

Figure 11.3. The teams table joined to the games table twice

The result of the query is shown in Figure 11.4. In short, we've joined the games table to the teams table twice, and thereby enabled two separate queries. The important point to note here, is that we need to use table aliases to accomplish this. In any query that references two representations of the same table, we must always use table aliases to distinguish them.

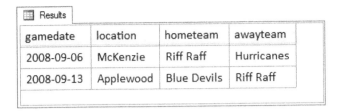

Figure 11.4. Team names in the result set

In addition, the query uses column aliases on two of the columns in the SELECT clause. (The column aliases hometeam and awayteam are actually the same names as the foreign key columns in the games table. This is a mere coincidence; any two different names will serve.) The purpose of the column aliases is to distinguish the home team from the away team. Without the column aliases, the result set would have two columns called name.

Joining a Table to Itself

We saw categories and entries in some detail in Chapter 3, in which the relationship between categories and entries was examined in the context of the various types of joins. Figure 11.5 shows the entries table, where the category column is a foreign key to the category column of the categories table, which is its primary key. This is, of course, not the whole entries table—it's missing some columns—just a simplified version for our purposes here. The categories table is shown in Figure 11.6.

entries	
category	title
angst	What If I Get Sick and Die?
humor	Uncle Karl and the Gasoline
advice	Be Nice to Everybody
humor	Hello Statue
science	The Size of Our Galaxy
computers	Windows Media Center Rocks

Figure 11.5. The entries table

categories	
category	name
advice	Gentle Words of Advice
angst	Stories from the Id
blog	Log on to My Blog
humor	Humorous Anecdotes
science	Our Spectacular Universe
computers	Information Technology

Figure 11.6. The categories table

Now let's say that we want to distinguish further between our categories of entries. We have a curious mix of different kinds of entries here—some are objective, analytical, and factual, whereas others are subjective, personal, and pensive. What we want to do is set up two new *super-categories*, General and Personal, as shown in Figure 11.7. This classification of our original categories into General and Personal would allow us, for example, to display entries from these categories using different themes.

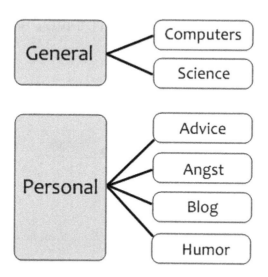

Figure 11.7. The new super-categories

Other than calling them super-categories, we can call them categories and demote the old categories to subcategories. The category/subcategory structure is implemented with a foreign key from the categories table to itself. Figure 11.8 shows the actual data once this relationship has been created. You can have a look at the SQL query that achieves this in the section called "The `categories` Table" in Appendix C. Notice that the new column, `parent`, contains values which are the same values as used in the `category` column—except in the first two rows. A category is determined to be a subcategory when it has a parent category value.

categories		
category	name	parent
general	Articles and Resources	
personal	Personal Stories and Ideas	
computers	Information Technology	general
science	Our Spectacular Universe	general
advice	Gentle Words of Advice	personal
angst	Stories from the Id	personal
blog	Log on to My Blog	personal
humor	Humorous Anecdotes	personal

Figure 11.8. The `categories` table with the new parent column

Figure 11.9 shows a portion of the data model diagram for the Content Management System application representing the relationship between categories and entries.

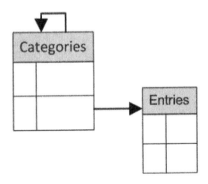

Figure 11.9. The relationship between categories and entries

You may be wondering about that funny-looking relationship from the categories table to itself. This is a **reflexive relationship** (sometimes called a recursive relationship). It's a one-to-many relationship because each category can have multiple subcategories, but each subcategory can have only one (parent) category.

Finally, we're ready to see an example of a query that joins a table to itself. We'll start with a query to list our categories and subcategories alphabetically:

```
                                    CMS_16_Supercategories.sql (excerpt)
SELECT
   cat.name AS supercategory
 , sub.name AS category
FROM
   categories AS cat
     INNER JOIN categories AS sub
       ON sub.parent = cat.name
ORDER BY
   cat.name
 , sub.name
```

The results of this query are shown in Figure 11.10.

supercategory	category
Articles and Resources	Information Technology
Articles and Resources	Our Spectacular Universe
Personal Stories and Ideas	Gentle Words of Advice
Personal Stories and Ideas	Humorous Anecdotes
Personal Stories and Ideas	Log on to My Blog
Personal Stories and Ideas	Stories from the Id

Figure 11.10. Results of the categories table joined to itself

So the categories table is being self-joined, or joined to itself, using a join condition which matches the foreign key of one row to the primary key of another row in the same table. The ON clause specifies that the sub row's parent column value must match the cat row's category column value. Figure 11.11 illustrates what's occurring in the join.

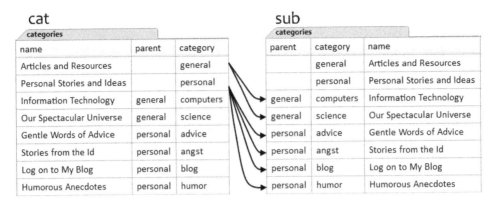

Figure 11.11. The `categories` table is being joined to itself

Choosing Table and Column Aliases

Did you notice that the above query uses `cat` and `sub` as table alias names, but `supercategory` and `category` as column alias names for display purposes? Which alias names you use in either case is up to you. You must use table aliases for syntax purposes, and you should use column aliases to distinguish the columns in the result set.

So are they super-categories and categories, or categories and subcategories? It's really up to you.

For more information on hierarchies, including examples of queries with several levels of subcategories, see the article *Categories and Subcategories* at http://sqllessons.com/categories.html.

The lines in the diagram above indicate the only pairs of `cat` and `sub` rows that actually match. It's an inner join, and since `NULL` equals no value, two of the `sub` rows are unmatched with any `cat` row. This is because the General and Personal categories do not themselves have parent categories.

Using categories and subcategories in a database is a common requirement. For instance, we often see them in a web site's navigation bar or site map. Our application's programming language helps us easily transform the result set in Figure 11.10 to the following HTML:

```
<ul>
  <li>Articles and Resources
    <ul>
      <li>Information Technology</li>
      <li>Our Spectacular Universe</li>
    </ul>
  </li>
  <li>Personal Stories and Ideas
    <ul>
      <li>Gentle Words of Advice</li>
      <li>Humourous Anecdotes</li>
      <li>Log On to my Blog</li>
      <li>Stories from the Id</li>
    </ul>
  </li>
</ul>
```

The transformation logic is a bit beyond the scope of this book, but involves looping over the rows of the result set and detecting control breaks in the super-category name—a technique introduced in the section called "ASC and DESC" in Chapter 8.

Finally, let's take our query one step further, and join the `categories` to the `entries` table as well:

CMS_16_Supercategories.sql (excerpt)

```
SELECT
  cat.name AS supercategory
, sub.name AS category
, entries.title
FROM
  categories AS cat
    INNER JOIN categories AS sub
      ON sub.parent = cat.category
    LEFT OUTER JOIN entries
      ON entries.category = sub.category
ORDER BY
  cat.name
, sub.name
, entries.title
```

Using a left outer join, we join the entries table to the result set of joining the categories table to itself. The result, shown in Figure 11.12, is a result set listing all entries with three columns: `supercategory`, `category`, and `title`. Because we used a left outer join to join to the `entries` table, we have a NULL in the `title` column for the `Log on to My Blog` category.

supercategory	category	title
Articles and Resources	Information Technology	Windows Media Center Rocks
Articles and Resources	Our Spectacular Universe	The Size of Our Galaxy
Personal Stories and Ideas	Gentle Words of Advice	Be Nice to Everybody
Personal Stories and Ideas	Humorous Anecdotes	Hello Statue
Personal Stories and Ideas	Humorous Anecdotes	Uncle Karl and the Gasoline
Personal Stories and Ideas	Log on to My Blog	
Personal Stories and Ideas	Stories from the Id	What If I Get Sick and Die?

Figure 11.12. Super-categories, categories, and titles

Implementing a Many-to-many Relationship: Keywords

Keywords are a very common feature of many different types of applications; you may see them implemented as **tags** in web applications where users *tag* entries with topic-related keywords. In our Content Management System application, entries may have one or more keywords, and the same keyword may be applied to multiple entries. So the relationship between entries and keywords is a many-to-many relationship. This relationship is shown in Figure 11.13.

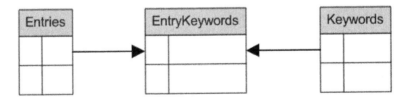

Figure 11.13. The relationship between entries and keywords in the CMS

However, when we're in the implementation stage of our data model, that is, when we're creating tables for the entities defined by our model, each many-to-many relationship must be broken down into two, one-to-many, foreign-key relationships. Knowing this, most data modellers simply introduce a relationship entity into the model. In this case, the relationship between entries and keywords is implemented via two one-to-many relationships, with the *EntryKeywords* entity—on the arrowhead end of both relationships in our ER diagram in Figure 11.13.

Lets first examine the data in our sample CMS application. Figure 11.14 shows the id (the primary key) and `title` columns from the `entries` table.

entries	
title	id
What If I Get Sick and Die?	423
Uncle Karl and the Gasoline	524
Be Nice to Everybody	537
Hello Statue	573
The Size of Our Galaxy	598
Windows Media Center Rocks	605

Figure 11.14. The `entries` table

Figure 11.15 shows the new `entrykeywords` table, where `entry_id` is a foreign key, referencing the id of the `entries` table, so this is just another typical one-to-many relationship. The SQL for the creation of this table can be found in the section called "The `entrykeywords` Table" in Appendix C.

entrykeywords	
entry_id	keyword
524	family
524	reckless
537	family
537	my three rules
598	astronomy
605	television
605	windows

Figure 11.15. The `entrykeywords` table

The primary key of the `entrykeywords` table is a composite key consisting of both columns, since we only want a keyword to be assigned to an article once. Any query which needs to return entries along with their keywords will have to perform a join between the `entries` and the `entrykeywords` tables, using the primary key and foreign key relationship depicted in Figure 11.16.

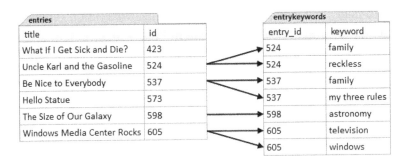

Figure 11.16. A join between the `entries` and `entrykeywords` table

In most situations, to achieve this result, a left outer join from `entries` to `entrykeywords` is used. You might like to use an inner join, however, if you're interested only in entries that have had at least one keyword assigned.

At this point, it would seem that our many-to-many relationship has been successfully implemented using only two tables, so why do we need a third? As it's implemented at the moment, we can insert rows into the `entrykeywords` table using whatever keywords we like; the `keyword` column in the `entrykeywords` is simply a data column, as opposed to a foreign key column. (It should still be a part of the primary key, though, so that we avoid inserting the same keyword more than once for each entry.)

This is another one of those delightful instances where the choice is up to you. As it stands any keywords can be inserted into the `entrykeywords` table. However, if your application should only allow a restricted set of keywords to be used, then you'll need to implement the second one-to-many relationship and make a third table for keywords.

This new `keywords` table will contain the list of keywords that can be associated with entries. Using a foreign key constraint, we can make sure that only keywords that are in the `keywords` table can be added to an entry. Of course, this will also mean that if a new keyword is introduced, it will have to be added to the `keywords` table first before it can be added to an entry.

We could implement the `keywords` table with two columns: an `id` column for the primary key (possibly a surrogate key, like an autonumber) and a `keyword` column for the keyword itself. The `entrykeywords` table should then be modified so that the `keyword` column becomes a foreign key column; that way it references the values from the `id` column in the new `keywords` table.

With an implementation like that, any query which needs to return entries along with their keywords will have to perform a join between the `entries` and the `entrykeywords` tables, and then between the `entrykeywords` table and `keywords` table, using the primary key and foreign key relationship. To me, this hardly seems worth the effort!

If all we're doing is ensuring that only the keywords in the `keywords` table are used for entries, it really only needs one column—the keyword column—as it's a perfect natural key; the surrogate primary key column is entirely redundant in this situation. Figure 11.17 illustrates the relationship between `entrykeywords` and a one-column keywords table.

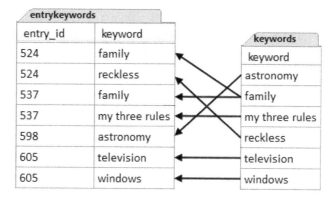

Figure 11.17. The relationship between `entrykeywords` and `keywords`

With the keywords table in place (and the foreign key relationship defined between the `entrykeywords` table to the `keywords` table), we simply add a new keyword to the keywords table, and then we can start assigning it to entries. We'll only be able to assign a new keyword to an entry if that keyword has been inserted beforehand in the keywords table. Since we're using a natural key (the keyword itself) instead of a surrogate key, we know that every foreign key value must have a matching primary key value. There's no need to perform a join operation to retrieve them, because they're going to be the same as the `keyword` values in the `entrykeywords` table.

The MySQL Function GROUP_CONCAT

MySQL has a wonderful aggregate function called GROUP_CONCAT. In a nutshell, it works on strings the same way that SUM works on numbers. The GROUP_CONCAT function concatenates the values in a character column, using an optional separator—the default being a comma.

This function is supremely useful in many situations where data from multiple relationships must be retrieved. It allows one of those relationships to be collapsed to one row per entity. Here's an example using entries and keywords:

(excerpt)

```
SELECT
  entries.title
, GROUP_CONCAT(entrykeywords.keyword) AS keywords
FROM
  entries
    LEFT OUTER JOIN entrykeywords
      ON entrykeywords.entry_id = entries.id
GROUP BY
  entries.title
```

The results of this query are shown in Figure 11.18. All of the keywords for each entry_id have been concatenated into a single value (but separated by commas within the single value), and placed in the row for the matching entry id value.

title	keywords
What If I Get Sick and Die?	
Uncle Karl and the Gasoline	family, reckless
Be Nice to Everybody	family, my three rules
Hello Statue	
The Size of Our Galaxy	astronomy
Windows Media Center Rocks	television, windows

Figure 11.18. The results using GROUP_CONCAT

We started with a many-to-many relationship in the original data model, but ended up implementing only half of the two one-to-many table relationships needed to support it. This is actually very common; the *one half of* a many-to-many structure is used for numerous other applications besides keywords and tags. As you work with databases, keep an eye open. Whenever you encounter a one-to-many relationship between two tables, ask yourself whether there needs to be another table—to complete the other half of a many-to-many relationship—and if a surrogate key is really necessary.

Wrapping Up: Special Structures

In this chapter, we learned about three types of special structures that occur often in applications:

1. two or more different relationships between the same two entities (showing how to join to a table twice)

2. a reflexive or recursive relationship (showing how to join a table to itself)

3. keywords in a many-to-many scenario (and whether a keyword table needs to be declared)

This concludes the chapters on database design, and also the book.

Don't forget that there's a web site that goes along with this book, located at http://www.sitepoint.com/books/sql1/, where you can also obtain the actual SQL script files used we've used.

There's a lot more to SQL than what we've covered in this book. SQL is like chess—you can learn the basics in a couple of hours, but it takes a long time to become a grand master. There is, however, only one way to become better: practice, practice, practice!

Appendix A: Testing Environment

In order to test your SQL, you need a testing environment. Even if you're working for an organization that creates web sites using databases (and therefore may have servers you can test on), you might want to have your own space, to see how more ambitious SQL queries work. Well, it's easy to set up your own testing environment on a laptop or desktop computer, but there are so many options it may take you a while to decide what to use.

Will you be using a Mac or PC? Do you need a specific database system, or are you free to assess what each one offers? How comfortable are you with source code text editing or with using the command line? What sorts of design tools will you use? It may be the case that you'll try out several combinations of database and script editor before you find one you like, but you should persevere.

The first step is to obtain a copy of the database system.

Download Your Database System Software

Choose a database system, and download and install the software. The more popular—but by no means only—database servers are listed here, including the URL of the web page where you can download them. These are all free versions that are ideal for practice.

MySQL Community Server

http://www.mysql.com/downloads/

Available for Windows, Mac OS X, and Linux.

PostgreSQL

http://www.postgresql.org/download/

Available for Windows, Mac OS X, and Linux.

Microsoft SQL Server Express

http://www.microsoft.com/express/sql/download/

Available for Windows.

IBM DB2 Express-C

http://www-306.ibm.com/software/data/db2/express/

Available for Linux and Windows.

Oracle Database Express Edition

http://www.oracle.com/technology/software/products/database/xe/index.html

Available for Linux and Windows.

Follow the installation instructions provided and if you have any difficulty, remember that you can always find help in the Sitepoint Databases forum at http://www.sitepoint.com/forums/forumdisplay.php?f=88.

The next step is to make sure you have access to *the manual*.

Bookmark or Download the SQL Reference

All database systems offer their SQL reference manual on the Web. Find your system's manual and bookmark it. It's invaluable for looking up those nasty—or useful, depending on the circumstance—deviations from standard SQL. Here are the links for the online manuals for the database systems listed above. You might also want to investigate obtaining the manual as a download, so that you don't have to be connected to the Internet to look up SQL syntax.

MySQL

http://dev.mysql.com/doc/refman/5.0/en/index.html

PostgreSQL

http://www.postgresql.org/docs/8.3/interactive/sql.html

Microsoft SQL Server

http://msdn.microsoft.com/en-us/library/bb510741.aspx

IBM DB2

http://publib.boulder.ibm.com/infocenter/db2luw/v9r5/
➡topic/com.ibm.db2.luw.container.doc/doc/c0052964.html

Oracle

http://download.oracle.com/docs/cd/B28359_01/server.111/b28286/toc.htm

Connect to the Database System

Communicating with the database system is accomplished via a *connection*, which must first be established. Once a connection is made, you send your SQL statements over this connection to the database system, and the results (or error messages) are sent back. There are two ways to establish a connection to your database: through the command line, or via a front-end application.

Command Line

Developers experienced in executing commands from the command line will need no instructions. If you lack the know-how, do yourself a favor and install a front-end application instead.

Front-end Applications

The benefits of using a front-end application are apparent the first time you use one:

- You never have to re-type an entire query to fix a simple error.

- It lists the tables in your database; allows you create, modify, and delete those tables; and also lets you browse the data they contain.

- It will help you write SQL queries, and in many cases will build join queries based on existing primary and foreign keys.

- It applies **code highlighting** to your queries. This means that the application understands SQL syntax and will apply different colors to the keywords, identifiers, and constants used in your queries.

- Those with more advanced interfaces let you build queries with drag-and-drop functionality.

Front-end applications are even easier to download and install than the database systems are. Many excellent third-party products exist, some free, some not. Here are some front-end applications to consider:

MySQL

MySQL Workbench is available for Windows:
http://dev.mysql.com/downloads/workbench/5.0.html.

MySQL GUI Tools are available for Windows, Mac OS X, and Linux:
http://dev.mysql.com/downloads/gui-tools/5.0.html.

PostgreSQL

pgAdmin is available for Windows, Mac OS X, and Linux:
http://www.pgadmin.org.

Microsoft SQL Server

Available for Windows, if you download the server package called **SQL Server 2008 Express with Tools**, you'll also receive SQL Server Management Studio Basic:
http://www.microsoft.com/express/sql/download/.

IBM DB2

The DB2 Developer Workbench is available for Windows and Linux, but you'll need to setup an IBM ID account to download it:

https://www14.software.ibm.com/webapp/iwm/
➥web/preLogin.do?lang=en_US&source=swg-dm-db2dwb

Oracle

Oracle SQL Developer is available for Windows, Mac OS X, and Linux:
http://www.oracle.com/technology/products/database/sql_developer/index.html

SQL Script Library

One final suggestion is to set up your own SQL **script library**, a simple text-based library of SQL code that you can reuse as the need arises. For example, you might wish to keep this template for returning unmatched rows:

```
FROM
  ltable
    LEFT OUTER JOIN rtable
      ON rtable.fk = ltable.pk
WHERE
  rtable.fk IS NULL
```

Appendix C contains the scripts to create the tables used in our sample applications. If you're building a similar application, copy those scripts into your script library and customize as necessary.

Scripts can also be generated by many front-end applications from existing database tables. This feature is often named Export, and will allow you to export database structure as DDL and/or existing data as DML (producing INSERT statements) into an SQL file. Doing this periodically is actually an effective backup strategy, although you would probably not mix these backup files in with your script library.

Using a comprehensive text editor can help, too, especially if your front-end application is weak in the text editing department. The code library would be the repository of your SQL queries—working in conjunction with either your text editor, your front-end application, or both.

Performance Problems and Obtaining Help

> When everything else breaks down, I don't hesitate to roam out of the pocket and do the boogaloo.
>
> —Fran Tarkenton

With so many different ways possible to write an SQL query, the number one criterion for writing good SQL is correctness. Performance plays a secondary role. Given that database systems all have competent optimizers, it shouldn't really matter which way you write your queries, as long as the results produced are correct. It matters little how fast a query runs, if it produces the wrong results.

However, in the real world, it sometimes does matter. If you end up having a performance problem with a query, there are three ways to solve it:

- analyze the execution plan
- gain external help
- implement proper indexing

Obtaining the Execution Plan

Many database systems offer help in this area, by letting you see the **execution plan** for a query—an outline of how the server's optimizer *plans* to execute the query—without actually running the query.

Some database systems have tried to make it simple for you to see the optimizer's execution plan. For example, both MySQL and PostgreSQL allow you just to stick the keyword EXPLAIN in front of the SELECT statement; Microsoft SQL Server's Management Studio Express, on the other hand, has the **Display Estimated Execution Plan** option, and so on.

Analyzing the information in the optimizer's execution plan is well beyond the beginner-to-intermediate level; it verges into DBA (database administrator) territory. But you may need to know at least how to produce the execution plan, especially if you're going to go looking for help elsewhere, so have a look in your SQL reference manual.

Seeking Help

Gaining external help can be done through the Sitepoint Forums. There is a main forum for Databases, and a second forum specifically for MySQL because of its popularity:

- Databases: http://www.sitepoint.com/forums/forumdisplay.php?f=88

- MySQL: http://www.sitepoint.com/forums/forumdisplay.php?f=182

If you do post your performance problem there (or in any other forum), you'll likely be asked whether you've indexed your tables properly, as this will almost always solve the performance problem. If you have, you'll probably next be asked to show your execution plan output—just in case you were wondering what to expect.

Indexing

Indexing is the number one solution to poor performance. We were introduced to indexes in the section called "WHERE Clause Performance" in Chapter 4. You should consult the documentation for your particular database system if you'd like to investigate indexes.

Appendix B: Sample Applications

For illustrative purposes, the SQL discussed in this book is based on several sample applications:

Teams and Games

This application keeps track of games played by sports teams. Each game has two teams who play each other, at a specific location. One team is designated the home team, and the other, the away team.

Content Management System (CMS)

In the Content Management System, online content is stored and retrieved via lists, displays, and searches. Comments, keywords, and categories of content are implemented.

Discussion Forums

The Discussion Forum application manages discussion threads consisting of related posts by registered forum members.

Shopping Carts

Shopping Carts are orders for specific items made by customers of an online store. Customers browse items for purchase from the site's inventory, and selected items are placed into a shopping cart.

Data Model Diagrams

Each of the sample applications is described with a data model diagram that gives a graphical overview of the entities, and the relationships between entities, in the application. Data modelling is a technique used in the early stages of application development to focus attention on the entities and their relationships within the scope of the application.

Translating a data model diagram into functional database table specifications is fairly straightforward. It involves creating primary and foreign keys in the tables, and we discuss this process in detail in Chapter 10. Each relationship ends up generating at least one foreign key. The diagram itself, though, is indispensable; just by looking at a data model diagram, you gain an immediate sense of what kind of data is in the application, and how it's related.

Here are the data model diagrams for the sample applications discussed in this book. See if you can acquire a sense of the cardinality of the various relationships—look for the arrowhead that indicates the one-to-many nature of the relationship.

Teams and Games

Figure B.1 shows the relationships between the entities in this application.

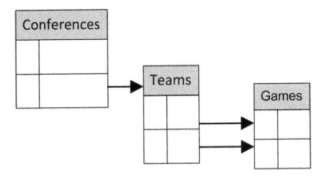

Figure B.1. The Teams and Games data model

Each team belongs to a *conference* (which could be a league, or a division). Each conference has multiple *teams*. This application is often implemented without the conference entity, if the teams all belong to just one league and there's no division of teams into separate groupings.

Teams play *games*, but there are two relationships between teams and games; one's for the home team, and the other's for the away team. Each team is related to many games where it's the home team, and many games where it's the away team. However, the same team cannot be both home and away for any given game.

Content Management System

Figure B.2 shows the relationships between the entities in this application.

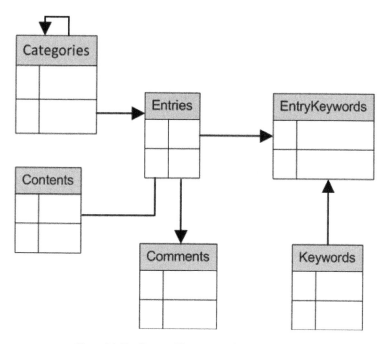

Figure B.2. The Content Management System data model

The main entity is the *entry* entity. An entry constitutes a web page, the basic unit of content. Entries belong to only one *category*, and each category can have many entries. Categories form a hierarchy of categories and subcategories, indicated by the reflexive one-to-many relationship from the categories entity to itself. A category that has a parent category is a subcategory.

Entries may have one or more *keywords*. At the same time, a single keyword may be applied to multiple entries, so this is actually a *many-to-many* relationship between the two entities. However, when tables are created for entities, each many-to-many relationship must be broken down into two one-to-many relationships. In this case, the many-to-many relationship between entries and keywords is implemented via two one-to-many relationships with the *entrykeywords* table, as illustrated above. In our example, we want to allow keywords to be assigned to entries without the database checking to see if they're an *allowed* keyword, so there's no specific keywords table mapping to the entity in Figure B.2.

Entries may have one or more *comments*. Each comment belongs to only one entry.

Entries have optional *contents*. When content is appropriate, it's stored in the contents table, which is in a *one-to-one* relationship with entries. A given entry has at most one content row, and each content row belongs to only one entry.

Discussion Forums

Figure B.3 shows the relationships between the entities in this application.

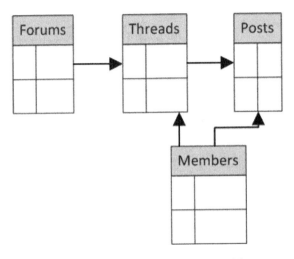

Figure B.3. The Discussion Forums data model

The Discussion Forums application allows registered *members* to make *posts* about various topics, organized into discussion *forums*. There can be one or more forums, and each forum consists of one or more *threads*. Each thread belongs to only one forum.

A thread consists of one or more related posts, and each post belongs to only one thread.

Both threads and posts are related to a member. For threads, it's the member who started the thread, and for posts, it's the member who made the post. Members can start multiple threads and make multiple posts.

Shopping Carts

Figure B.4 shows the relationships between the entities in this application.

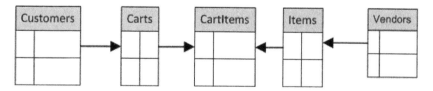

Figure B.4. The Shopping Cart data model

Customers of an online store place orders for items from an inventory (of items) that they can browse. Each separate order is called a shopping *cart*, and a customer can have more than one cart. Each cart belongs to only one customer.

A cart consists of multiple *items*. An item can be ordered in multiple carts. The many-to-many relationship between carts and items is implemented using the intermediary table `cartitems`. Each cart item belongs to only one cart and is for only one item. The *cartitem* entity allows for a quantity to be specified, so that, for example, three widgets can be ordered in a particular cart.

Each item is supplied by a specific *vendor*, and vendors can supply more than one item.

Appendix C: Sample Scripts

The following scripts are used to create, populate, and alter the tables belonging to the applications in this book, as described in Appendix B.

The samples are presented in the form of scripts, SQL statements saved as a source or text file using the file extension `.sql`. These files are available at the web site for this book: http://www.sitepoint.com/books/sql1/. Each script file is meant to be executed, and you can do this quite simply in the command line, or by importing the script into your front-end application. Also included in the code archive are scripts containing the SQL statements discussed in the book. Each script also contains commentary relating to its purpose and position in the book.

TIMESTAMP and DATETIME

All the scripts in this chapter use the `TIMESTAMP` data type to hold date and time values. If your database system does not support this data type, you should use the `DATETIME` data type instead and change the scripts accordingly.

Row Constructors

All the scripts in this appendix that `INSERT` rows into a new table use row constructors to add them in one step. If your database of choice does not support row constructors, you'll need to insert each row individually, as shown in Chapter 1.

Teams and Games

The Teams and Games application uses three entities: *teams*, *games*, and *conferences*. They're represented in two tables called `teams` and `games`.

The `teams` Table

The `Teams` table has three columns and three rows, and is first met in Chapter 1. Here's the DDL to create the table:

Teams_02_INSERT.sql *(excerpt)*

```
CREATE TABLE teams
(
   id            INTEGER      NOT NULL  PRIMARY KEY
 , name          VARCHAR(37)  NOT NULL
 , conference    CHAR(2)      NOT NULL
        CHECK ( conference IN ( 'AA','A','B','C','D','E','F','G' ) )
);
```

Note that the `CHECK` constraint appearing above is discussed in Chapter 9. If your database lacks support for `CHECK` constraints, you'll need to delete it. To populate the `teams` table we run the following:

Teams_03_DELETE_INSERT.sql *(excerpt)*

```
INSERT INTO teams
   ( conference , id, name )
VALUES
   ( 'F' , 9 , 'Riff Raff' )
 , ( 'F' , 37 , 'Havoc' )
 , ( 'C' , 63 , 'Brewers' )
```

Later in Chapter 11, the teams table is repopulated:

```
                                              Teams_07_Games.sql (excerpt)
DELETE FROM teams;

INSERT INTO teams
  ( id , name , conference )
VALUES
  ( 9 , 'Riff Raff'   , 'F' )
, (11 , 'Savages'     , 'F' )
, (15 , 'Blue Devils' , 'F' )
, (24 , 'Hurricanes'  , 'F' )
;
```

The games Table

The games table has four columns and two rows, and is first met in Chapter 11:

```
                                              Teams_07_Games.sql (excerpt)
CREATE TABLE games
(
  gamedate   DATETIME    NOT NULL
, location   VARCHAR(37) NOT NULL
, hometeam   INTEGER     NOT NULL
, awayteam   INTEGER     NOT NULL
);

INSERT INTO games
  ( gamedate , location , hometeam , awayteam )
VALUES
  ( '2008-09-06' , 'McKenzie'  ,  9 , 24 )
, ( '2008-09-13' , 'Applewood' , 15 ,  9 )
;
```

Content Management System

The Content Management System application uses six entities: *entries*, *categories*, *comments*, *contents*, *entrykeywords*, and *keywords*. They're represented in five tables, with *entrykeywords* and *keywords* being wrapped up into one table called entrykeywords. A view called entries_with_category is also created for demonstration purposes.

The entries Table

The entries table has six columns and five rows. It's first introduced in Chapter 2:

CMS_01_Title_and_Category_of_Entries.sql *(excerpt)*

```
CREATE TABLE entries
(
  id           INTEGER      NOT NULL   PRIMARY KEY
, title        VARCHAR(99)  NOT NULL
, created      TIMESTAMP    NOT NULL
, updated      TIMESTAMP    NULL
, category     VARCHAR(37)  NULL
, content      TEXT         NULL
);

INSERT INTO entries
  (id, title, created, updated, category)
VALUES
  (423,'What If I Get Sick and Die?',
      '2008-12-30','2009-03-11','angst')
, (524,'Uncle Karl and the Gasoline',
      '2009-02-28',NULL,'humor'),
, (537,'Be Nice to Everybody',
      '2009-03-02',NULL,'advice'),
, (573,'Hello Statue',
      '2009-03-17',NULL,'humor'),
, (598,'The Size of Our Galaxy',
      '2009-04-03',NULL,'science')
;
```

A second script provides the extended content for one of the entries:

```
                        CMS_02_Display_An_Entry.sql (excerpt)
UPDATE
  entries
SET
  content =
      'When I was about nine or ten, my Uncle Karl, who would''ve
      been in his late teens or early twenties, once performed
      what to me seemed like a magic trick.

      Using a rubber hose, which he snaked down into the gas tank
      of my father''s car, he siphoned some gasoline into his
      mouth, lit a match, held it up a few inches in front of his
      face, and then, with explosive force, sprayed the gasoline
      out towards the lit match.

      Of course, a huge fireball erupted, much to the delight of
      the kids watching. I don''t recall if he did it more than
      once.

      The funny part of this story? We lived to tell it.

      Karl was like that.'
WHERE
  id = 524
```

A sixth row is added to the table to demonstrate right outer joins in Chapter 3:

```
               CMS_07_Categories_RIGHT_OUTER_JOIN_Entries.sql (excerpt)
INSERT INTO entries
  (id, title, created, updated, category)
VALUES
  (605,'Windows Media Center Rocks','2009-04-29',NULL,'computers')
```

Once the contents table has been created, the content column in the entries table is removed:

```
               CMS_14_Content_and_Comment_Tables.sql (excerpt)
ALTER TABLE entries DROP COLUMN content
```

Finally, in Chapter 11, the table receives an index and foreign key (if you're using MySQL, you'll need to index the foreign key first):

CMS_15_Add_FK_To_Entries.sql *(excerpt)*

```
ALTER TABLE entries
ADD INDEX
  category_ix (category)
;


ALTER TABLE entries
ADD CONSTRAINT
  category_fk
    FOREIGN KEY (category)
      REFERENCES categories (category)
        ON DELETE CASCADE
        ON UPDATE CASCADE
;
```

The `categories` Table

The `categories` table has two columns and initially five rows. It's first seen in Chapter 3 and then altered in Chapter 11:

CMS_05_Categories_INNER_JOIN_Entries.sql *(excerpt)*

```
CREATE TABLE categories
(
  category    VARCHAR(9)    NOT NULL   PRIMARY KEY,
  name        VARCHAR(37)   NOT NULL
);

INSERT INTO categories
  ( category, name )
VALUES
  ( 'blog'  , 'Log on to My Blog' )
, ( 'humor' , 'Humorous Anecdotes' )
, ( 'angst' , 'Stories from the Id' )
, ( 'advice' , 'Gentle Words of Advice' )
, ( 'science' , 'Our Spectacular Universe' )
;
```

Later, in Chapter 11, a sixth category is added:

CMS_15_Add_FK_to_Entries.sql *(excerpt)*

```
INSERT INTO categories
  ( category, name )
VALUES
  ( 'computers' , 'Information Technology' )
```

Finally, a new column, index, and foreign key are added to the table to demonstrate how a table can be joined to itself. (Again, if you're using MySQL, you'll need to index the foreign key first.) This creates a *pseudo-hierarchy* of items stored within the table:

CMS_16_Supercategories.sql *(excerpt)*

```
ALTER TABLE categories
ADD COLUMN
  parent VARCHAR(9) NULL
;

ALTER TABLE categories
ADD INDEX
  parent_ix (parent)
;

ALTER TABLE categories
ADD CONSTRAINT
  parent_fk
    FOREIGN KEY (parent)
      REFERENCES categories (category)
;

INSERT INTO categories
  ( category, name )
VALUES
  ( 'general' , 'Articles and Resources' )
, ( 'personal' , 'Personal Stories and Ideas' )
;

UPDATE
  categories
SET
  parent = 'general'
```

```
WHERE
  category in ( 'computers', 'science' )
;

UPDATE
  categories
SET
  parent = 'personal'
WHERE
  category in ( 'advice', 'angst', 'blog', 'humor' )
;
```

The `entries_with_category` View

The `entries_with_category` view is created in Chapter 3. The script to create it will only work in versions of MySQL from version 5.0.1:

CMS_10_CREATE_VIEW.sql (excerpt)

```
CREATE VIEW
  entries_with_category
AS
SELECT
  entries.title
, entries.created
, categories.name as category_name
FROM
  entries
    INNER JOIN categories
      ON categories.category = entries.category
```

The `contents` Table

The `contents` table has two columns and one row initially, copied from the `entries` table. It's first mentioned in Chapter 5. Note that you must create the `entries` table and populate it before running this script:

CMS_14_Content_and_Comment_Tables.sql (excerpt)

```
CREATE TABLE contents
(
  entry_id   INTEGER   NOT NULL  PRIMARY KEY
, content    TEXT      NOT NULL
```

```
);

INSERT INTO contents
  ( entry_id , content )
SELECT
  id
, content
FROM
  entries
WHERE
  NOT ( content IS NULL )
;
```

Once the contents table has been created and populated, the contents column of the entries table is no longer needed:

CMS_14_Content_and_Comment_Tables.sql *(excerpt)*

```
ALTER TABLE entries
  DROP COLUMN content
;
```

The comments Table

The comments table has six columns and three rows. It's first met in Chapter 5:

CMS_14_Content_and_Comment_Tables.sql *(excerpt)*

```
CREATE TABLE comments
(
  entry_id   INTEGER     NOT NULL
, username   VARCHAR(37) NOT NULL
, created    TIMESTAMP   NOT NULL
, PRIMARY KEY ( entry_id, username, created )
, revised    TIMESTAMP      NULL
, comment    TEXT        NOT NULL
);

INSERT INTO comments
  ( entry_id, username, created, revised, comment )
VALUES
  ( 524, 'Steve0', '2009-03-05', NULL ,
      'Sounds like fun. Must try that.')
, ( 524, 'r937'  , '2009-03-06', NULL ,
```

```
                  'I tasted gasoline once. Not worth the discomfort.')
, ( 524, 'J4s0n' , '2009-03-16','2009-03-17',
        'You and your uncle are both idiots.')
;
```

The entrykeywords Table

The entrykeywords table has two columns and seven rows. It's first seen in Chapter 11:

CMS_17_Entrykeywords.sql *(excerpt)*

```
CREATE TABLE entrykeywords
(
  entry_id    INTEGER     NOT NULL
, keyword     VARCHAR(99) NOT NULL
, PRIMARY KEY ( entry_id, keyword )
, CONSTRAINT entry_fk
    FOREIGN KEY (entry_id)
      REFERENCES entries (id)
);

INSERT INTO entrykeywords
  ( entry_id, keyword )
VALUES
  (524,'family')
, (524,'reckless')
, (537,'my three rules')
, (537,'family')
, (598,'astronomy')
, (605,'windows')
, (605,'television')
;
```

Discussion Forums

The Discussion Forums application, used in Chapter 7, has four entities: *forums*, *members*, *threads*, and *posts*; they're represented in four tables of the same name. All four are created in the same script, but we've separated them here for clarity.

The `forums` Table

First, the `forums` table, which has two columns and three rows:

Forums_01_Setup.sql *(excerpt)*

```
CREATE TABLE forums
(
  id           INTEGER      NOT NULL  PRIMARY KEY
, name         VARCHAR(37)  NOT NULL
, CONSTRAINT forum_name_uk
    UNIQUE ( name )
);

INSERT INTO forums
  ( id, name )
VALUES
  ( 10001 , 'Search Engines' )
, ( 10002 , 'Databases' )
, ( 10003 , 'Applications' )
;
```

The `members` Table

The `members` table has two columns and five rows:

Forums_01_Setup.sql *(excerpt)*

```
CREATE TABLE members
(
  id           INTEGER      NOT NULL  PRIMARY KEY
, name         VARCHAR(37)  NOT NULL
, CONSTRAINT name_uk
    UNIQUE ( name )
);

INSERT INTO members
  ( id, name )
```

```
VALUES
  (   9 , 'noo13' )
, (  37 , 'r937' )
, (  42 , 'DeepThought' )
, (  99 , 'BarbFeldon' )
, ( 187 , 'RJNeedham' )
;
```

The threads Table

Now the threads table—it has four columns and four rows:

```
                                            Forums_01_Setup.sql (excerpt)

CREATE TABLE threads
(
  id          INTEGER      NOT NULL  PRIMARY KEY
, name        VARCHAR(99)  NOT NULL
, forum_id    INTEGER      NOT NULL
, starter     INTEGER      NOT NULL
, CONSTRAINT thread_name_uk
    UNIQUE ( id, name )
);

INSERT INTO threads
  ( id, name, forum_id, starter )
VALUES
  ( 15 , 'Difficulty with join query', 10002 , 187 )
, ( 25 , 'How do I get listed in Yahoo?', 10001 ,   9 )
, ( 35 , 'People who bought ... also bought ...' , 10002 ,  99 )
, ( 45 , 'WHERE clause doesn''t work', 10002 , 187 )
;
```

The posts Table

Finally, the posts table. Note that you should remove the DEFAULT and CHECK constraints if your database does not support them. It has eight columns and seven
rows, each of which has been added in its own INSERT statement for clarity:

```sql
CREATE TABLE posts
(
  id         INTEGER      NOT NULL  PRIMARY KEY
, name       VARCHAR(99)  NULL
, thread_id  INTEGER      NOT NULL
, reply_to   INTEGER      NULL
, posted_by  INTEGER      NOT NULL
, created    TIMESTAMP    NOT NULL  DEFAULT CURRENT_TIMESTAMP
, revised    TIMESTAMP    NULL      CHECK ( revised >= created )
, post       TEXT         NOT NULL
);

INSERT INTO posts
  ( id, name, thread_id, reply_to,
      posted_by, created, revised, post )
VALUES
  ( 201 , 'Difficulty with join query' , 15, NULL , 187 ,
      '2008-11-12 11:12:13', NULL, 'I''m having a lot of trouble
      joining my tables. What''s a foreign key?' )
;

INSERT INTO posts
  ( id, name, thread_id, reply_to,
      posted_by, created, revised, post )
VALUES
  ( 215 , 'How do I get listed in Yahoo?', 25, NULL , 9 ,
      '2008-11-15 11:20:02', NULL, 'I''ve figured out how to submit
      my URL to Google, but I can''t seem to find where to post it
      on Yahoo! Can anyone help?' )
;

INSERT INTO posts
  ( id, name, thread_id, reply_to,
      posted_by, created, revised, post )
VALUES
  ( 216 , NULL , 25, 215 , 42 , '2008-11-15 11:37:10', NULL,
      'Try http://search.yahoo.com/info/submit.html ' )
;

INSERT INTO posts
  ( id, name, thread_id, reply_to,
      posted_by, created, revised, post )
VALUES
```

```
  ( 218 , 'That''s it!' , 25, 216 , 9 , '2008-11-15 11:42:24',
      NULL, 'That''s it! How did you find it?' )
;

INSERT INTO posts
  ( id, name, thread_id, reply_to,
      posted_by, created, revised, post )
VALUES
  ( 219 , NULL , 25, 218 , 42 , '2008-11-15 11:51:45',
      '2008-11-15 11:57:57', 'There''s a link at the bottom of the
      homepage called "Suggest a site"' )
;

INSERT INTO posts
  ( id, name, thread_id, reply_to,
      posted_by, created, revised, post )
VALUES
  ( 222 , 'People who bought ... also bought ...' , 35, NULL ,
      99 , '2008-11-22 22:22:22', NULL, 'For each item in the
      user''s cart, I want to show other items that people
      bought who bought that item, but the SQL is too hairy
      for me. HELP!' )
;

INSERT INTO posts
  ( id, name, thread_id, reply_to,
      posted_by, created, revised, post )
VALUES
  ( 230 , 'WHERE clause doesn''t work' , 45, NULL , 187 ,
      '2008-12-04 09:37:00', NULL, 'My query has WHERE
      startdate > 2009-01-01 but I get 0 results, even though
      I know there are rows for next year!' )
;
```

Shopping Carts

The Shopping Carts application uses four tables to represent *customers*, *items*, *shopping carts*, and *cartitems*, the items in each cart: `customers`, `carts`, `cartitems`, and `items`. All of them are introduced in Chapter 4. A fifth table, `vendors`, is introduced in Chapter 10 to represent those who are selling the items.

The `items` Table

The `items` table has four columns and eighteen rows:

Cart_01_Comparison_operators.sql (excerpt)

```sql
CREATE TABLE items
(
  id      INTEGER      NOT NULL PRIMARY KEY
, name    VARCHAR(21)  NOT NULL
, type    VARCHAR(7)   NOT NULL
, price   DECIMAL(5,2) NULL
);

INSERT INTO items
  ( id, name, type, price )
VALUES
  (5021,'thingie'         ,'widgets',  9.37 )
, (5022,'gadget'          ,'doodads', 19.37 )
, (5023,'dingus'          ,'gizmos' , 29.37 )
, (5041,'gewgaw'          ,'widgets',  5.00 )
, (5042,'knickknack'      ,'doodads', 10.00 )
, (5043,'whatnot'         ,'gizmos' , 15.00 )
, (5061,'bric-a-brac'     ,'widgets',  2.00 )
, (5062,'folderol'        ,'doodads',  4.00 )
, (5063,'jigger'          ,'gizmos' ,  6.00 )
, (5901,'doohickey'       ,'widgets', 12.00 )
, (5902,'gimmick'         ,'doodads',  9.37 )
, (5903,'dingbat'         ,'gizmos' ,  9.37 )
, (5911,'thingamajig'     ,'widgets', NULL  )
, (5912,'thingamabob'     ,'doodads', NULL  )
, (5913,'thingum'         ,'gizmos' , NULL  )
, (5931,'contraption'     ,'widgets', 49.95 )
, (5932,'whatchamacallit' ,'doodads', 59.95 )
, (5937,'whatsis'         ,'gizmos' , NULL  )
;
```

In Chapter 4, before we experiment with AND and OR in the WHERE clause, we have to supply prices to the items that have a price of NULL:

Cart_04_ANDs_and_ORs.sql *(excerpt)*

```
UPDATE
  items
SET
  price = 22.22
WHERE
  name IN ( 'thingamajig', 'thingamabob', 'thingum' )
;

UPDATE
  items
SET
  price = 93.70
WHERE
  name = 'whatsis'
;
```

In Chapter 10, the vendors table is created, and then a foreign key column and reference to that table is added to the items table linking items to their vendors.

Cart_17_Vendors.sql *(excerpt)*

```
ALTER TABLE items
ADD COLUMN
  vendor_id INTEGER NULL
;

ALTER TABLE items
ADD INDEX
  vendor_ix (vendor_id)
;

ALTER TABLE items
ADD CONSTRAINT
  vendor_fk
    FOREIGN KEY (vendor_id)
      REFERENCES vendors (id)
        ON DELETE CASCADE
        ON UPDATE CASCADE
;
```

```
UPDATE
  items
SET
  vendor_id = 17
WHERE
  name < 't'
;

UPDATE
  items
SET
  vendor_id = 19
WHERE
  name > 'w'
;

INSERT INTO items
  ( id, name, type, price, vendor_id )
VALUES
  ( 9901, 'gift wrapping', 'service', 5.00, NULL )
, ( 9902, 'discount coupon', 'service', -10.00, NULL )
;
```

The customers Table

The customers table has four columns and eight rows. Note that the first seven rows use the default value of the shipaddr column, but the eighth uses its own and so is added using its own INSERT statement:

Cart_04_ANDs_and_ORs.sql *(excerpt)*

```
CREATE TABLE customers
(
  id        INTEGER      NOT NULL PRIMARY KEY
, name      VARCHAR(99)  NOT NULL
, billaddr  VARCHAR(255) NOT NULL
, shipaddr  VARCHAR(255) NOT NULL DEFAULT 'See billing address.'
);

INSERT INTO customers
  (id, name, billaddr)
VALUES
  (710,'A. Jones','123 Sesame St., Eureka, KS')
```

```
, (730,'B. Smith','456 Sesame St., Eureka, KS')
, (750,'C. Brown','789 Sesame St., Eureka, KS')
, (770,'D. White','246 Sesame St., Eureka, KS')
, (820,'E. Baker','135 Sesame St., Eureka, KS')
, (840,'F. Black','468 Sesame St., Eureka, KS')
, (860,'G. Scott','357 Sesame St., Eureka, KS')
;

INSERT INTO customers
  (id, name, billaddr, shipaddr)
VALUES
  (880,'H. Clark',
     '937 Sesame St., Eureka, KS', 'P.O. Box 9, Toledo, OH' )
;
```

The `carts` Table

The carts table has three columns and ten rows:

Cart_04_ANDs_and_ORs.sql (excerpt)

```
CREATE TABLE carts
(
  id          INTEGER    NOT NULL PRIMARY KEY
, customer_id INTEGER    NOT NULL
, cartdate    TIMESTAMP  NOT NULL
);

INSERT INTO carts
  (id, customer_id, cartdate)
VALUES
  (2131,710,'2008-09-03 00:00:00')
, (2461,820,'2008-09-16 00:00:00')
, (2921,730,'2008-09-19 00:00:00')
, (2937,750,'2008-09-21 00:00:00')
, (3001,750,'2008-09-23 00:00:00')
, (3002,730,'2008-10-07 00:00:00')
, (3081,880,'2008-10-13 00:00:00')
, (3197,770,'2008-10-14 00:00:00')
, (3321,860,'2008-10-26 00:00:00')
, (3937,750,'2008-10-28 00:00:00')
;
```

The `cartitems` Table

The `cartitems` table has three columns and fifteen rows. Note that you should remove the `DEFAULT` and `CHECK` constraints if your database does not support them:

Cart_04_ANDs_and_ORs.sql *(excerpt)*

```sql
CREATE TABLE cartitems
(
  cart_id  INTEGER  NOT NULL
, item_id  INTEGER  NOT NULL
, qty      SMALLINT NOT NULL  DEFAULT 1 CHECK ( qty <= 10 )
);

INSERT INTO cartitems
  (cart_id, item_id, qty)
VALUES
  (2131,5902,3)
, (2131,5913,2)
, (2461,5043,3)
, (2461,5901,2)
, (2921,5023,3)
, (2921,5937,2)
, (2937,5913,1)
, (3001,5912,3)
, (3001,5937,2)
, (3002,5901,1)
, (3081,5023,3)
, (3081,5913,2)
, (3197,5932,1)
, (3321,5932,3)
, (3937,5913,3)
;
```

The vendors Table

This script creates the vendors table. It has two columns and two rows. We never get around to doing much with the vendors table, other than pointing out that items don't have to belong to a vendor.

Cart_17_Vendors.sql *(excerpt)*

```sql
CREATE TABLE vendors
(
  id      INTEGER       NOT NULL PRIMARY KEY
, name    VARCHAR(21)   NOT NULL
);

INSERT INTO vendors
VALUES
  ( 17, 'Acme Corp' )
, ( 19, 'Ersatz Inc' )
;
```

Appendix D: SQL Keywords

The following are—or were—reserved words in at least one version of the SQL standard.[1] The purpose of this appendix is primarily to alert you to some of the words that you should *not* use as an identifier, for example, for a table or column name.

Of course, the final arbiter of whether you'll have a problem using any word you choose is not this list, but the SQL reference manual for your particular database system. In fact, your database system may have its own, additional reserved words—so don't use those, either:

```
ABSOLUTE, ACTION, ADD, AFTER, ALL, ALLOCATE, ALTER, AND, ANY,
ARE, ARRAY, AS, ASC, ASENSITIVE, ASSERTION, ASYMMETRIC, AT,
ATOMIC, AUTHORIZATION, AVG, BEFORE, BEGIN, BETWEEN, BIGINT,
BINARY, BIT, BIT_LENGTH, BLOB, BOOLEAN, BOTH, BREADTH, BY, CALL,
CALLED, CASCADE, CASCADED, CASE, CAST, CATALOG, CHAR, CHAR_LENGTH,
CHARACTER, CHARACTER_LENGTH, CHECK, CLOB, CLOSE, COALESCE,
COLLATE, COLLATION, COLUMN, COMMIT, CONDITION, CONNECT,
CONNECTION, CONSTRAINT, CONSTRAINTS, CONSTRUCTOR, CONTAINS,
CONTINUE, CONVERT, CORRESPONDING, COUNT, CREATE, CROSS, CUBE,
CURRENT, CURRENT_DATE, CURRENT_DEFAULT_TRANSFORM_GROUP,
CURRENT_PATH, CURRENT_ROLE, CURRENT_TIME, CURRENT_TIMESTAMP,
CURRENT_TRANSFORM_GROUP_FOR_TYPE, CURRENT_USER, CURSOR, CYCLE,
DATA, DATE, DAY, DEALLOCATE, DEC, DECIMAL, DECLARE, DEFAULT,
DEFERRABLE, DEFERRED, DELETE, DEPTH, DEREF, DESC, DESCRIBE,
DESCRIPTOR, DETERMINISTIC, DIAGNOSTICS, DISCONNECT, DISTINCT, DO,
DOMAIN, DOUBLE, DROP, DYNAMIC, EACH, ELEMENT, ELSE, ELSEIF, END,
EQUALS, ESCAPE, EXCEPT, EXCEPTION, EXEC, EXECUTE, EXISTS, EXIT,
EXTERNAL, EXTRACT, FALSE, FETCH, FILTER, FIRST, FLOAT, FOR,
FOREIGN, FOUND, FREE, FROM, FULL, FUNCTION, GENERAL, GET, GLOBAL,
GO, GOTO, GRANT, GROUP, GROUPING, HANDLER, HAVING, HOLD, HOUR,
IDENTITY, IF, IMMEDIATE, IN, INDICATOR, INITIALLY, INNER, INOUT,
INPUT, INSENSITIVE, INSERT, INT, INTEGER, INTERSECT, INTERVAL,
INTO, IS, ISOLATION, ITERATE, JOIN, KEY, LANGUAGE, LARGE, LAST,
LATERAL, LEADING, LEAVE, LEFT, LEVEL, LIKE, LOCAL, LOCALTIME,
LOCALTIMESTAMP, LOCATOR, LOOP, LOWER, MAP, MATCH, MAX, MEMBER,
MERGE, METHOD, MIN, MINUTE, MODIFIES, MODULE, MONTH, MULTISET,
NAMES, NATIONAL, NATURAL, NCHAR, NCLOB, NEW, NEXT, NO, NONE, NOT,
NULL, NULLIF, NUMERIC, OBJECT, OCTET_LENGTH, OF, OLD, ON, ONLY,
```

---

[1] Sometimes, a word is "unreserved" by a subsequent version of the standard.

```
OPEN, OPTION, OR, ORDER, ORDINALITY, OUT, OUTER, OUTPUT, OVER,
OVERLAPS, PAD, PARAMETER, PARTIAL, PARTITION, PATH, POSITION,
PRECISION, PREPARE, PRESERVE, PRIMARY, PRIOR, PRIVILEGES,
PROCEDURE, PUBLIC, RANGE, READ, READS, REAL, RECURSIVE, REF,
REFERENCES, REFERENCING, RELATIVE, RELEASE, REPEAT, RESIGNAL,
RESTRICT, RESULT, RETURN, RETURNS, REVOKE, RIGHT, ROLE, ROLLBACK,
ROLLUP, ROUTINE, ROW, ROWS, SAVEPOINT, SCHEMA, SCOPE, SCROLL,
SEARCH, SECOND, SECTION, SELECT, SENSITIVE, SESSION, SESSION_USER,
SET, SETS, SIGNAL, SIMILAR, SIZE, SMALLINT, SOME, SPACE, SPECIFIC,
SPECIFICTYPE, SQL, SQLCODE, SQLERROR, SQLEXCEPTION, SQLSTATE,
SQLWARNING, START, STATE, STATIC, SUBMULTISET, SUBSTRING, SUM,
SYMMETRIC, SYSTEM, SYSTEM_USER, TABLE, TABLESAMPLE, TEMPORARY,
THEN, TIME, TIMESTAMP, TIMEZONE_HOUR, TIMEZONE_MINUTE, TO, TRAILING,
TRANSACTION, TRANSLATE, TRANSLATION, TREAT, TRIGGER, TRIM, TRUE,
UNDER, UNDO, UNION, UNIQUE, UNKNOWN, UNNEST, UNTIL, UPDATE, UPPER,
USAGE, USER, USING, VALUE, VALUES, VARCHAR, VARYING, VIEW, WHEN,
WHENEVER, WHERE, WHILE, WINDOW, WITH, WITHIN, WITHOUT, WORK,
WRITE, YEAR, ZONE
```

Index

A

ADD CONSTRAINT keyword, 228
aggregate, 109
aggregate function, 30
aggregate functions, 109, 120, 140, 141–149
    COUNT (*), 146–149
    COUNT (DISTINCT), 144–146
    ignore NULLs, 144
    without GROUP BY, 142–144
aggregate functions and GROUP BY clause, 117
aggregate row, 109
aggregation, 29
ALTER statement, 7, 10
AND and OR
    combining, 89–90
    compound conditions with, 86
    use parentheses when mixing, 90
ASC (keyword), 32
ASC and ORDER BY clause, 164–166
attributes (data modelling), 213–219
autonumbers (surrogate key), 234–235

B

BETWEEN operators, 83–86
BIGINT (data type), 185, 186, 193
Binary Large Objects (BLOBs), 117
BLOB column, 198–199

C

cardinality, 215
cart_id, 105

cartitems table, 105, 283
carts table, 282
carts.id, 109, 163
CASE function, 152–154
case-sensitivity, 9
CAST function, 153
categories table, 47, 270–271
    full outer join, 63–67
    inner join, 48–56
    left outer join, 56–61
    one-to-many relationships, 50
    right outer join, 61–63
category column, 47, 242
CHAR column, 194–195
CHAR_LENGTH, 153
CHARACTER column, 194
character data types, 194–200
    CHAR, 194–195
    CLOB and BLOB, 198–199
    NCHAR and NVARCHAR, 198
    numeric or character, 196–198
    string functions, 199–200
    VARCHAR, 195–196
Character Large Objects (CLOBs), 117
CHECK constraints, 209–210
clauses, 4, 19–20
CLOB column, 198–199
COALESCE function, 151–152
code highlighting, 255
coding style, 4
Collations, 81
column, 3, 7
column alias, 30, 244
column alias or aggregate expression, 128

column constraints, data types (SQL), 208–210
  CHECK constraints, 209–210
  DEFAULT, 209
  NULL or NOT NULL, 208
column name, 3
column names
  qualifying, 54–55
columns, 25, 28, 33, 184
  grouping, 137
  numeric data type, 184
  selecting, 135–138
columns with certain large data types, 117–122
columns, order of, 8
comments table, 273
Common Era calendar, 200
comparison operators, 79–82
composite key, 221
compound condition, 75
compound conditions with AND and OR, 86–90
  combining AND and OR, 89–90
  truth tables, 87–89
concatenation operator, 154–155
condition (WHERE clause), 28
conference (column), 8
Constants, 3, 13
CONSTRAINT keyword, 222
Content Management System (CMS), 24, 25–27, 46, 118, 214, 259, 261–262, 268–274
contents table, 272–273
contents.content (TEXT column), 120
conversions in numeric calculations
  numeric data types, 193
correlated subqueries, 93–96

correlated subquery, 97
correlation, 93
COUNT (DISTINCT), 144–146
COUNT function, 120, 144, 146
COUNT(*), 30, 146–149
COUNT(entry_id) aggregate function, 122
COUNT(items.name), 138
CREATE statement, 7–9, 12
CREATE TABLE statement, 8, 9, 183
cross join, 38, 44–45
current/previous logic, 166
CURRENT_DATE - INTERVAL 5 DAY, 85
CURRENT_DATE (keyword), 85
CURRENT_DATE (time function), 207
CURRENT_TIME (time function), 207
CURRENT_TIMESTAMP (time function), 207
customer table, 87
customers table, 281–282
customers.name, 109
customers.name column, 137

D

data, 6
Data Definition Language (DDL), 6–11, 22
  ALTER statement, 7, 10
  CREATE statement, 7–9, 12
  DROP statement, 7, 10
  starting over, 10–11
Data Manipulation Language (DML), 6, 11–20, 22
  DELETE statement, 18
  INSERT statement, 12–15
  SELECT statement, 18

UPDATE statement, 15–17

data model diagrams, 259–260

data modelling, 212–219

    entities and attributes, 213–214

    entities and relationships, 214–219

data retrieval, 2, 19–20

data types, 180

data types (SQL), 183–210

    character data types, 194–200

    column constraints, 208–210

    numeric data types, 185–194

    overview, 184

    pros and cons of non-standard data
        types, 186

    temporal data types, 200–208

    wrapping up, 210

database design, 2, 211

database designer, 214

database development, 10

database environments, 2

database objects, 6

database optimizer, 100

database structure, 6

database system, 189

database system software, 253–254

database system, connecting to the, 255–256

database systems, 21, 204

DATE, 206

DATE (keyword), 201

DATE (temporal data types), 200–203

    input format, storage format and display format, 201–203

date arithmetic, 85

DATE data type, 200

date functions (temporal data types), 207–208

date values, inserting, 201–203

DATETIME, 265

DB2, 7, 15, 22, 156, 185, 254

DECIMAL, 187–188

decimal data type

    latitude and longitude, 190–191

    precision, scale and accuracy, 190

decimals

    numeric data types, 187–191

DEFAULT (column constraints), 209

DELETE statement, 18

deprecated (data type), 188

derived tables, 70–71

DESC (keyword), 32

DESC and ORDER BY clause, 164–166

designated database administrators
    (DBAs), 9

detail query, 104

detail rows, 104, 135–136

Discussion Forum application, 138–140

    forums table, 139

    members table, 139

    posts table, 140

    threads table, 139–140

Discussion Forums, 138

Discussion Forums application, 213, 217, 221, 223, 224, 262, 275–278

    forums table, 275

    members table, 275–276

    posts table, 276–278

    threads table, 276

Display Estimated Execution Plan, 258

displaying query results on a Web Page, 27

DISTINCT (keyword), 144

dot notation, 48, 54

drill-down SQL, 113–114

DROP statement, 7, 10

E

entities (data modelling), 213–219
entities and relationships (data modelling), 214–219
entity-relationship (ER) diagram, 214–219
entity-relationship (ER) modelling tools, 219
entries table, 25–27, 268–270
    full outer join, 63–67
    inner join, 48–56
    left outer join, 56–61
    one-to-many relationships, 50
    right outer join, 61–63
    some of it is hidden, 49
entries_with_category view, 272
entrykeywords table, 247, 248, 249, 261, 274
equals sign = (keyword), 3
error
    full outer join, 64
execution plan for a query, 257
EXISTS conditions, 96–99
exponent, 191
EXTRACT, 153

F

floating-point data type, 193
floating-point numbers
    numeric data types, 191–193
FOREIGN KEY keyword, 228
foreign keys (relational integrity), 224–232
    declaring, 230

how they work, 225–226
must reference a key, 227–230
NULL, 230
ON DELETE and ON UPDATE, 231–232
using, 226–232
forums Table, 139
forums table, 275
FROM (keyword), 3
FROM clause, 1, 19–20, 24–27, 33, 115, 133, 134, 180, 182
    derived tables, 70–71
    more than one table using JOINS, 37–45
    one table, 37
    real world joins, 46–67
    result set, 73
    subqueries, 70–71
    testing, 105
    views, 67–69
    Why start with?, 36–37
    wrapping up, 71
front-end applications, 255–256
full outer join, 38, 42–43
    categories and entries, 63–67
    union queries, 64–67
FULL OUTER JOIN (keyword), 64

G

games table, 239, 267
granularity, 137
GROUP BY
    using ORDER BY with, 175–176
GROUP BY clause, 20, 29–31, 34, 103–123, 133, 135, 159, 163, 166, 182
    and aggregate functions, 117

columns with certain large data types, 117

group rows, 125–126

HAVING without a, 128–132

how it works, 115–117

in context, 114–115

rules for, 117–122

subquery, 118, 120

wrapping up, 122–123

GROUP BY queries, 104

group condition, 127

group row, 109

group rows, 29, 104, 115–117, 136–138

GROUP_CONCAT, 250

Grouping, 104

grouping columns, 137

H

HAVING clause, 20, 29–31, 34, 125–132, 133, 134, 182

Are thresholds database or application logic?, 130–131

use of common aliases in the, 131–132

wrapping up, 132

HAVING filters group rows, 125–132

HAVING without a GROUP BY clause, 128–132

threshold alert, 129–132

help, SQL, 257–258

I

IBM DB2, 254, 256

IBM DB2 Express-C, 254

id (column), 8

id (identifier), 3

ID number, 25

Identifiers, 3

case-sensitivity, 9

identity (relational integrity), 212, 235

primary keys, 219–221

IN conditions, 91–93

with subqueries, 92–93

indexed retrieval, 101

indexes

WHERE clause performance, 100–102

Indexing, 258

inner join, 38, 39

all columns are available after a join, 52–53

categories and entries, 48–56

difference between outer join, 43

qualifying column names, 54–55

table aliases, 56

when a join is executed in a query, 54

INSERT statement, 12–15

INTEGER, 9

integers

numeric data types, 185–186

intervals (temporal data types), 206–207

IS NULL test, 99, 100

items table, 78, 105, 279–281

items.name, 163

J

JavaScript, 167

join condition, 38

joined tables, 37–67

all columns are available after a join, 52–53

cross, 44–45

difference between inner and outer joins, 43

full outer, 63–67

inner, 39–40
joining a table to itself, 240–246
joining to a table twice, 237–240
left outer, 56–61
outer, 40–43
query, 55
real world, 46–56
right outer, 61–63
types of, 38–39
when a join is executed in a query, 54

K

keys (*see* foreign keys (relational integrity);natural keys (relational integrity);primary keys (data modelling)surrogate keys (relational integrity))
keywords, 3, 246–251, 261, 285–286

L

left outer join, 38, 40–41
    categories and entries, 56–61
LEFT OUTER JOIN, 99, 100
    avoid using COUNT(*), 149
LIKE operator, 82

M

major-to-minor sequencing
    ORDER BY clause, 162
mantissa, 191
manuals, database, 21–22
many-to-many relationship, 216, 226, 246–251, 261, 263
many-to-one relationship, 215
mastering SQL, 2
MEDIUMINT, 186

members table, 139, 275–276
Microsoft SQL Server, 254, 256
Microsoft SQL Server Express, 253
MONEY (data type), 188
multiple row constructors, 15
MySQL, 7, 22, 64, 76, 156, 185, 186, 201, 205, 229, 230, 250, 254, 256
    CONCAT function, 155
    SUBSTRING_INDEX, 155
MySQL Community Server, 253
MySQL DDL, 219

N

name (column), 8
name (identifier), 3
natural keys (relational integrity), 232–235
    autonumbers, 234–235
    using, 234
NCHAR column, 198
non-standard data types, 186
NOT (keyword), 75
NOT EXIST condition, 98–99
NOT IN condition, 98–99
NOT NULL (column), 208
NOT NULL (name column), 9
NULL, 9, 77
NULL (column), 208
NULL (outer joins), 60
NULL or NOT NULL (column constraints), 208
NULL value, 220
NULL values, 169–173, 180
NULLIF function, 153–154
NULLs by design, 144
NUMERIC (decimal data type), 187–188
numeric data types, 185–194

conversions in numeric calculations, 193

decimals, 187–191

floating-point numbers, 191–193

integers, 185–186

numeric functions, 193–194

numeric functions

numeric data types, 193–194

numeric identifiers, 212

numeric operators, 154

NVARCHAR column, 198

O

"One-to-Zero-or-Many" relationships, 107

ON clause, 39

ON DELETE clause, 231

ON UPDATE clause, 231

one-to-many relationship, 50, 215, 226, 242

one-to-many relationships, 247, 261

one-to-many table relationships, 250

one-to-one relationship, 216

online SQL reference manuals, 22

operator (keyword), 3

operators

BETWEEN, 83–86

comparison, 79–82

concatenation operator, 154–155

LIKE, 82

numeric, 154

SELECT clause, 154–156

temporal, 155–156

operators (WHERE clause), 79–86

Oracle, 7, 22, 156, 254, 256

Oracle Database Express Edition, 254

ORDER BY clause, 20, 32–33, 34, 108, 161–182

ASC and DESC, 164–166

dealing with problems, 169

detecting groupings in applications, 166

expressions, 176

how it works, 162–173

major-to-minor sequencing, 162

performance, 167–168

scope of, 173–181

sequence of values, 168–169

special sequencing, 176–177

syntax, 162

using with GROUP BY, 175–176

when it seems unnecessary, 168

with UNION queries, 178–181

wrapping up, 182

ORDER BY expressions, 176

ORDER BY syntax, 162

outer join, 40–43

(*see also* full outer join; left outer join; right outer join)

difference between inner join, 43

produce nulls, 60

OUTER JOIN (keyword), 40

outer table, 61

P

parsing an SQL statement, 36–37

pattern matching, 82

performance problems, SQL, 257–258

PostgreSQL, 7, 15, 22, 185, 253, 254, 256

posts table, 140, 276–278

precision (decimals), 187

primary keys (data modelling), 219–221

Q

qualifying column names, 54–55
queries
    correlated subqueries, 93–96
    execution plan, 257–258
    GROUP BY, 104
    subqueries, 92–93
    UNION, 178–181
queries, union, 64–67
query
    SQL (Structured Query Language), 99,
        257
query results on a web page, 27
query, join, 55
query, when a join is executed in a, 54

R

range test, 83
real world joins, 46–67
REFERENCES keyword, 228
referential integrity, 228
reflexive relationship, 242
relational integrity, 211–236
    data modelling, 212–219
    foreign keys, 224–232
    identity, 212
    natural versus surrogate keys, 232–235
    primary keys, 219–221
    UNIQUE constraints, 221–223
    wrapping up, 235–236
result set, 20
right outer join, 38, 41–42
    categories and entries, 60–63
row, 7, 12
row constructor, 14–15
row constructors, 265

rows
    detail, 135–136
    group, 136–138

S

sample applications, SQL, 259–263
scalar functions, 141, 149–154
scale (decimals), 187
script, 11
SELECT (keyword), 3, 157
SELECT *, 156–157
SELECT * (keyword), 105
SELECT clause, 5, 19–20, 24–27, 33,
        106, 120, 133–159, 240
    Discussion Forum application, 138–
        140
    functions, 140–154
    operators, 154–156
    SELECT *, 156–157
    SELECT DISTINCT, 157–159
    sequence in execution, 134–135
    Which columns can be selected?, 135–
        138
    wrapping up, 159
SELECT DISTINCT, 157–159
SELECT SQL statement, 161
select star (*), 105
SELECT statement, 2, 18–20, 23–24, 33,
        133, 135, 183
    clauses, 19–20
    data retrieval, 19–20
    tabular structure, 20
self-documenting, 55
semantics, 5
sequence of values
    ORDER BY clause, 168–173
Sequencing, 104

Shopping Cart, 104

shopping carts, 76–79, 263, 279–284

   cartitems table, 283

   carts table, 282

   customers table, 281–282

   items table, 279–281

   vendors table, 284

sitemap

   application for left outer joins, 59

SMALLINT, 185, 186

SMALLINT column, 208

SMALLINT values, 204

special sequencing

   ORDER BY clause, 176–177

special structures, 237–251

   implementing a many-to-many rela-
      tionship, 246–251

   joinging a table to itself, 240–246

   joining to a table twice, 237–240

   wrapping up, 251

splittime column, 205

SQL (Structured Query Language), 1

   aggregate functions, 141–149

   functions, 140–154

   help, 257–258

   keywords, 285–286

   language, 2

   online reference manuals, 22

   performanve problems, 257–258

   query, 2, 99, 257

   sample applications, 259–263

   scalar functions, 149–154

   script, 11

   standards, 2, 20–22

   structure, 1

   syntax, 7

   tabular structures, 1, 7, 13, 20

   testing environment, 253–258

   trying out the sample, 24

   trying out your, 7

   types of statements, 2

SQL data types (*see* data types (SQL))

SQL or Sequel, 2

SQL reference, 254

SQL reference manual, 201, 258, 285

SQL scalar functions

    commonly available in all database
       systems, 149–154

SQL script library, 256–257

SQL Server, 7, 22, 185, 186, 201

SQL Server 2008 Express with Tools, 256

SQL standard, 198, 201

SQL statement, parsing an, 36–37

SQL statements, 1, 7, 22, 133, 161

   clauses, 4

   Data Definition Language (DDL), 6

   Data Manipulation Language (DML),
      6

   keywords, identifiers and constants,
      2–3

   overview, 1–6

   script, 11

   syntax, 5–6

   types of, 2

SQL, drill-down, 113–114

SQL-1999, 185

SQL-2003 standard, 185

standards, SQL, 2, 20–22

starting over, 10–11

string functions (character data types),
    199–200

strings, 13

structure, SQL, 1

Structured Query Language (SQL), 1

subqueries, 70–71

subquery, GROUP BY clause, 118, 120–122

subselects (union queries), 65

SUBSTRING function, 149–151

surrogate keys (relational integrity), 232–235

   and redundancy, 234

   autonumbers, 234–235

   UNIQUE constraint, 235

syntax, 5–6

T

table, 3

table aliases, 56, 244

table name, 3

table scan, 101

tables

   (*see also* joined tables)

   creating, 39

   single, 37

tables, multiple, 37

tables, single

   FROM clause, 37

tabular structure, 1, 7, 13, 20, 73, 105

tags, 246

teams (identifier), 3

Teams and Games application, 266–267

teams and games data model, 260

teams table, 8, 239, 266

temporal data types, 184, 200–208

   DATE, 200–203

   date functions, 207–208

   intervals, 206–207

   TIME, 203–205

   TIMESTAMP, 205–206

temporal operators, 155–156

temporary table, 115

testing environment, SQL, 253–258

TEXT column, 28

threads table, 139–140, 276

threshold alert, 129–132

thresholds, database or application logic, 130–131

TIME, 206

TIME (temporal data types), 203–205

   times as duration, 204–205

   times as point in time, 205

time as duration, 204

TIME data type, 200

TIME values, 205

times as points in time, 205

TIMESTAMP, 265

timestamp (temporal data types), 184

TIMESTAMP (temporal data types), 205–206

TINYINT, 186

TINYINT values, 204

truth tables, 87–89

U

UNION (keyword), 65

UNION ALL, 67

union queries

   full outer join, 64–67

UNION Queries

   ORDER BY with, 178–181

UNIQUE constraint

   NULL, 230

UNIQUE constraints (relational integrity), 221–223, 235

   dealing with keys in application code, 223

UNKNOWN (WHERE clause), 75, 79, 88

UPDATE statement, 15–17

V

VARCHAR, 9
VARCHAR column, 195–196
vendors table, 284
Views, 67–69

W

web development
   views, 69
WEEKDAY (date function), 207
WHERE (keyword), 3
WHERE clause, 20, 28–29, 33, 115, 133,
      134, 168, 182
  compound conditions with AND and
     OR, 86–93
  conditions, 74–75
  correlated subqueries, 93–96
  EXIST conditions, 96–99
  operators, 79–86
  performance, 99–102
  shopping carts, 76–79
  wrapping up, 102
WHERE condition, 74–75
  conditions that are true, 74
  when 'Not True" is preferable, 75
wildcard characters, 82
Wordpress, 25

Y

YYYY-MM-DD format, 202

What's Next?

Web designers: Prepare to master the ways of the jQuery ninja!

JQUERY: NOVICE TO NINJA

By Earle Castledine &
Craig Sharkie

jQuery has quickly become the JavaScript library of choice, and it's easy to see why.

In this easy-to-follow guide, you'll master all the major tricks and techniques that jQuery offers—within hours.

Save 10% with this link:

www.sitepoint.com/launch/customers-only-jquery1

Use this link to save 10% off the cover price of *jQuery: Novice to Ninja,* compliments of the SitePoint publishing team.

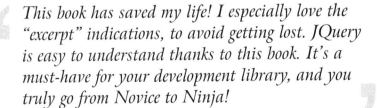

This book has saved my life! I especially love the "excerpt" indications, to avoid getting lost. JQuery is easy to understand thanks to this book. It's a must-have for your development library, and you truly go from Novice to Ninja!

Amanda Rodriguez, USA

Create mind-blowingly beautiful and functional forms with ease

FANCY FORM DESIGN

**By Jina Bolton, Tim Connell &
Derek Featherstone**

No longer do you need to worry at the thought of integrating a stylish form on your site.

Fancy Form Design is a complete guide to creating beautiful web forms that are aesthetically pleasing, highly functional, and compatible across all major browsers.

Save 10% with this link:

 www.sitepoint.com/launch/customers-only-forms1

Use this link to save 10% off the cover price of *Fancy Form Design,* compliments of the SitePoint publishing team.

> *Overall it's a good book, entertaining, well-written, not overly long, (and) full of immediately practical examples that anyone familiar with form design and development can use.*

Gary Barber, 17 Jan 2010

How About ...

HTML email simplified, seriously

CREATE STUNNING HTML EMAIL THAT JUST WORKS!

By Mathew Patterson

This step-by-step guide is perfect for front-end web designers looking to expand their range of services to clients. You'll be able to take your CSS and HTML skills, and deploy them to build beautiful, effective, and compatible HTML emails.

Save 10% with this link:

 www.sitepoint.com/launch/customers-only-htmlemail1

Use this link to save 10% off the cover price of *Create Stunning HTML Email That Just Works!*, compliments of the SitePoint publishing team.

 I have been searching for a book about HTML email design and have finally found it! I just read the entire thing in about 2 hours.

Russell , 6 May 2010

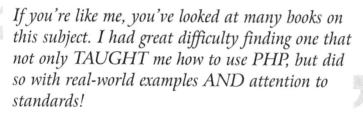

How About ...

The first guide to tapping into the endless capacity of the cloud

HOST YOUR WEB SITE IN THE CLOUD: AMAZON WEB SERVICES MADE EASY

By Jeff Barr

Stop wasting time, money, and resources on servers that can't grow with you. Cloud computing gives you ultimate freedom and speed, all at an affordable price.

Save 10% with this link:

 www.sitepoint.com/launch/customers-only-cloud1

Use this link to save 10% off the cover price of *Host Your Web Site in the Cloud,* compliments of the SitePoint publishing team.

About Jeff Barr

In his role as the Amazon Web Services Senior Evangelist, Jeff speaks to developers at conferences, as well as user groups all over the world.